The Mummy at the
Dining Room Table

Jeffrey A. Kottler

Jon Carlson

The Mummy at the Dining Room Table

Eminent Therapists Reveal Their Most Unusual Cases and What They Teach Us About Human Behavior

JOSSEY-BASS
A Wiley Imprint
www.josseybass.com

Published by Jossey-Bass
A Wiley Imprint
989 Market Street, San Francisco, CA 94103-1741   www.josseybass.com

Jossey-Bass books and products are available through most bookstores. To contact Jossey-Bass
directly call our Customer Care Department within the U.S. at 800-956-7739, outside the U.S.
at 317-572-3986 or fax 317-572-4002.

Jossey-Bass also publishes its books in a variety of electronic formats. Some content that
appears in print may not be available in electronic books.

Library of Congress Cataloging-in-Publication Data

The mummy at the dining room table: eminent therapists reveal their most unusual
cases and what they teach us about human behavior/[edited by] Jeffrey A. Kottler,
Jon Carlson.—1st ed.
    p. cm.
    ISBN 0-7879-6541-3 (alk. paper)
    1. Psychotherapy—Popular works.   2. Psychotherapy—Case studies.
I. Kottler, Jeffrey A.   II. Carlson, Jon.
    RC480.515   .M865   2004
    616.89'14—dc21

                                 2002152132

Printed in the United States of America
FIRST EDITION
HB Printing   10 9 8 7 6 5 4 3 2 1

—⌇— Contents

The Mummy at the Dining Room Table

To our children: Cary, and Kirstin, Matt, Karin, Ben, and Kali, hoping they have learned the lessons we've tried to live, that is, to learn from mistakes after acknowledging them.

⸺ᴡ⸺ Introduction

You will not recognize anyone you know in this book (great efforts have been made to disguise their identities), but you may certainly see aspects of yourself reflected in their incredible stories. The people profiled in these cases were faced with difficult and unusual challenges, not so different from those you may have confronted in your own life. What is different are the ways these individuals attempted to cope with their demons, the perseverance they displayed, and their good fortune to end up under the care of an extraordinary therapist.

Although the stories in this book are indeed quite amazing and unusual, this is not a book that glorifies the most bizarre aspects of human behavior. It is instead a collection of tales about psychotherapy relationships that were as transformative for the therapists as they were for their clients. These are stories of compassion and caring, tales that demonstrate the kind of commitment practitioners make to their craft. This is not a book that intentionally makes heroes and heroines of therapists (although there are plenty of quite amazing and creative strategies by some of the greatest practitioners alive). Rather it is a book that celebrates the courage of individuals who, in the face of overwhelming and debilitating problems, manage to overcome these challenges through hard work and continual trust in their professional helpers.

WHY THESE CASES?

In the field of human behavior, we have seen more than our fair share of unusual and challenging cases. Many of these have not only shaped the development of psychotherapy but also captured public interest. Sigmund Freud's case of Anna O. was seminal in the evolution of psychoanalysis. Here was a young woman presenting symptoms of blurred vision, difficulty swallowing, and a paralyzed right arm, but with no physical causes for these problems. Freud and his colleague

Josef Breuer found themselves not only challenged to treat the first case of hysteria but also enamored by the peculiarities of Anna's condition. (Breuer became a little too enamored with Anna, but that's another story.)

In more recent times, the story of *Sybil*, the first documented case of multiple personality disorder, was a runaway best-seller. Clinicians were not the only ones who were interested in reading about this woman with sixteen distinct personalities and how her therapist managed to deal with the challenge. The same is certainly true of other books that have followed in the tradition of presenting strange cases for popular consumption. *The Man Who Mistook His Wife for a Hat* spawned a whole industry of stories about people who have weird neurological, psychological, or behavioral disorders.

We wondered why strange behavior holds such fascination not only for the public at large but also for members of our profession. There are reasons why we remember particular cases, even after twenty or thirty years, but forget others. There is also some meaning in the choice we make to discuss one case out of the thousands we have seen in our lives. Why do we consider one patient more unusual or distinctive than all the others?

In some cases, the therapists picked the patient who represented the first of something—the first success or failure, the first representative of a diagnostic entity (a borderline or schizophrenic disorder, for example). More often, the cases selected were those that were high in "novelty," meaning that they were just so different from anything or anyone else the therapist had seen before or since. Nevertheless, which case each of us chose says as much about who we are as it does about the people we describe.

WHY THESE THERAPISTS?

Consider that therapists, as a group, are among the most articulate and verbally expressive people around. As a profession, we are well trained and highly experienced in all the nuances of communication, problem conceptualization, and interpersonal relationships. We are good talkers and experts at explaining complex ideas in understandable terms. What we do for a living, essentially, is persuade people to do things they don't want to do, and convince people to surrender sacred (but self-destructive) beliefs they have held all their lives.

Now consider further that among this population of professionals who are the most skilled talkers around, there is a subgroup—the top fraction of 1 percent—who are still even more articulate. These are people who have developed theories followed by all the rest. They are the ones who write the books and manuals that guide other clinicians. These are the therapists you see on talk shows, read about in articles, or hear interviewed on the radio. These are the best and brightest members of a profession that already represents some of the most intelligent, perceptive, sensitive, and interpersonally effective people. These are the people whose voices you will hear in this book.

Our collection of stories come from thirty of the most prominent and well-regarded therapists. They live in different parts of the world. They are trained in different disciplines of psychology, psychiatry, counseling, family therapy, and social work. They represent radically different approaches to therapy: psychoanalytic, cognitive-behavioral, constructivist, feminist, humanistic, systemic, and all the rest. It could probably be said that many of the therapists in this book don't so much *follow* a particular theoretical orientation as much as they have *invented* one. Between them, they have written most of the major books in the field that guide all other therapists.

In this book, you will have the opportunity to hear the greatest living theorists and practitioners talk about their strangest cases. In each story, you will not only gain an intimate look at how individuals have chosen to adapt in unique ways to adversity in their lives but also get an inside peek at how some of the greatest minds of our generation sort out the complexities of the situation in such a way as to cure their clients' presenting problems. As never before, you will learn about how therapists work with their most challenging clients, and you will gain a deeper understanding of human suffering.

FROM UNUSUAL TO BIZARRE

As we began collecting the stories, we soon realized that there was no universal way to structure these interviews or the chapters that resulted from them. We started out with an interview protocol—we even sent a list of prospective questions to the participants ahead of time. We thought our lead question was fairly straightforward: tell us about the most unusual case you have ever worked with. We expected to hear stories about bizarre variations in human behavior, and of course we did. But some therapists elected to interpret the assignment in a different way: rather than focusing on what it was about their patients that was truly strange, they may have also looked at the cases in terms of their most unusual features. In other cases, what was most memorable was not so much people's bizarre behavior, but rather the unusual circumstances the patients found themselves in that required them to act in amazingly resourceful ways.

Each of our conversations was unique, guided not just by where we wanted it to go but by the direction that the master therapist wanted to take. Considering that we were working with rather strong-willed, articulate folks, it was not easy to keep things along the predictable track we had in mind originally. This means that each chapter is different from the rest, not only in the variety of material presented but also in aspects of its style and structure. Some therapists came to the conversation completely open, loose, and flexible, willing to go wherever it might lead. Others had actually written out their case ahead of time and wanted to read it to us before we talked about its implications. Still others insisted we stick with the prearranged agenda that had been prepared ahead of time.

One thing that struck us right away was the diverse ways that famous therapists conceptualized this subject. Originally we explained that we were collecting stories about "unusual" cases they had seen. This word did not resonate with all the people we spoke with. Some went in the direction of their own perceptions, preferring the word *memorable* to describe their case; others liked the more descriptive nature of the word *bizarre.* Then other therapists quibbled with any of these choices and instead substituted *unforgettable, haunting, interesting,* or *strange.* No matter which word we selected to introduce what we were after, there was a high likelihood that the therapist would change it to something else.

Regardless of the particular label attached to the patient, what all the cases have in common is that they challenged the therapist by presenting clinical problems for which he or she was unprepared. These are thus stories about not only the development of suffering patients but also seminal experiences in the lives of their therapists. In some cases, whole theories evolved as a direct result of these cases.

SOME CAUTIONARY NOTES

There was great concern about preserving the confidentiality and privacy of the people profiled in this book. In some cases, the patients are now deceased. In other instances, the therapists received permission from the individuals to talk about their cases. In all instances, names and identifying features have been changed, as have some of the characteristics and settings, in order to disguise patients' identities. As is true for physicians, therapists' first rule of practice is to do no harm. If these patients thought that that there was a resemblance between them and the people depicted in the book, we would hope that they would feel proud to know how important they were in the lives and work of their therapists.

We hope that these stories convey how much compassion and caring these therapists felt for their clients. If some of the voices of our contributors appear cynical or judgmental, or even appear to poke fun at the expense of others, we wish to accept full responsibility for taking things too far. In truth, what made these conversations so revealing and insightful was the informality, the looseness, the playfulness with which we prompted our colleagues and friends.

For you, the reader, it will seem as if you are listening in to the most intimate, private conversations between trusted colleagues, but with this privilege comes an understanding of its context. It is a reality that therapists talk about their most unusual cases just as plumbers, accountants, and surgeons talk about their own; it is a significant way that professionals in any field become better at what they do—we learn from every conceivable variation that can occur, and adjust our methods to fit more flexibly in the future.

All of these stories are utterly and completely true—no matter how unbelievable they may sound. Although some dialogue has been reconstructed, the essence of the cases, and what they have to teach, have been preserved.

ACKNOWLEDGMENTS

We are grateful to Alan Rinzler, our third "partner" in this process, whose keen therapeutic wisdom and editing skills helped shape these stories into such powerful tales of transformation.

Thanks to Jean Naggar, our agent.

We are indebted to Laurie Johnson, who transcribed all the interviews and then handled all the voluminous correspondence with our participants.

And to the contributors themselves—some of the best therapists and most distinguished theoreticians in the world—we are most grateful to them for donating their time to be interviewed and reviewing the stories afterwards. They were paid nothing for their efforts. They receive no authorship credit. Their only reward was the enjoyment they have received as a result of talking to us about an unsettling aspect of their work. They participated in this project because they believe strongly that others can learn much from their most unusual cases.

Finally, we wish to acknowledge the incredible courage and commitment of the people profiled in these stories. They sought help, persevered, and often triumphed over great odds to recover from past traumas. They demonstrate not only the amazing richness and diversity of human behavior but also the resilience that makes it possible for any of us grow beyond our present limits.

Jeffrey A. Kottler
Huntington Beach, California

Jon Carlson .
Lake Geneva, Wisconsin

CHAPTER ONE

Jeffrey A. Kottler

The Man Who Wanted His Nose Cut Off

The examining room was empty except for two chairs and a desk. There was a sink off in the corner, a vestige of the days when this part of the hospital housed medical cases rather than an outpatient psychiatric clinic. I was an eager doctoral student, preparing to begin the first day of my internship.

I was more than a little nervous about greeting my first patient. Although I had been working as a counselor for a few years, my clients had been mostly young children and college students. Now I was about to begin working with folks who had considerably more severe problems.

I could hear my patient being escorted into the examining room before I could see him. He made some sort of jangling sound as he walked, almost as though he were in chains. It turned out that I wasn't far wrong: his neck and wrists were encircled by strands of beads and chains, dozens of them.

I took a deep breath and prepared to hear the story of my very first patient. This was the beginning of my new career, and I was determined to do the best job I could. I just hoped that he presented the sort of problem that I could address. Little did I imagine how poorly his expectations would match my capabilities.

THE LAB COAT

"So," I began in my most welcoming voice. "How can I help you?"

"Well, Doc, I was hopin' you could take care of the smell."

"The smell?" I asked the very anxious man, not sure what he was talking about.

"Yeah. Cain't you get the scent? It's turbul."

"Turbul?" I pronounced the word carefully, exactly as he had.

"Turbul. Just turbul."

"Oh, *terrible.* You mean *terrible?*"

My voice was a little excited because I finally understood what this man was saying. I was neither a staff doctor nor even a graduated psychologist but a mere intern. Nevertheless, the hospital administration made us wear these white lab coats to give us an air of respectability. Etched on the pocket of mine was the name of some long-departed physician who was kind enough to leave his coat behind. I must admit that it did make me feel a bit more as though I belonged in the place. But I was nervous, maybe even more so than the patient sitting in front of me.

The man was dark skinned and wore many different layers of clothes, each of which clashed with the others. Striped shirt. Checkered pants. A vest. Mismatched socks. And then, of course, the chains and beads. He appeared to have randomly reached into a box for his daily wardrobe. Maybe he had.

Although his appearance was striking, even regal, it was the beaded cornrows of hair that drew my attention. He looked African, or maybe Jamaican, but his accent was clearly that of rural Virginia. This was not surprising, as we were *in* rural Virginia, but what I did find strange was that he kept taking long whiffs of air, grimacing, and then gagging deep in his throat. Because this was my first day on the job, I was wondering how I'd call for help if he passed out. I remembered from television shows something about calling "code blue," but maybe that was for cardiac arrest.

"You were saying there was a turbul, er, terrible, smell." I had learned my lessons well—when you don't know what else to say, repeat what you just heard.

The man only nodded, his beaded hair jangling.

"What sort of smell?" I probed. By now I was imitating him, sniffing the air in deep breaths. All I could sense was the antiseptic hospital odor and my own sweat from trying way too hard to do a good job with my first patient.

"You cain't smell the cowdoc?"

"The cowdock?" I was wracking my brain trying to figure out what a cowdock was, not realizing that he was haunted by the smell of a cow and addressing me as "Doc." This was so much of a problem for him that he couldn't concentrate on anything else.

As I tried to gather basic information, I learned that Manny lived on a family farm quite a distance from town. It wasn't often that he came into the city, but lately he was so distracted that he couldn't get much work done.

"And so," I stalled, trying to figure out what he wanted from me, "you smell cows on the farm?"

"Course I smell 'em on the farm. That's way they is."

"I see," I said, not seeing at all. "The cows are on the farm."

It's a good thing my supervisor wasn't watching, because this was *really* embarrassing. I'd been talking to my patient for fifteen minutes, and all I'd learned so far was that he smelled cows on the farm where he lived. Considering they had a small herd of cattle at their place, so far this discovery was not particularly useful.

"The cows is everywhere," Manny elaborated. "They's smell is everywhere."

"And can you smell the cow right now?"

Manny looked at me with disappointment, as if to let me know that I'd let him down. He had been hoping I could smell them too.

Now I was in a bit of a bind. His presenting complaint was that he was experiencing a disturbing, chronic imaginary bovine scent. This sounded like a job for an ear, nose, and throat specialist or, at the very least, a neurologist. But for some reason he had been sent down to our unit, probably because any physical cause had already been ruled out.

I took a deep breath, as much to calm myself as to once again rule out that there were no cow smells in the examining room.

"What can I do to help you?" I asked Manny in my most empathic, invitational voice. This was one thing I could do very well.

Manny looked at me as though I were an idiot and then shook his head because I was so slow witted. "Well, Doc," he said carefully, making sure that I could understand him, "I want you to cut off my nose."

"You want me to cut off your nose?" I felt foolish not because of the content of what we were talking about but because I was so clueless about what else to say or do to help this poor, suffering man.

Manny just looked at me placidly and nodded his head. I was transfixed by the swinging beads on the end of his long braids. We just sat that way for some time, each taking the measure of the other. I had no idea what was going on inside his mind, but I was going through the list of options I could think of for where to go next. Should I schedule him for surgery to have his nose removed? Should I order another neurological workup? Maybe a psych evaluation? Then I remembered that *I* was the psychological evaluator. *I* was the one who was supposed to be assessing this man's mental status and planning some sort of treatment that would alleviate his distressing symptoms. There were a lot of things that I was willing to do to help people, especially with my very first patient, but I drew the line at cutting off noses. Besides, I wasn't allowed to do that sort of thing even if they did issue me a lab coat with the title *doctor* on it.

Clearly there was some psychological reason for this man's persistent scent disorder. If there was no medical origin for the condition, then it had to be because of some underlying emotional problem or past trauma. That much I could figure out on my own. But how was I supposed to get to the bottom of this situation in the few sessions that I was allowed to see my patients?

Although these events took place over twenty-five years ago, before the advent of "brief therapy," we were only permitted to do assessments and then administer some sort of psychological "Band-Aid" before sending people back into the world. Cutting off a patient's nose was just the sort of direct, decisive treatment that would appeal to the hospital's efficiency review committee. But as attractive as this option may have seemed at the time, I had chosen my profession because I enjoyed playing detective and getting at the root of matters. Whereas the likes of Freud had months, if not years, to resolve things, I was challenged to do so in just a few sessions. At least these intake sessions were booked as double-sessions, ninety minutes, so I had time to explore the situation a little deeper.

THE SECRET

"Could you tell me something about what you do?" This was a very good, open-ended question. Because I had no idea what else to do next with Manny, I decided it was time to get to know his phenomenological world, so to speak. I clearly needed more background information in order to get a handle on the source of his smell disorder.

"Lives on a farm," Manny told me in his compact speech.

For the next half hour or so, I asked a series of questions about where he lived exactly, who he lived with, what he did for work and for fun. This is what I learned: although he was in his mid-twenties (I peeked at his chart since I couldn't tell how old he was from looking at him), Manny still lived at home on his family farm. They grew their own food and some cash crops. They had chickens. And of course they had cows, or I guess that would be cattle. Being a city boy, born and raised in Detroit, I was more than a little fascinated by life on a farm, as I didn't know the first thing about it except for what I'd seen as a child on the television show *Green Acres*.

Manny had spent all his life on the farm and had seemed happy there, if a little isolated (the nearest neighbors were not close). Among his jobs was to take the cows (cattle?) out to pasture and bring them back when they were done with supper. In the meantime, he had plenty of time to wander around and occupy himself any way he chose. He was a little sketchy about what that might involve, so I pressed him further.

"So, Manny, what else do you do for fun? I mean, besides being with your family. Do you have a girlfriend or anything?"

Manny shrugged and looked down. He shook his head and looked up at me for a minute, then averted his eyes again. Was this a signal to pursue the topic further or leave it alone? I couldn't tell. There was something there, though.

Although eccentrically dressed, Manny was not an unattractive man. In fact, he was well built and rather impressive looking, and at the height of his dating years, so it seemed reasonable to find out more about his love life.

"You don't have a girlfriend then?"

Another shake of the head, this time a definite one. It was so beautiful to watch the beaded cornrows swing musically back and forth, I thought about asking a third time just to watch the show.

"There's something you're not telling me, Manny," I ventured. For the first time in our conversation, he seemed closed off. Until this point he had been open to whatever I might ask him, or whatever avenue we might venture down, but now he was retreating. I could feel it. Then I could see clear evidence: his long arms hugged himself, and he leaned forward on his knees, as if to present a smaller target for my probes.

"I *sade* I don't have no gurlfren'!" For the first time, Manny startled me by raising his voice. Although he looked quite gentle, I still checked my escape route to the door.

"I heard you, Manny," I said softly. "I just want you to know that we can talk about anything you want."

As I tell the story now, it may seem as though things proceeded in a logical, sequential manner, as if I followed some systematic procedure designed to unlock whatever secrets were hidden from view. In fact as a beginner to this craft, even if an enthusiastic one, I just bumbled along, asking questions that came to mind. Through luck, or just plain persistence and earnestness, I eventually did hear a more complete version of what Manny did with his days. I also heard more than I wanted to about why he didn't exactly have a girlfriend. But what I was learning about this work is that once you open up a door, you have no choice but to walk through it. Because I insisted that we get to the bottom of things—the source, as it were—for his problems, we both had little choice but to follow this line of inquiry to the end.

It seems that Manny had tried dating for a while. He had courted a neighbor a few times. He had gone out on a few dates with a city girl he met during one of his trips to town. But he found these encounters frustrating, if not unsatisfying. When I asked him what he meant by that, Manny explained that you have to treat girls so carefully. You have to sweet-talk them and bring them gifts and take them out and spend money on them. And even with all that investment of time and money, there was still no certainty that a guy would end up "getting lucky." I don't think he used that expression, "getting lucky," but it was some other quaint euphemism for sex.

Although I was recently married, Manny and I were about the same age, and I had sympathy for his plight. I could remember all too well the painful, laborious dating rituals that I would go through in order to "get close" to a woman I liked. I thought about telling him that I could relate to his frustration. Then I could give him a motivational speech about being patient, taking risks, venturing outside of his comfort zone. I had been learning cognitive therapy at this time, so I was eager to confront his irrational fears of failure. I had it all mapped out in my head and felt excited that I had finally discovered something I could do for him. But still: I *knew* I was missing something.

"Manny, you were saying that you don't date much anymore."

"No, done gave that up."

"I see."

We waited. This time I was determined to outlast him. As much as I wanted to latch on to his reluctance to date anymore and attack his core dysfunctional beliefs, I had been listening to him. Even with my lack of experience, I could tell that Manny had a story to tell, and it was more important for me to listen than to talk. Even many years later, I still think this is often the biggest mistake we therapists make: trying to fix things too quickly because of our own sense of helplessness.

THE LADDER

After a period of time that felt like several minutes but was probably twenty or thirty seconds, Manny told me what he did in his spare time and why it wasn't strictly true that he didn't have a girlfriend. You see, Manny really did have a very active sex life, although I don't think it could strictly be called a "love" life. But maybe that's just my judgment, because this was so far beyond what I had ever imagined. I understand, now, that these situations may not be so unusual on farms.

"You were saying, Manny, that you don't see many women."

"Dat be true," he agreed, nodding his head.

There was something not quite right here. The expressions on Manny's face were so transparent; in some ways, he reminded me of a child who had been caught telling a lie. He was actually looking down and scraping the toe of his untied work boot against the linoleum floor.

"But there's something you're not telling me about that," I ventured carefully. I didn't want to spook him by pushing too hard.

"Yessuh, they is."

"And do you mind telling me what that might be?"

"Yessuh, I do mind."

"OK then," I tried again. "Manny, you said you wanted me to cut off your nose, but before we can explore that, I've got to find out more about what's going on."

He looked at me suspiciously, then continued to rub the toe of his boot against the floor. I gave him all the time he needed while he decided whether he could trust me enough to tell me what was wrong.

"Well, there's this cow I see. Mertle's her name."

He sees cows on a farm? What is he telling me here? All I could think to do was repeat what he said.

"Yessuh, she's duh best of duh lot. We been gettin' together fo a spell."

"You've been getting together with this cow, with . . . Mertle's her name?"

"Thas it." He grinned happily, delighted that I remembered her name.

I was still confused about what he was telling me. Then it dawned on me what he was really talking about: Manny was having sex with a cow named Mertle. No, more than that—he seemed sweet on her.

"So, Manny, what you're telling me is that you, ah, you . . . get . . ."

"Thas right. Me and Mertle. We do it when I's feel the need."

He could see me struggling with this, but as embarrassed as he felt for himself, he felt sorrier for me. He could tell how hard I was working to try to help him, and he seemed to appreciate that a lot.

"I see," I said, and unfortunately I could now see this all too clearly. But I also had a hundred questions. How does one have sex with a cow, I wondered? After all, cows are kind of big, and people are kind of small by comparison. And how did Manny decide on Mertle as his partner? And more to the point, how did he ever get started with this sort of thing?

During his adolescence, Manny learned about sex from watching the horses and cows during mating season. (It was news to me that they *had* a season.) He would sit and watch the improbably erect stud horse mount the mare and have a go with wild abandon. Manny couldn't help but picture some day when he would have his own girlfriend to have sex with. Yet after many rejections, Manny had all but given up trying to woo young maidens and had recently turned his efforts toward those of the bovine persuasion.

It is great testimony to my composure, my highly professional demeanor, my superior sensitivity, that I didn't fall to the floor in laughter or shock. Although I couldn't quite believe what I was hearing, I sat stoically, my standard shrink look (I really did practice in front of the mirror) frozen in place. I nodded my head as casually as if he had just told me that he liked eggs for breakfast.

"So," I reflected back to Manny in what I hoped was a steady voice, "what you're saying is that you and this cow . . . I mean, Mertle, have been seeing one another for some time?"

Manny looked me right in the eyes, checking my reactions carefully, and then nodded.

So *this* was the source of the cow smell that was following him around everywhere. I had a solid grounding in psychodynamic theory, so it wasn't any great stretch to link his symptoms to underlying guilt he was feeling about his rather unusual dating behavior. I did consider that it would probably be unwise to explore Oedipal feelings he might have toward his mother, as he might take offense at the implication that she resembled a cow. First, however, I needed to learn more about what was going on.

OK, true confession time. I was dying of curiosity about this situation. Just how does someone have sex with a cow? I mean, they really are rather large beasts.

I decided to get some of my questions answered. I was discovering that one of the really great things about being a therapist is that you get to ask people all sorts of very personal questions and they don't get mad or anything. Most of the time, if you can manage to appear unconcerned, as though you've heard this sort of thing many times before, people will tell you their deepest secrets. I was reveling in this power and decided to find out just how far I could go. To be honest, though, I had some questions as to what extent I was pursuing this for my own curiosity and how much of it was related to helping my patient.

"So, Manny," I said in a casual voice, "how do you get up there to do it with Mertle?"

"Jes use a ladda. I got me a step-ladda dat I keep. We sometime use it for fixin' fenceposts and such."

"OK," I answered. I had no idea where to go with this next. "So you get up on your stepladder . . ."

"Thas right." Manny smiled shyly. He seemed to feel better telling me about these secret trysts.

I still couldn't get a handle on how all this took place. How did he get the damn cow to stay still? Did he have to keep moving the ladder around? Did the cow enjoy this sort of thing? I even wondered if I was supposed to report Manny's activity to whatever government agency controlled cruelty to animals. I knew I had to report suspected and confirmed instances of sexual abuse of children, but this was in a whole other category that had never been covered in my training.

I figured that I was now way past the point at which the information Manny was giving me was useful to his case. But I still had one more question I wanted to ask: Just how did he settle on Mertle as his favorite cow? What was it about her that seemed especially alluring to him?

Well, maybe this is far more than you want to know about this story. For me, it was like passing a car accident or seeing a scary movie. Part of me wanted to avert my eyes from the horror of it all, yet something compelling, almost irresistible, caused me to peek through the fingers covering my eyes. As much as I wanted to change the subject and move on, I couldn't stop myself from asking far too many questions about the mechanics of how one has sex with a cow. I couldn't believe the things I was learning.

Throughout Manny's description of his sexual behavior, he presented a fairly compelling rationale for why his "dating" choice was preferable over other options. He explained that he didn't have to win cows' affections or spend money on them. They never rejected him. I had some questions about that, wondering if they let him nearby when they weren't in season, so to speak, but I realized that I had already gotten far deeper into this topic than I wanted to. At that particular moment, I was wondering how the hell I was ever going to write this up in my progress notes. What was I going to tell my supervisor?

Well, at least I found one possible explanation for Manny's presenting complaints. It looked like we wouldn't have to cut off his nose after all if I could help him come to terms with his behavior.

Because our time was running out, I thanked Manny for being so forthcoming about his situation and promised him that we would continue the following week. On that note, we ended our first meeting. I, of course, immediately ran out of the room to tell my fellow interns about the amazing first session I had just lived through.

THE PERFUME

Next week, Manny greeted me warmly with a huge grin. I hadn't noticed the previous session how much gold was in his mouth. I could see the white centers of each tooth framed in inlayed gold. I also observed that his wardrobe was more subdued, a sign I would have taken optimistically as improvement if it were not for the intense smell of cheap cologne.

I could barely catch my breath through the sweet, sickly stink of English Leather or some other common scent. I don't think this product was ever intended to be worn in such quantity, and from the overpowering smell it would seem that Manny had drenched himself in the whole bottle. He looked pleased with himself.

At first, I believed it was my superior clinical skills from the previous session that had brought out Manny's new golden smile. It must have been the empathic bond I had forged with my first patient. Or maybe it was the professional way I had conducted myself, outfitted so sharply in my lab coat.

"I see that you are feeling better," I began the conversation. This let him know I was an astute observer of his internal condition.

Manny just smiled even brighter. The fluorescent overhead lights were ricocheting off his golden teeth. In those days, the "gas-permeable" contact lenses I wore made my eyes especially light sensitive, so I blinked a lot. I was worried that if I closed my eyes for too long I might miss something important.

"I also notice that you are wearing a lot of perfume today."

"It's cologne."

"Right. Cologne. It's kind of strong." I shrugged apologetically as I said this, scooting my chair back a tad further so I could breathe to the side. I was feeling a little dizzy.

"Damn right," Manny agreed. "Used all I had."

"Uh huh." I was waiting for Manny to explain why he was wearing so much cologne, but he seemed far more patient than I was. Then again, he didn't have to answer to a supervisor who demanded to know why I hadn't yet come up with a diagnosis for the case, much less a treatment plan. I had pleaded that I needed more time for "data gathering." I knew that recommending nasal amputation would not be well received by the tweed-jacketed, pipe-smoking, Van Dyke–bearded psychiatrists and psychologists who sat around the conference table during our case conferences.

"You were saying that you used all the perfume you had," I prompted again.

"It's cologne. Told you that."

Now I was grinning too, but stupidly. This was getting nowhere. I tried again. "Maybe you could explain to me why you are wearing so much cologne today."

"Duh cow smell. It gone now." Manny looked very proud of himself.

"You mean that you don't smell the cows anymore?"

A nod.

"Does that mean after our last conversation you decided to, uh, not continue your . . . with the ladder?" I couldn't bring myself to mention the cow-sex out loud. But it seemed that my first therapeutic contact was so potent that Manny no longer had his annoying symptoms. Man, am I good or what?

When he looked at me with some discomfort I realized that my assumption was incorrect. In fact, Manny had continued to have cow-sex during the week since our last meeting. Nothing had changed in that regard.

What was different, though, was that Manny had found a way to disguise the smell that had been lingering for so long. He had cured his own problem without the need for surgical intervention. He could now contentedly continue his bovine affair without the annoying guilt and cow smell.

"Duh best part, Doc," he told me before he solemnly shook my hand and walked out the door for the last time, "is dat you won't have to cut off my nose after all. I could tell you didn't really want to do dat."

THE LESSONS

Although it has been many years since I saw Manny, I hope that he eventually made the transition to having a relationship with one of his own kind. I would like to think that, in some small way, talking to me about his story, letting his secret out, helped him move on to a more appropriate level of human interaction. I was certain of one thing, however, and that was that there was no way he could afford the amount of cologne it would take to douse himself every day and cover the haunting smell.

Manny never returned to the clinic after the second session, at least while I was still working there. That is one of the burdens of being a therapist for me—so often I don't learn the end of the story. Clients just go away. They leave and never return. They don't respond to follow-up letters or phone calls. And so we are left to make sense of what happened on our own, or sometimes through the inventive theories of our supervisors.

When I presented Manny's case to the group of psychiatrists and psychologists at our weekly case conference, of course they had a field day. This was a distinguished assemblage of prominent faculty in the medical school, most of them dressed identically—not in white lab coats but in vested suits as clones of Sigmund Freud. Even the one woman psychiatrist present wore a vested suit (although not the requisite beard).

This was a competitive group, so they would argue among themselves about the most advantageous medication for the patient, as well as about cases they had seen in their own practices that were far more interesting than the one we were reviewing. I tried to tell them that Manny would not be returning, that he had chosen perfume over Clozaril,

Prolixin, Fluanxol, or one of their other favorite anti-hallucinatory drugs, but they were too immersed in their discussion to hear me. They seemed disappointed, if not critical, that I had not thought to invite one of them to meet my curious case.

UNDERWEAR

I ask myself today what legacy Manny left for me. For one thing, I wish I could banish from my memory the altogether too vivid image of Manny approaching a particularly delectable-looking cow with the ladder under his arm. I certainly learned, and rather quickly at that, how to keep my judgments under control. In fact, my very next assigned case was a faculty member at the university who had his own secret to confess. Having already survived my first patient while managing to keep my composure, I found it no greater challenge to remain unflustered when the instructor revealed that he dressed in his wife's underwear and felt uncontrollable urges to run outside his house. In my naïveté, and because I couldn't think of anything else to say, I responded impulsively.

"I see. So what is it you'd like me to help you with?"

"Excuse me?" he said, genuinely puzzled.

"Well," I answered carefully, realizing now that I had better have a good explanation for my casual response. "You said that you have some kinky sexual preferences. So do a lot of people. You like to dress up in women's underwear. So what? I was just wondering what it is about this behavior that you'd like to change?"

It wasn't *what* I said, of course, but *how* I said it that indicated to the young professor that I genuinely felt no horror after hearing his confession. Sure, his behavior was a bit unusual, especially the part about his obsessive fantasies of running through his neighborhood wearing a bra and panties, but hey, I'd heard a lot stranger things just sitting in a bar.

The professor examined me very, very carefully, looking for any sign of disgust or even critical judgment. But I'd already spent time with Manny. I was not merely pretending to be neutral but actually felt that way inside. I had now learned one of the most important therapist skills: how to stop judging people. After what I'd already heard, people could tell me *anything* without getting a strong reaction from me.

When I met with this instructor the next week, he said that the recurrent fantasies had now stopped. It was his theory that my acceptance of him felt so wonderful that his shame diminished significantly. During the preceding week, he had even confessed his secret to one of his friends, who had reacted in much the same way that I had. In fact, the guy had shared his own weird sexual preference.

When we met for the last time two weeks after that, the instructor told me, almost with regret, that he no longer felt the urge to dress up in his wife's underwear. In some ways, this felt like a loss to him, as if he were leaving something behind that, although perhaps unhealthy, was still comforting. He had been "cured" of his problem essentially by the power of human acceptance. Because I didn't judge him critically or react negatively to his disclosure, he began to accept himself as a man who sometimes enjoyed putting on lady's underwear, as some men do. The "cure" in this case was not so much stopping the behavior—although frequency diminished significantly—as accepting that he was not a bad, demented person just because he enjoyed a source of stimulation that was harmful to nobody.

I have never forgotten this lesson, at least as it affects my work. What has continued to remain a struggle for me, however, is that I don't often practice in my personal life what I do with my clients, at least with regard to this dimension. Once someone walks through my office door, I can listen to whatever he or she says with hardly any negative reaction. Heck, I have interviewed serial killers on death row and heard their murderous confessions without reacting visibly (or even internally) to what I heard. But once outside the professional arena, I can be as critical, catty, and condescending as the best of them. Someone doesn't live up to my unusually high standards, and I shake my head in disappointment. Someone moves more slowly than I think he or she should, and I become extremely impatient. The truth that I don't like to admit is that I have not (yet) learned to transfer my total acceptance and noncritical judgment of others in my office to those in my personal life who matter most.

As you can no doubt tell from this confession, I am no more forgiving of my own weaknesses than I am of others' lapses—at least those of people who are not my clients. But one of the wonderful things about the work I do is that I am constantly reflecting on what I do, how I do it, and how I can live my life more fully functioning. It all started with Manny.

CHAPTER TWO

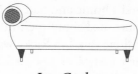

Jon Carlson

The Mummy at the Dining Room Table

In preparation for writing my contribution to this book, I tried to figure out just how many therapy sessions I've done in my life. I figure it has been somewhere close to fifty thousand hours over thirty years that I've spent with couples, families, and individuals. Choosing just one or two cases that seem most bizarre or unusual was really hard for me, but certainly some do stand out. Let's begin with a few short cases, then we'll go on to the main event.

THE MAN WHO WORE DIAPERS

In taking inventory of my notable cases, I recall one man who really stood out. Quite literally.

Li'l Ricky was a forty-one-year-old man whose presenting problem was that he felt compelled to wear diapers in public. I don't mean that he wore them underneath his clothes; I mean that he would take off all his clothes and just wear a diaper while walking around outside. This was no easy task, considering that he weighed somewhere over four hundred pounds.

This alarmed his family, of course. His parents were both factory workers who never owned a home and had no relatives other than Li'l Ricky. They were very concerned about their future and worried about who would take care of their son. Li'l Ricky was born when the couple had been in their early forties, at a point when they had accepted that they would have a childless life. They were delighted to have a child, even though both would have preferred a girl.

Li'l Ricky's parents were quite distraught about the way in which their wayward son had developed. They had tried everything they could think of to curtail his diaper outings, but nothing seemed to work. Finally they decided to just lock him in his room at night so he wouldn't embarrass them further by parading around in public with his huge blubbery belly hanging over the lip of the diaper.

As I began to talk with Li'l Ricky, it became apparent that what he really wanted most was to be a woman. He was secretly building a small guillotine device to cut off his penis so that he could have his wish. As he began to trust me, he confided that he was hoping to do this in my office. The only way I could think of to dissuade him was to plead that my secretary refused to clean up the mess this procedure would make. He seemed to buy this excuse, at least until such time that he could afford to have a proper sex-change operation. As a gesture of good faith, he brought me his half-built penile guillotine device. I'm no expert on such matters, but it looked to me as though it very well could have been operational.

Li'l Ricky definitely needed some guidance. He needed help moving out of his childlike role and taking on the responsibilities of adulthood. In order to do this, he needed skills and a job. Because he seemed to have considerable artistic ability, as manifested by his miniature guillotine construction, I suggested he might wish to seek employment using these skills. Indeed, he did eventually land a job as a graphic artist. And he managed to show up to work each day without wearing a diaper—at least one that was visible. When I last saw him, he was still living at home with his parents, but with penis still intact.

But this was not really my strangest case.

A NEW SOURCE OF REFERRALS

A couple of years ago, I got a rather unusual phone call.

"Is this Dr. Carlson?" a disembodied voice asked. I thought maybe it was a speaker phone.

"Yes it is. How can I help you?"

"I'm calling from the state UFO chapter."

Was this a fraternity, I wondered, or some sort of professional organization I had joined but for which I had forgotten to pay dues? I belong to so many of these associations that I can't keep them all straight.

"UFO?"

"Yes," the voice said rather haughtily, as if I were some kind of idiot because I didn't immediately recognize who this was. "You know, UFO, unidentified flying objects. We monitor these activities in the state, log the sightings, provide support for those who may have been abducted."

"Abducted?"

"Yes. As a matter of fact, I'm calling because I'm wondering if you work with people who have had encounters."

"Encounters?"

"Yes, encounters. We wondered if you have ever helped people who have seen aliens or been abducted by them."

"Uh, no," I admitted. "I haven't had much experience in that area."

"Well, that's fine. Not many professionals have, I suppose. It *is* a rather new specialty. But I'm certain you will see more and more such individuals as the number of encounters increases. And you can believe me when I tell you, Doctor, they *will* increase."

"I guess I'll just have to take your word for that."

"Ah hum. Well, what we were wondering, though, is whether you would be willing to see referrals in this area."

"Sure," I replied cheerfully. Heck, I will see almost anyone who walks in the door—the stranger the better as far as I'm concerned. That's one of the things I enjoy most about my work.

A woman of roughly average appearance soon showed up at my office. I don't know what I expected from someone who had spent time on other planets, as well as rocketing between them, but she was quite pleasant and, to my surprise, quite intelligent. She had spent the better part of seven years in college, amassing over two hundred credit hours without yet declaring a major or even coming close to graduation. I suppose I could say that she lacked focus. But this was hardly why she was coming to see me.

The woman had both a son and a daughter. The son would break down doors in the house. She would put him in his room, and he would get angry and kick down the doors. Before I could find out much more about this strange behavior, the woman informed me that her daughter had recently left town because the carnival had come through. She had met and fallen in love with a guy who worked for the carnival. He had told her that he was a trapeze artist, but it seemed more likely that he was just one of the guys who set up and maintained the equipment.

OK, I thought, trying to get all this down in our first couple of meetings. This woman hangs out with aliens. One of her children just joined the circus, and another likes to kick down doors. But there was more.

In addition to living with her husband and angry son, she had also invited her lover to move in with them. She would spend the night with her husband on Tuesdays, Thursdays, and Saturdays, and then would stay in the boyfriend's room on Mondays, Wednesdays, and Fridays. They would rotate Sundays.

"That sounds like an equitable arrangement," I observed, otherwise at a loss for words.

"We think so," she agreed. "But I'm not here to talk about that. I came here because they say that I need to talk about the aliens."

"All right. Let's begin."

And so our therapeutic relationship was launched. The therapy did include vivid descriptions of her abductions. The treatment, however, involved helping her with her more earthly concerns. She was eventually able to establish a different structure with her family. She ended the affair and had the boyfriend move out. She got her son on medication. She refused to allow her daughter to return home unless she was able pay rent or was willing to return to high school.

I felt pretty good about the progress we made, but the one thing that I couldn't seem to fix was her alleged contact with aliens. No matter what I tried, she insisted that these extraterrestrial relationships were out of her hands. Compared to the other things she had to deal with, though, I figured this was the least of her problems.

But hers really isn't the case I want to talk about either. I have another one, a better one, involving a family I am certain I will never forget.

THE ROCK

The first thing I noticed about Trina was how nervous she seemed. Her eyes darted from one end of the room to the other, looking left, right, almost as though she were checking for someone who might be hiding. Except for this marked apprehension—and let's face it, most people who come to see me are a little anxious—she appeared personable and attractive, although a little overweight. The only thing I found a bit disconcerting was that she had a tendency to jiggle her foot a lot when she talked. In a peculiar way it was as if her foot movements were connected to her brain activity, reflecting what she was thinking or talking about at the time.

Trina's nervousness seemed to extend to the ways she managed her life so carefully. She was particularly compulsive about being punctual. She always came to sessions early. Whatever time of day our appointments were scheduled, I would hear her entry into the waiting room ten, fifteen, sometimes thirty minutes before the appointed time. So I was surprised one day when she didn't show up at the scheduled time.

I was catching up on paperwork when Trina finally appeared, almost half an hour late.

"I'm *so* sorry," she apologized. "I'm so, so sorry."

"Hey, no big deal," I said. "So, what would you like to talk about today?"

"I just couldn't help it," she pleaded, returning again to her unforeseen lateness. I noticed that her foot was making large circular motions as she spoke.

"No problem," I reassured her once again.

"I just saw this rock in the middle of the road. I passed it while I was driving here."

"Uh huh," I said, not at all sure where this was going.

"I just couldn't get the image out of my head of that rock just sitting there. I had almost arrived here—I was just a few miles away—when I knew I had to drive back there to that place and pick up the rock."

"You drove all the way back toward your home to pick up a rock?" I hoped I didn't sound as incredulous as I felt. I didn't want to hurt her feelings.

She nodded her head sadly and then reached into her pocket to reveal the rock, as though wanting to show me the evidence. It looked pretty ordinary to me, just a rock about five inches in diameter.

FAMILY PHOTOS

Once we got past the rock—I placed it carefully on my desk—she continued to fill me in on her family history. It was easy to get lost in all the details. She thought her mother was probably a lesbian, and her father was an abusive alcoholic. She told me about her brother who was gay and her sister who lived by herself on a farm where her closest neighbor was five miles away. Then, in the midst of all this family information, she mentioned that if only she could lose some weight, she thought she might be able to get along better with her husband.

Trina's husband came to see me next. He was a large, hulking man with a crew cut, who seemed even more nervous than his wife. Throughout the whole time we visited, he kept his hands clasped, wringing them in a washing motion. I had this nearly irresistible impulse to hand him some soap.

"Well," Jake filled me in, "my wife's family is pretty strange, maybe more than mine, but we got our share of weirdos too."

"I'm not sure what you mean," I encouraged him; from the motion of his hands and Trina's accompaniment with her jiggling foot, I knew this was going to be a good story.

"You see, my sister . . . ?"

"Uh huh."

"See, she's got this daughter."

"That would be your niece," I said helpfully.

"Right. My niece. Anyway, the daughter just got engaged to this boy."

"Tell him her name, Jake," Trina piped in. Then to me: "Her name is Melba, like the cracker." She laughed nervously and bobbed her foot. "With a name like that, what do you expect."

"You should talk," Jake snapped at his wife, "with that family *you* got."

"You were saying that your niece just got engaged," I said, trying to get the story back on track.

"Right," Jake said, wringing his hands some more. "So we were all at my sister's house one day when she tells us this. Everybody was all excited and all—"

"Sure they were," Trina interrupted, "'cause nobody thought that girl would *ever* get married."

"I was saying," Jake continued, giving his wife a look that told her to let him finish. I couldn't help but agree with him. I was still wanting to find out where this was all going. And I still had to get back to Trina's family history.

"Where was I?" Jake asked.

"You were telling him about that crazy Melba cracker."

"Right. So, anyway, we're all sitting around. And my sister asks us if we want to see a picture of the boyfriend. So everybody said sure. We knew that woman was just so excited that her daughter was getting married. So she pulled this picture out of her purse, like she carried the damn thing in there all the time, just in case somebody might want to take a look at Melba's new fiancé."

"So tell him already," Trina jumped in impatiently. She looked at me with this huge grin, telling me this was going to be really good.

"All right. All right. Pipe down. So, anyway, I look at the picture and, truth to say, he's not a bad-looking ugly. Certainly not a model or anything, but a nice face."

"Tell him the rest," Trina said, her foot pumping.

"Well sir, in the picture, the guy had his pants down around his ankles. And he had this huge hard-on sticking straight out at full mast."

"A hard-on?" I said, not sure if I had heard him right.

"Yeah, he had this huge dick sticking straight out. And my crazy sister was so proud that her daughter was marrying this guy. She carries around this picture of him and his cock everywhere she goes. Probably pulls it out at the grocery store and shows it to the cashier, or anyone else she can find."

"Well, there's nothing like a proud mother-in-law," I mentioned, not knowing what else to say.

LONG-LOST AUNT

"So," Jake said to his wife, "now why don't you tell the doctor some more about your crazy family." He didn't like all this attention on him and wanted me to get back to Trina, since she was supposedly the one I was helping. Of course, the wife is almost always the identified patient, the one who brings the couple into therapy; but even though the problems usually have to do with both the husband and wife, I've learned not to challenge this too early, or the husband won't come back.

"OK, Trina," I encouraged her, "you were saying that your own family background was difficult."

"Don't forget to tell him about your brother and your aunt and all," Jake nudged her.

"I got this brother of mine who is sort of homosexual, he means. And my aunt who is sort of shy," Trina said.

"Your aunt doesn't feel very comfortable around others?"

Trina laughed nervously. Her foot started bobbing up and down so hard I thought she might lose her shoe. "Yeah, you could say that." Nervous laugh again. "She pretty much keeps to herself a lot, she and her family. The truth is I don't have much family around." She looked sad as she disclosed this.

"They don't get out much?" I prompted. I wasn't sure where this was going, but by the barometer of her foot, this story was going to top even that of Jake's niece and her fiancé.

"No, they pretty much stay inside. They're all kind of eccentric, you could say." Then Trina just stopped abruptly, as though she would go no further. She gave her husband a warning look, and this time he did not challenge her.

The therapy progressed reasonably well after that. I helped them learn to listen and to stop interrupting one another, so they developed better communication. I noticed that their nervous gestures seemed to diminish over time. But the one thing that was most frustrating for Trina was that she did not lose much weight. We also determined that she was fairly isolated. She had few friends and very little contact with anyone in her family. So we reached the point where Trina didn't think she would make further progress unless she was able to communicate with her family and understand them a lot better.

First, Trina tried to talk to her gay brother. He had been out of touch with everyone because he had never really felt accepted. Though he was happy to see her, he didn't have much to convey about the rest of the family. Then she called her sister, who had a lot of information, but it wasn't very useful or new. So finally she thought she would try the only other relative left alive, her aunt who she had told me was so shy. Trina hadn't seen or heard from this aunt in years, so she called her house but never got an answer. The few times that someone did pick up the phone—one of the kids—he said she was busy and couldn't come to talk. The aunt had seemed to disappear, never showing up at family functions with her husband and young kids. It was most peculiar.

Finally, Trina decided she would pay a surprise visit. She contacted her brother for support, and they both drove out to the house to check on things. They knocked on the door, but they were told firmly by her husband that their aunt couldn't come to the door. They continued to call and stop by, but each time, the uncle shooed them away and said the aunt was just not available.

THE MYSTERY

Exasperated and worried, Trina persisted in her efforts to make contact with her long-lost aunt.

"So we went back there again and again," Trina told me when we were alone in a session together. When Jake wasn't present, she would ordinarily be less nervous and more forthcoming. But by the look of her agitated foot, she was more anxious than I'd ever seen her.

"Finally, we called the police to check on things."

"So you were really worried."

"Wouldn't you be? I mean I hadn't seen her in years. And the longer I thought about it, I realized that I hadn't even talked to her on the phone in such a long time. We had been really close at one time, but then, all of a sudden, she just stopped all contact with me, with everyone."

"You were saying you called the police."

"Yeah, they went over there to find out what was going on. They knocked on the door, but my uncle wouldn't let them in the house. They threatened they'd get a search warrant, but he told them to go ahead. My uncle, his kids, were all standing at the door but they just wouldn't let anyone inside the house. When the police asked about my aunt, they said she was in the bath, and that was that. Then they slammed the door. The police had no choice but to leave."

"So," I said, "I guess that means you'll just leave this thing alone?"

"Hell no! I will not. There's something strange going on over there at the house, and I mean to find out what it is." With that, our session ended.

THE MUMMY

Trina returned to the next session alone again. She seemed to be a little more anxious than usual. I was in a playful mood and asked, "Another rock in the road?"

"Huh?"

"You just seem especially upset about something today. I wondered if you found another rock on the road."

"No, no rocks." She looked very sad.

"So then, what's going on?"

"Well, you won't believe this, but they found my aunt."

"That's great!"

"No, I mean the police found her."

"What do you mean? Was she lost?"

"No, actually she's dead."

"Dead?"

"Yeah, the police got a warrant and they went inside the house and they found her. She was dead." Tears began to fall down Trina's face. She was so upset even her foot stopped moving.

We sat for a while together, allowing her to grieve, and then I asked her what happened.

"She's been dead a long time," Trina said through the tears.

"You mean it had been several days?"

The foot started jiggling again. "No, I mean a long time."

"What's a long time?"

"Well, seven years actually."

"Wait a minute. Let me get this straight. The reason you haven't seen your aunt in so long is because she's been dead all these years?"

Trina just nodded her head.

"Well, was she buried in the house or something? I mean, what happened? A dead body would make an awful smell. Didn't the neighbors suspect anything?" I was filled with a dozen other questions, but then I realized I was more concerned about my own curiosity than her welfare.

"Well, what happened apparently is that my uncle and some weird dental doctor made her into a mummy."

I wasn't sure whether I should pursue the part about the dentist or the part about the mummy. "Go on."

"Really, she was a mummy just like you'd see on TV, stuffed and wrapped in some kind of coating. It's like in one of those old scary movies with the yellow wrinkly skin all around her. She even had hair on her head."

Apparently, the aunt had been having a series of medical problems that were not responding to traditional medicine, so she had consulted some fringe health practitioner who happened to be a dentist by training. He treated the aunt with a series of colonic enemas consisting of lemon juice and other substances that apparently became toxic through prolonged exposure. The aunt eventually died of these treatments.

Distraught with grief, the husband decided to have his wife embalmed and made into a mummy. That way, he and the children would not lose her presence and might be aided in their grief. So the aunt had been kept in the house all these years. They often propped her up at the head of the dining room table during mealtimes. This way she could oversee their family gatherings just as she had done when she was alive. Then, at night, the husband would carry his mummified wife to bed with him so they could sleep together. In the morning, the whole family would help get her dressed. They'd comb her hair—carefully, because it was starting to come out in tufts. Then they'd insert her in her favorite chair in front of the TV so she could watch the soaps and game shows during the day while they were all gone at school and work.

"So, what happened?" I asked Trina.

"What do you mean?"

"You know," I prodded her, "with your aunt's family." She had so many weird stories about her family, she would sometimes forget to finish them.

"Oh, that. Well, they buried my aunt and took the kids into protective services. But I think it was just a few months later that they went back to live with their father and the dentist."

"You mean the guy who killed his wife?"

"That very one."

MAKING SENSE OF STRANGE CASES

Although my client sounds peculiar, she was actually a very nice woman. I liked her a lot and looked forward to our sessions. In spite of her eccentricities, and those in her family, she was reasonably successful at buying houses with her husband, fixing them up, and then selling them at a profit. She did the same thing with boats, then with cars. She was always buying and selling things, which didn't make for a lot of stability in her life. During the time that I worked with her, she was probably in nine or ten different houses.

Even after Trina and her husband left treatment, I still kept thinking about them. I wondered what had happened to the mummy family as well. But as Jeffrey mentioned in his story, that's the frustrating thing about doing therapy—people sometimes leave before we are ready to let them go.

When I encounter really weird stuff like this case, I always wonder what the purpose is of this behavior. How does it work for the person?

The mummy was a difficult one to understand. Apparently, the family just found it hard to let their mother go. As long as she was present, she was holding them together. The other strange thing about the case was that when psychological evaluations were done on everyone in the family, they all turned out to be pretty normal.

CHAPTER THREE

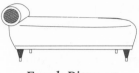

Frank Pittman

Buzzy Bee's Oral Fixation

Frank Pittman is one of the leading voices of moral authority in the profession. In his columns for Psychology Today *and* Psychotherapy Networker, *as well as in his books about commitment in relationships, Pittman is not shy about expressing his views about what is good for people (as you will see in this chapter).*

Trained originally as a psychiatrist, Pittman embraced a family systems approach to his work early in his career. He has also devoted a significant amount of effort trying to understand the ways that boys and men are socialized into their gender roles. Consistently in his writing and speaking about issues of fidelity and intimacy, Pittman emphasizes the importance of being morally responsible for one's choices and behavior.

At first glance, you might imagine that his emphasis on taking responsibility for one's behavior is consistent with a more behavioral approach, yet Pittman is very much a student of history and a respecter of larger family systems. In fact, in his popular movie reviews, he commonly examines contemporary films in the context of their historical origins and how they reflect our culture.

A few of his best-known books include Turning Points: Treating Families in Transition and Crisis; Private Lies: Infidelity and the Betrayal of Intimacy; Man Enough: Fathers, Sons, and the Search for Masculinity; *and* Grow Up! How Taking Responsibility Can Make You a Happy Adult.

In addition to being incredibly articulate, Pittman is just mischievous and provocative enough that he is often consulted by national talk shows when they want a mature, sober voice of authority about mental health issues.

—*w*—

Pittman told us that his most memorable case goes back forty years to his psychiatric residency in the early 1960s. As was not atypical for the times, he was going through intensive training to become a psychoanalyst who would specialize in long-term, individually based treatments.

"I can't get Buzzy Bee out of my head," Frank began the conversation.

"Buzzy what?"

"Not what. Who. Buzzy Bee was his name." This was the name by which Pittman thought about the one patient who has haunted him beyond all others.

"I first worked with Buzzy for a couple years, then went to Denver to do some work keeping families out of hospitals. When I returned to Atlanta six years later as chief of psychiatric services for the big public hospital where I'd first seen him, Buzzy showed up again, and I ended up working with him for another twenty years."

"So this was brief therapy," Jeffrey commented. "A lesser man would have taken at least forty years to cure this guy."

Pittman laughed appreciatively. "Well," he continued modestly, "I don't know whether he got anything out of the therapy or not, but I sure learned a lot."

"So tell us about it already," we said impatiently.

Frank Pittman is not a man to be rushed. With his soft Southern accent and gentlemanly manner, he is a born storyteller. He insisted on going at his own pace and telling the tale in his own way.

"I am really disappointed in myself when I encounter some people whose problems are so familiar that I go on automatic pilot. Unless it is something I am hearing for the first time, unless it is something that challenges me, I fear that not only am I wasting my own time but theirs also. I'm just not being stimulated by what people are going through, however unique it might seem to them at the time."

Before he resumed the narrative, Pittman wanted to explain how all behavior, especially sexual behavior, is shaped by our earliest experiences of what is attractive. Even though he is a seasoned family systems therapist, his psychoanalytic roots are still deeply embedded in his thinking.

"I remember a guy whose wife was complaining because he was screwing around so much. This was his fifth wife. He came in and explained that he had sex with lots of people. He had had sex with all of his wives of course, plus several thousand other women, a couple hundred men, and even a few people who were going through sex-change operations."

Although we laughed appropriately, Pittman is not actually amused by this sort of thing. Commitment and fidelity are important themes in his work with couples.

"In addition to all his sexual partners, the guy tells me that his first sexual experience was with the next-door neighbor's mule when he was twelve. He said that despite all the people that he had had sex with, he still gets a hard-on whenever he sees a cute mule. So I found out early on that people's initial sexual experiences really kind of mark them and signal what they are going to be attracted to. I think of that often when I think about Buzzy."

THINGS ARE DIFFERENT GROWING UP IN THE COUNTRY

"Buzzy Bee was an illiterate sixth-grade dropout from rural Alabama," Pittman continued. "I know rural Alabama. I grew up there, in a family different from Buzzy's but probably just as crazy. It is a good place to be crazy—nobody notices. Anyway, Buzzy's father had left with another woman and hadn't been heard from since. His mother was retarded and on welfare. They lived in a little cabin with a dirt floor. The mother had never gone to the movies in her life. She certainly had never read a book. There was no television or anything of that sort. But they did have a grandfather who was a Holy Roller preacher obsessed with sex. He was a domineering, controlling old man who was erratic and unpredictable, and he instilled fear in his family. He would come out to their house and give lectures about the horrors of sex and then he'd beat them."

Ironically, all this talk about sex stirred up Buzzy and his older sister. This was rural Alabama, and there were not many other kids around for miles, and not a lot of entertainment, so they started having sex together. A lot.

After conversing about sex with mules and then incest, Pittman commented on a book he was reviewing about sex.

"I just realized how different sex seems for people who come from the rural South," Pittman observed. "You have to understand: when you grow up in the country there are not a lot of people around, and things are different."

We laughed again, and Pittman joined us, but there was also an edge to what he said. "So Buzzy had an incestuous relationship with his older sister by the time he was nine. He started giving blow jobs to boys at school for money when he was ten. They kicked him out of school because they couldn't stop him from giving blow jobs; apparently, this was the only thing he'd ever done that anyone appreciated. So he dropped out of school and supported himself as a male prostitute from the time he was twelve to age sixteen, when he got into serious trouble."

"You mean he wasn't in trouble yet?"

"This was a small town in Alabama, and guys just don't go around offering everybody oral sex on demand. Buzzy would go from door to door and ask if he could give people blow jobs. It was the only skill that he had developed so far in his life."

Buzzy was eventually run out of town. He ended up living in Atlanta, where he met Sue, who was fifteen at the time. Although only sixteen himself, Buzzy got her pregnant and married her and moved in with her parents.

"It was around Christmastime, and he didn't have any money to buy presents, so he offered his father-in-law a blow job. That led to an affair with his wife's father that went on for a few years."

"OK, Frank." Slow down, we warned him, trying to take all of this in. Buzzy's only skill in life was giving oral sex to other men. He was married but having an affair with his wife's father. We were trying to sort all this out when Pittman added more, far more to the story.

By this time, Buzzy was now eighteen, with a new baby, still unable to find a job because he is illiterate and has no other skills except his oral fixation. Sue's mother now discovered that her son-in-law was sleeping with her husband *and* her daughter. This didn't go over too well, so she kicked Buzzy out of the house. Sue was not crazy about the idea either and decided she wanted nothing further to do with this strange guy who couldn't read and write, couldn't hold a job, and certainly couldn't be trusted.

Sue's parents divorced. On top of all that, Buzzy was now homeless, unemployed, and unable to see his child. This brought on an anxiety attack. He began hyperventilating and thought he was having a heart attack. He was brought to the hospital, which was when Pittman first saw him.

THE PATIENT AND SUPERVISOR

Remember, during the first phases of his treatment with Buzzy, Pittman was in a psychoanalytic residency. That meant that his strong inclination was to look at cases from the perspective of a Freudian who would no doubt notice that this was a rather severe case of oral fixation.

"He was the sweetest, dumbest, most agreeable child," Pittman said of his first impression of Buzzy. "But he was eighteen and the father of a two-year-old. I started working with him, put him on some Sinequan, a tricyclic antidepressant. I got him to use birth control. I helped him a bit with his reality testing about what was socially acceptable and what was not." In other words, he told Buzzy it was probably not a good idea for him to keep offering blow jobs to other men. People might get the wrong impression.

"He was horrified that people would think he was homosexual. Just because he was giving these people blow jobs, it didn't mean that he was gay. He insisted he was definitely heterosexual. This was a matter of considerable pride.

"My supervisor didn't really think this was a treatable case but was trying nonetheless to teach me psychoanalytic technique. So I would pretend to do it my supervisor's way while I was doing something I didn't want my supervisor to know about. I was providing all sorts of reality testing and really reparenting for Buzzy. I was trying to give him what a father would have provided."

Pittman didn't realize that this was what he was doing at the time, but in reflecting back on the case, he realized that he was trying to undo the influence of the crazy, sex-obsessed grandfather. "I saw Buzzy with his wife a few times, which was a big no-no to my supervisor. I even helped him get a job driving a milk truck. He got back on his feet.

"The real difficulties began when he and Sue reconciled. Sue's mother was so vengefully angry at her husband for having this affair with his son-in-law that she was violently opposed to Sue reconciling with Buzzy."

The mother blackmailed Sue: She had to end the relationship with Buzzy, or the mother would break off all future contact with her. This was strong leverage because the mother was providing most of the child care for their little girl.

"It also didn't help matters much," Pittman added, "that I was following the direction of my psychoanalytic supervisor when this case clearly did not fit those parameters."

"I'm just trying to picture the parameters that this would fit," Jon said.

"I was doing some couples therapy. As it turned out, I was just too chicken to call in Sue's mother, much less Sue's father, or the retarded mother back in Alabama, or the psychotic Holy Roller grandfather. I had the idea of doing so, but then I feared he'd come in handling a snake or two."

Pittman was referring to the now accepted practice of inviting into session as many members of the family system as possible. This allows for the most possible leverage in producing changes that go beyond an individual person to the whole underlying family structure. It also helps take the heat off one person by looking at everyone's contributions to the shared problems.

In addition to holding the joint sessions between Buzzy and Sue, Pittman spent an inordinate amount of time trying to combat Buzzy's obsessive guilt about possibly being gay. These thoughts were so disturbing to Buzzy that they virtually took over his life. He heard voices accusing him of being gay.

"It is interesting looking back on this now and realizing that my patient and my supervisor were both obsessed in matters of sexual identity and sexual feelings. Neither one of them seemed to have any concept of functioning responsibly or acting like a grownup. The big question for both of them was whether Buzzy was somehow innately homosexual. Maybe he had a misshapen brain that made him homosexual, or perhaps this was a result of being molested as a child by his older sister. Another possibility was that he was a psychopath of some sort."

Pittman reminded us that this was forty years ago, when there were some very different ways of looking at these issues.

"There was very little concept of sex as being something learned. Sexual attractions—whether toward men or women or tall blondes or short brunettes or mules or chickens—were thought to come from innate nature rather than life experiences. And this is what we ended up devoting most of our work toward. Buzzy was feeling that God was going to get him for having any sort of thoughts and feelings that were different from those he was 'supposed' to have.

"What was so fascinating was how similar my psychoanalytic supervisor was to Buzzy's grandfather. They were both obsessed with what people's feelings are, with not 'lusting in your heart.' The effort is to get the feelings right, while the behavior itself gets treated as if it is beyond your control."

Pittman had a great time working with Buzzy. He enjoyed the novelty of the case and the challenges it presented. In supervision, there was a lot of debate over diagnosis, about whether this was a case of paranoid schizophrenia, mental retardation, sociopathy, or a half-dozen other possibilities. "I learned a lot," Pittman confided, and then said dryly, "and after all, this was my residency."

Pittman was also feeling pretty good about the progress so far.

"I had gotten Buzzy off the streets. He was out of the male prostitute business, into the milk delivery business. I had done enough couples therapy to get him back with his wife and baby. I had provided him with an adult male figure who could find something of value in him other than sex. Once he was stabilized on medication, he stopped having hyperventilation episodes. So I thought I had done a pretty good job."

WHAT WAS MISSED

We applauded Pittman's efforts, especially so early in his career and with such a complex case. But he was reluctant to take too much credit for what he viewed as limited success.

"Yeah, I guess so. But I missed so much because I really had been getting him to focus on his thoughts and feelings rather than getting him to engage in social learning by focusing on the world around him."

Pittman explained about the nature of the field during the early 1960s. All the focus was on psychology and biology and individual behavior, but very little attention was devoted to sociology and the larger context in which behavior takes place. In this case, context was everything—because of both where Buzzy grew up and his family circumstances.

"It seems so strange when I look back on it—the hours that I sat there with him as we tried to decide who he felt attracted to and who he was not attracted to. There was so much shame about what was going on in his head. All of this was bullshit and utterly beside the point. It was as beside the point as that guy and his mule."

Pittman was referring back to the promiscuous man who had hundreds of affairs as a way to distance himself from his marriage and his family. His behavior was not about having sex but about running away from intimacy and about avoiding responsibility and growing up.

"The guy with the mule was not really doing anything to help his children. He never really felt like an adult, so he was always at the dawn of puberty. He had just sprouted his first pubic hair overnight, and he wasn't quite sure what direction it pointed in. But the therapy that was commonly taught and practiced in the 1960s somehow assumed that people had a solid core of mental health, had incorporated all the world's store of social reality testing and wisdom, and knew far more than they really did about how life worked. It was presumably all inside us, and it is the therapist's job to free them up from whatever hang-up or perversity keeps us from using all that wisdom."

Pittman paused for a moment, then added: "Guys like Buzzy and the muleman may have the best of intentions but a faulty instruction book. They have brains, bodies, and genitals but no idea how to use them as grown men. What the man with the mule needed was the same thing that Buzzy and so many other immature men need—a father who can teach them how to be men."

In looking back on his work with Buzzy and so many other men during those decades, Pittman regrets that he didn't yet have the understanding and courage to tell them what he knew, to pass on his wisdom. The psychoanalytic stance was instead to be withholding and enigmatic.

"Even today, I don't know whether Buzzy was schizophrenic, but he was certainly an inadequate personality. I don't know whether that was innate or whether he had severe attention deficit disorder, which I think was probably the case. But what he needed most was for someone to tell him how to behave and what to do."

SIX YEARS LATER

Buzzy went out into the world, reconciled with his wife, holding a reasonable job driving a milk truck and restraining himself from acting out on his oral fixation. Pittman went off to a job in Colorado and lost touch with Buzzy for six years until he returned to Atlanta to begin the hospital administrative job.

"Buzzy reappeared. He and Sue had been off and on. She started to look like her father to him, so he continued his obsessions about that affair. He was finding that having sex with Sue made him feel more homosexual rather than heterosexual because she kept reminding him of her father."

During the years he had been away, Pittman had referred Buzzy to another therapist. "This therapist was trying to decide whether Buzzy was really homosexual or not. He was trying to push him back into a homosexual identity, which was scaring Buzzy to death. So he broke off the therapy and was left to his own devices."

Pittman believes that human beings are not just bisexual but omnisexual. "We can all have sex successfully with men, women, children, machines, animals, and certain kinds of plants. Even mules. It hardly matters what we are attracted to. We end up being attracted to whoever or whatever has given us sexual pleasure most recently. I believe that trying to find some deeper meaning in that is disempowering. It leaves people at the mercy of their impulses rather than being able to make their own choices."

This point of view is important to understanding Pittman's next point. Buzzy dropped out of treatment with his new therapist because he saw where things were going, that he was inevitably going to be labeled that which he most dreaded. Pittman blamed himself for buying into this dichotomy instead of realizing that these categories of homosexual-heterosexual were irrelevant.

In order to affirm his masculinity and heterosexuality, Buzzy got involved with another (married) woman. This relationship was much easier for him because he had not had sex with the woman's father. He was also still living with Sue at the time and still driving a milk truck.

He was picking up milk one day when another truck ran over him, injuring him to the extent that he could no longer do any heavy lifting. He was in the hospital with a crushed pelvis and broken hips when he again contacted Pittman for help.

"Dorcas, his latest sex partner, was pregnant and about to have his baby. His wife, Sue, didn't know about this, so he was in quite a fix.

"I got all of that story out in the open. I helped him and Sue to deal with all this. I met with Buzzy and his sister to work through that old incestuous relationship. I got him into vocational rehabilitation, and they sent him to barber school. I worked with him and Sue for the next few years, as Sue came to accept his child with Dorcas and even to help him in doing things for that child as well. He didn't have enough money yet, since he was still in barber school. It all got pretty crazy because he was still at the mercy of whatever he was feeling, and from time to time he would run back and forth between Sue and Dorcas. Sweet Sue, so eternally loyal and tolerant and so wise and competent (and self-sacrificing), outlasted Dorcas, who went back to her husband but accepted whatever help Buzzy could offer their daughter. Neither Buzzy nor I could ever get Sue to give up on him."

BARBER TO HAIR STYLIST

Buzzy graduated from barber school. He began group therapy to help stabilize himself. He began practicing his new trade, and things went pretty well for the next few years. His daughter graduated from high school, the first person in his family ever to do so, and this was a source of never-ending pride to him. Pittman found it incredible and extremely gratifying that Buzzy could help raise children, considering that Buzzy was still such a kid himself and continued to act that way. After his affair with Dorcas ended, he took up next with Penny, a hairdresser with whom he worked. Buzzy had high hopes that this latest girlfriend could keep him on the straight and narrow path, so to speak.

"Buzzy never did anything homosexual again," Pittman explained, "but he couldn't get his life with Sue back. When he didn't feel man enough with Sue, he would get involved with various women who reaffirmed his masculinity. Meanwhile I was trying to teach him that if he wanted to be a man, he could affirm his masculinity through responsibility, not through sex. To be a father and a husband means someone who shows up on time. I was trying to retrain him to think in this way, but, being fatherless, it was very, very difficult for him. People who are not real bright tend to remember the first thing they learn on any subject and forget what comes next."

It went better with Penny, who taught him to read and write a little bit and helped him in other ways. He was doing well as a barber, but then business turned bad. This was the 1970s, when barbers went out of fashion and everyone wanted "hair stylists" instead.

"The problem for Buzzy," Pittman said with a chuckle, "is that he didn't want to become a 'hair stylist' because that just seemed too gay. He wanted to stay a barber because that was manly. He struggled with this a lot, but he never, despite all of our efforts—and this had been going on for years by now—developed any sense of himself. He left the therapy group. He couldn't pay his bills. The barbering business got worse. He left the group abruptly and didn't return again for some time. He was ashamed of himself for not making enough money, and he ran away from Penny as well."

Over the next ten years, Buzzy would show up occasionally in the midst of some crisis or other. He could rarely pay for therapy, but that was fine with Pittman.

"I couldn't get him to stay in the group because he felt too guilty about not being able to pay for it. I would come to my office in the morning, and there would be a box of old classical records that he had picked up at garage sales and dropped off at my office as payment. Every year or so, there would be something like that waiting for me. He would call me to tell me good news about his daughters and to reassure me he was being a good father. Sometimes he would call if there was a major crisis with him, and I could sometimes talk him into coming to see me.

"Sue, who never married again but had success as an X-ray technician (she could see through anybody), hovered over him no matter what woman he was sleeping with, and no therapist could talk her into giving up on him. Buzzy would get into a fix of some sort and would run back to her. And she would take him in and help him out every time. She would call me to say that he was moving from one barber shop to another or from one woman to another. Then last year—he was almost sixty—I got a call from Sue, who told me that Buzzy had died from a heart attack. As he was dying, he had asked her to call me and tell me that he had never forgotten me, that he never went back to his old ways, and that he had been a good father to both his daughters. He just wanted me to know."

LOOKING BACK

Pittman had spent over forty years off and on with Buzzy Bee, almost all of their adult lives. Frank still has regrets about what he didn't know and didn't understand at the time. He thinks about all the ways he could handle such a case differently today.

"I would have stood firm with the idea that his obsession about his sexual orientation didn't matter and it didn't mean anything. Sex takes place in your 'nads [gonads], and that leaves traces in your brain. It's not the other way around."

We remarked that for such a simple-minded person, Buzzy was certainly a complex case. He didn't know how to act like a proper schizophrenic.

"He didn't know how to act like a nonschizophrenic," Pittman said, returning to the theme he introduced earlier about the role of therapists to teach people how to act. "He would hear voices; he would get these paranoid ideas that people were looking at him and declaring him homosexual. He was a handsome child when I first met him, but as he was getting older, he feared he was losing his looks. He was afraid that people would think he looked gay. He grew a beard to appear more manly. This was an obsession that was with him for a lifetime. And as with so many other people I have seen who are consumed with schizophrenia, the better you get to know them, the less there is that barrier between sanity and insanity. If nobody teaches you how to be a man, if you don't have any models, then you are always faking it. You are always in a somewhat paranoid position and you can very easily look very crazy."

This was clearly a seminal case in Frank Pittman's professional development. Buzzy really was the most memorable patient he had ever seen, not just because of his strange behavior and obsessions, not just because of the amount of time they spent together, but because of everything he learned about doing therapy.

"I now move in a whole lot closer with people. I'm less afraid of adopting them. I'm less afraid of imposing my reality on people. I assume that people do the things they do because they don't know the difference—they have the best of intentions and a faulty instruction book. They are misinformed how to live a life. It's my job to learn from all of my other patients how you can screw up, and how you can recover, and then make whomever I am seeing more aware of what the possibilities are. Any of my patients who have got any sort of issues related to sexual identity have heard about Buzzy, have heard about the guy with the mule, and between the two of them, those two stories pull it all together."

DON'T ASK

The story was over now, and we were all silent. There was a reverence that we all felt toward this case. With all the complexities and twists and turns in the story, we felt uncertain about where we should go next. Frank broke the silence first.

"If you ever have sex with a man or a woman or a child or a mule, you will never forget it; it will impact what you feel thereafter. I once saw a guy who could only have sex with one-legged women. He said that if you ever have sex with a one-legged woman, you will never be satisfied with two legged-women instead."

"And that's because?"

Pittman laughed. "Don't ask." Returning to our previous topic, Frank remarked what a wonderful guy that Buzzy was in spite of his eccentricities. People loved this guy. He always gave everything he had to anyone who was nice to him. Sue told me that Dorcas, Penny, Buzzy's sister, and both his daughters had all been at the funeral. They all cut him a lot of slack. They did not expect him to be like normal people. You can't expect people to be normal if they never knew anyone normal growing up.

"I saw a guy who I also think about along with Buzzy and the mule man, another man who had grown up in a strange family. His father was sleeping with the daughter. His mother would put on a striptease show for this guy and his brothers while the three would sit on the floor and masturbate. Eventually, this guy had sex with everybody in the family, except his own sister, so after the rehearsal dinner when the sister was getting married, they had sex as well. This guy's father was also a Holy Roller preacher obsessed with sex, but he believed that the best way to control such feelings is to act on them. He sincerely thought that was the best way to deliver yourself from temptation."

Pittman didn't find it the least surprising that when this guy became a doctor, he would invite the nurses, his patients, and all the medical students of both genders to have sex with him.

"This was very upsetting to his wife, so I worked with him for a while and he stopped doing it. Rather than exploring why he did it, or what sort of feelings he might have that would lead to this behavior, I just explained to him that he had been misinformed. This is not the way people do things. This is not socially acceptable, and he is going to get into trouble. That had some meaning for him, while all the therapy that he had before then had focused on what his feelings were and what sort of trauma might have led to those feelings. Nobody slapped his hand and told him to stop it. Which is one of the things I do."

CHAPTER FOUR

Arnold Lazarus

An Oedipal Dilemma

As the theorist who first coined the term behavior therapy, *Arnold Lazarus has spent much of his distinguished career broadening the base of his thinking to embrace other approaches to human change. His Multimodal Therapy was one of the first, if not the most enduring, integrative therapeutic systems. In its assessment process, Multimodal Therapy combines a focus on behavior with cognitive, emotional, sensory, interpersonal, imaginal, and physiological features.*

Lazarus first developed his method during his early years as a psychologist in South Africa in the 1960s. After a decade of practice, he published his ideas about a more eclectic approach in Behavior Therapy and Beyond *(1971). Subsequent to joining the faculty at Stanford, Yale, and Temple universities, he settled at Rutgers University for most of his career.*

Lazarus has published eighteen books and over 250 professional papers covering a variety of clinical interests. Some of his best-known works include The Practice of Multimodal Therapy *and* Brief But Comprehensive Psychotherapy: The Multimodal Way. *Lazarus has also written several popular books for the public, including* I Can If I Want To; Marital Myths Revisited: A Fresh Look at Two Dozen Mistaken Beliefs

About Marriage; and The 60 Second Shrink: 101 Strategies for Staying Sane in a Crazy World (which he coauthored with his son, Clifford N. Lazarus).

Lazarus is a distinguished-looking professional with snowy gray hair and a slim, regal presence. His sharp wit and distinctive South African accent make it necessary to concentrate more than usual on what he says, lest your attention wander and you miss something amusing or important.

When we asked Lazarus about his own qualifications to be included in a book about the most unforgettable cases of famous therapists, he responded with his usual good humor. "As you know, there is a huge difference between experience and expertise. We all know experienced therapists—that is, colleagues who have been around for a long time—and yet we may regard them as mediocre at best. Truly effective therapists, in my opinion, are people who exude warmth, confidence, caring, understanding, genuine concern, and who are intelligent, wise, tactful, and persuasive."

He would be too modest to say so, but this is an exact description of Arnie Lazarus. What did surprise us, however, is that for someone who is best known for his contributions to behavior therapy and cognitive therapy, he now sounds more like a relationship therapist, which of course, is what we all are anyway.

—⁓—

"If you want to talk about strange," Lazarus began, "then there is one case that comes to mind, but I rather hesitate to tell you."

Of course he had us hooked. Knowing how long Lazarus has been in practice and how many difficult cases had been referred to him by less experienced and expert practitioners, we knew there was a potential gold mine in his head.

"Go ahead," Jon encouraged. Both of us held our breath for the long seconds it took for Lazarus to decide whether to go on or not.

"I've always had difficulty," he said, "when I am asked to focus on one thing when a slew of them come to mind. I have seen thousands of people over the years, and most of them are totally forgotten, since my senile dementia is now very advanced."

We laughed appreciatively. Arnie's memory, just like his command of language, is flawless.

THE REUNION

"OK," Lazarus starts, then takes a breath. He isn't sure if he wants to talk about this case or not. We don't want to push him, but neither do we want to let him off the hook if he is willing to open up and talk about this peculiar case.

"This woman comes to see me," he starts again. "She is in her forties—late forties—and the story goes that her father had abandoned the family when she was about two months old. She had heard her mother talk about what a bastard he was, but she decided as an adult to look up her daddy. She did indeed track him down. He was, by that time, in his seventies and working on his fourth marriage.

"What happened was that she basically wanted to find out why her father left, and other pedestrian details. One thing led to another, and the two of them started screwing."

Lazarus continued with the narrative, but neither of us was hearing him at that point. He was so matter-of-fact in the way he was telling the story that we were still wondering if we heard him right. Did he just say that his client had begun a sexual relationship with her father?

"Talk about Oedipus schmedipus," we next heard Lazarus say as we rejoined the story. "So, the reason she comes to me for therapy is that she is feeling very guilty because here she is having an affair with her father. On top of that, she tells me that she had never had such good sex, never had so many orgasms, and that the guy can screw like a rattlesnake."

We are laughing now, part of it the result of shock (and we thought we'd heard it all!) and part of it because we can't get the image out of our heads of what a rattlesnake must look like while it is screwing.

"She was very, very conflicted," Lazarus adds—unnecessarily. "She was certainly unhappy about it, but here is the upside: the lady is married to a guy who barely ekes out a living. Daddy has megabucks, and he starts buying her jewelry and clothes. He picks up a lot of the rent and gets her a car. The husband, and everyone else, thinks that this is a repentant father who feels bad. It appears all very innocent to see the father showering his long-lost daughter with money and gifts."

Lazarus paused for a moment, then asked, "Shall I go on?"

"Sure," Jon answered in a squeaky voice, panicked at the very thought that he might leave us hanging.

"Then what happens," Lazarus continued with a lilt in his voice. He was teasing us, knowing he had us spellbound. He told us that the father had a plan that the two of them should dump their respective spouses and move in together, the seventy-year-old father and his forty-seven-year-old daughter/lover.

"It was at this point," Lazarus said, "that she was kind of thinking that things might have gone a little too far."

Lazarus stopped the story for a minute to back up to what he considered the crucial turning point. He stressed that all the while he was listening to this incredible story, he was wondering to himself what he was supposed to do with her.

"What do I say to her? What would most of my colleagues say? Do I read her the morality act? Do I whip out the Bible? What do I do?"

We were wondering exactly that. We were thinking about what we would say to a client who brings us such a predicament. We were also feeling very grateful that this was Arnie's case and not our own. And we were dying to find out just what he did do with her. This time he didn't keep us waiting long.

"Look," Lazarus said to his client, "let's examine this thing closer. The truth of the matter is that psychologically this is not your father. He is your father solely from a biological perspective. So while indeed there is this affair going on that might shock some people, in a sense it is not within the context of a genuine father-daughter relationship."

Now *that* was a creative reframing of a situation that would have never occurred to us. Lazarus introduced the idea that because she never knew the man before, because she met him as an adult, she had never thought of him as a father, nor did he think of her as a daughter. In that sense, the two of them were just strangers who met, had a brief affair, and then decided to end it. Now if the father wanted to buy her presents, there was no reason to feel guilt.

The intervention worked well, and the woman felt immediately relieved. Not so our intrepid therapist, who was worried that maybe he had gone too far, that his moral neutrality might be subject to criticism. Even during our conversation, as he relived the case, Arnie felt some hesitance about whether it was OK to tell the story, and especially the part about his role in forgiving her. There are many professionals who would justifiably believe that this old man was exploiting and abusing his daughter, especially after abandoning her since infancy. Even though she was a consenting adult in this relationship, she was hardly on an equal footing with him in terms of power.

LISTENING WITHOUT JUDGMENT

Although Lazarus is known far and wide as one of the major action-oriented theorists, he admitted that in this case he was more like Carl Rogers, the originator of humanistic, relationship-oriented therapy. Lazarus listened to his client without judgment. Once she confessed her terrible secret, he responded with acceptance of her as a person and with forgiveness for her behavior that he labeled as less than sinful and more as an understandable mistake. This was especially understandable in light of the ways she had been exploited by her father.

We asked Lazarus about whether the client might tell a different version of the story than the one he had told. What would she say that was different?

Lazarus pondered for a while and then said, "Nothing that I can think of."

"Nothing?" We were surprised by that answer. In these times when so-called constructivist therapies (those that help people look critically at their lives) are increasingly popular, it is common to talk about multiple realities and different perceptions of the same events. Besides, after all these many years, how could he know what she'd think? We were surprised again when he told us that he had recently seen her again when she returned for treatment.

"I had the occasion to see her again because of problems with her husband. She discovered that he had an affair, and this has created turmoil in the marriage. So I saw them together for a while as a couple. When I saw her alone, she reminded me of this story, as if I would have forgotten. She admitted that she couldn't very well be critical of his lover since she was the one who had the affair to beat all affairs. Nevertheless, she was still upset over her husband's dalliance."

Lazarus was still intrigued with the question we had asked about what she might have said that was different from his version of the story. He speculated that she might have heard something a little different from what he meant.

"For example," we pointed out, "that my therapist said that it was OK for me to have an affair with my father . . ."

". . . because from a psychological perspective he wasn't really my father," Lazarus finished.

"He even wrote me a note telling me it was OK, in case anyone asked."

"Notarized," Lazarus joked.

"Did you find it surprising that she came back to see you?" Jon asked Arnie.

"She knew Arnie would forget the case anyway," Jeffrey interjected.

Rather than finding this amusing, Lazarus turned uncharacteristically serious. It was obvious that what he was about to say was very important to him.

"No, I wasn't surprised she came back. I would bump into her from time to time, and there was always a big hello, like she was really glad to see me. She trusted me. She knew that I respected her, that I never looked down on her, or judged her in any way. She felt accepted by me in a way that she never had by her father, or most of the people in her life."

Of course, the only issue was hardly the respect Lazarus felt toward his patient, as if she [were the one who] had single-handedly committed a sin deserving of guilt. Even if she had set about trying to seduce the old man as a way to punish him, the father was more than a little culpable.

DIFFERENT PATHS

Given the moral issues implicit in this challenging case, we asked Lazarus what he would have done differently if the woman walked in for help today. As it turns out, he had talked with a number of trusted colleagues about the case over the years, curious what they would have done in these circumstances. Perhaps not surprisingly, the reactions he heard ran the gamut from a full validation of his own strategy to utter horror that he would have proceeded in such a way as to virtually endorse her behavior. Then there were others who wondered why he focused exclusively on her behavior and not that of her father. This, of course, is what usually happens when we consult with colleagues—not just with unusual cases but sometimes the most common sort. Ask a dozen different therapists what they would do in almost *any* situation and you'll likely get an assortment of different reactions.

Although Lazarus can understand why some therapists might take issue with his approach, it amazes him that some so-called professionals can be so judgmental of others.

"Do they think it would have been helpful to her to berate her? If this had become a repetitive thing, that she sought out relatives with whom she could have sex, then we would have a problem. But this was clearly a one-time unique deal for her. So why pathologize it?"

In looking back on how he handled things, he really couldn't think of anything he would have done differently. For Lazarus, the main question he asked himself was whether anyone was harmed by what was done. He also concluded that this relationship had not been indicative of any other underlying pathology.

Out of genuine curiosity, because we ourselves were still stumped about how we would have handled things, we asked what alternative plans Lazarus had heard from his colleagues. It is always interesting to compare notes about how others would deal with a particular therapeutic challenge.

"I think most people I talked to would have indicated to her that this was really a very unfortunate action to have taken. Did she have to go so far as screwing the guy instead of just being friendly and daughterly? They would have also looked in greater detail at whether what she did represented her as a sexual being. How was this part of some ongoing pattern?"

Another obvious avenue to pursue was the power inequality in this relationship. The father was hardly an innocent, passive recipient of the sexual advances. And it was never really clear who initiated the sexual advances. In any case, the father represented an idealized object of longing for the daughter, someone she had thought about her whole life, someone she tracked down just so she could find out why she had been abandoned. She was clearly needy, vulnerable, and yearning for attention. He literally screwed her a second time.

Lazarus mentioned that there are many "moralists" in the field who are interested not only in helping their own clients but also in policing the ranks of the rest of us to make certain that we are living up to their particular notions about what is good for people.

The discussion now turned from Lazarus back to us. Lazarus asked Jon what he would have done with this woman's case.

"I would feel like a deer caught in the headlights," Jon confessed. "What do I do now? I like what you did, Arnie, in terms of looking at the impact of the behavior. Who was harmed? I guess I would be curious at the reasons for them getting involved in that way."

Jeffrey admitted that he probably would not have thought about reframing things the way that Lazarus had. Of course, in those days reframing as a common strategy had not yet been formally invented.

"The part that would have struck me the most," Jeffrey said further, "was the anger that she must have felt toward her father. I don't know if she seduced her father or if her father seduced her, but I'd be interested in what meaning the relationship had for both of them."

We both agreed that we would never have ended up anywhere near where Lazarus did.

WHAT'S TO BE LEARNED?

A case this memorable clearly must have some impact on the therapist afterwards. We asked Lazarus to talk about the enduring effects on him and on the way he works.

"I hope the thing that others would learn from this is to really think through the issue of any judgmental, moralistic, or pejorative things that they may say or feel toward others. The first and foremost guiding principle should be, did any harm come of this? And if the answer is yes, then it would be a very different situation from the one I presented. But if the answer is no, then let's not make an issue about it."

This reminded Lazarus about another case, but then when you've been in practice as long as he has, *everything* reminds you of a case. In this particular situation, a distraught woman came to see him who had been involved in sex play as a child. She enjoyed the games they had played and looked forward to them.

"Then," Lazarus said, "she goes to college and learns that what happened was a dreadful thing. Now she feels terribly guilty. So she comes to therapy saying she didn't know why she felt so guilty because she didn't feel bad until she learned she was supposed to feel guilty."

In a manner similar to the earlier case, Lazarus took a position that since no harm was done, there was little reason to feel bad about what happened.

"I tried to assuage her of any guilt and told her to look at it as an innocent thing, a kind of prelude of her own awakening sexuality. It didn't mean that she was a bad person. The guiding light is always whether or not there was any harm done to the victim."

MULTIPLE VERSIONS OF THE STORY

We returned to the earlier question about what might the client have remembered differently about the time they spent together. So often, we might be proud of the way we frame something or interpret a situation, or of the creative way that we confront somebody or dispute his beliefs. Yet when we hear the client's version of what happened in therapy we are surprised by what he remembers. He often has a very different story to tell that bears little resemblance to our own narrative.

"You're so right," Lazarus agreed. "That reminds me of another case. It goes back to my days in South Africa. I was seeing a guy who was very anxious."

"Look," the man said to Lazarus, "I am going to tell you something, and I am pretty sure I know what is going to happen. You are going to kick me or grab a broomstick and beat me over the head and tell me to get the hell out."

Lazarus prepared himself for the awful secret he was about to hear. He considers himself a very open-minded guy, and even among the population of therapists on earth, he is on the far end of the continuum when it comes to being accepting—as we've already seen. Nevertheless, he knew a whopper was coming, and he wanted to make certain that he didn't convey any shock or disgust that might alienate his client. He was fairly sure the man was going to admit he had strangled someone.

"OK," Lazarus prompted him in a carefully modulated voice. "What would you like to tell me?"

After sputtering and hedging for quite some time, the man finally blurted out that he had had sex with a black woman.

"Go on," Lazarus encouraged him.

"That's it," the man said, and then looked down in shame.

Lazarus reminded us that this was back in the days of apartheid in South Africa, when interracial sex was defined as an act of immorality.

"I said to him that this was an arbitrary decision that this crazy place we live in has made. I have worked in London. I went to Paris for the weekend. Wherever I went I saw plenty of blacks and whites together. South Africa is just a cultural anomaly. Why would you take it to heart? Well, this was so reassuring to the guy. It's a similar kind of thing to the woman's case I mentioned earlier. I think his version of the story would be that he expected to be castrated. Instead, what he got from me was the reassurance that there was nothing wrong with him, but that the society was sick."

Although we agree with most of what Lazarus is saying, we also recognize that there are those in our field who believe that therapists need to take a stronger moral position so society doesn't go to hell. They are very outspoken critics of those professionals who support and accept their clients even when those clients are doing things that go against cultural norms. And in the first case presented, it is entirely possible that someone *was* harmed, namely the daughter by her father, who first abandoned her and then screwed her. Literally.

Lazarus agrees 100 percent with the position that people should not be permitted to harm themselves or others. He cites child abuse, selling drugs, and similar behaviors as examples. In these and similar situations, therapists can and must take a strong position to stop clients from continuing their destructive behavior. But he makes a strong distinction between the behavior described in the case examples he talked about and the kind he finds most harmful.

What Lazarus did that was most therapeutic for the client who had sex with her father was less related to his trademark interventions and more connected to the accepting, caring stance he had adopted with her. He made her feel safe. He reassured them that they were not horrible human beings just because they were engaging in behavior about which others might disapprove. Most of all, he let his client know that just because she might have had the affair to beat all affairs, she was still a good person.

CHAPTER FIVE

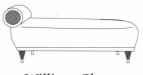

William Glasser

The Urge to Eat
from Garbage Cans

William Glasser is, quite simply, one of the most influential educators and therapists who ever lived. Beginning in the 1960s when he first developed Reality Therapy, he was among the first to develop a relatively brief method for helping people address a wide range of personal problems, from depression and addictions to lifestyle issues.

By concentrating on the consequences of one's behavior and the choices one makes, Glasser provided a framework for helping people move toward taking constructive action in their lives. His classic books Reality Therapy *(1965),* Positive Addiction *(1976),* Reality Therapy in Action *(2000), and* Counseling with Choice Theory *(2001) educated several generations of practitioners about his theory. Reality Therapy has since become so popular that Glasser Institutes have sprouted up all over the world, from Australia and Hong Kong to Russia and the Middle East. At this point practically every therapist makes use of some aspect of his approach.*

As if his contributions to therapy were not enough, Glasser has been just as influential in the field of education. Through his books Schools Without Failure *(1969) and* The Quality School *(1990), he expanded his "choice theory" to design education and discipline strategies that both empower children and make them more responsible for their behavior.*

He has accomplished similar goals by developing "choice theory communities" in which civic and corporate cultures are restructured in such a way as to emphasize more cooperative and self-determined actions.

Although trained originally as a psychiatrist, Glasser has spent most of his professional life working in the areas of education, counseling, addictions, organizational behavior, and public health. He has also concentrated more recently on improving marital relationships, in his books What Is This Thing Called Love? *(2000) and* Getting Together and Staying Together *(2000). Although now close to eighty years old, Glasser is still quite active as a speaker and writer, continuing to refine his ideas and apply choice theory to new settings.*

⟶

Bill Glasser's voice has a playfulness and accessibility that one would not expect in someone of his mature years and lofty position in the profession. Although known primarily for his reality-based, practical methods, he is actually quite sentimental and loving when he talks about the people he has helped in his life. These are not just patients of his but, as you'll see, members of his extended family.

THE LAST PATIENT HE EVER SAW

Glasser began the conversation by matter-of-factly mentioning that he was going to talk about the last patient he saw before he closed his office. "But," he said enigmatically, "I did not actually see her in my office."

This was a young woman, about twenty-one years old, from a family that Glasser knew intimately. He had seen both her sister and father previously.

"I was playing tennis with her pediatrician," Glasser said. "The family took the young woman to him rather than to me." This bothered Glasser, not only because they made a poor choice but because this particular physician was especially unsympathetic toward the practice of psychiatry. Nevertheless, because the pediatrician had been unable to do anything for the patient, he urged the family to contact Glasser for a consultation.

"This woman had what they nowadays would call an eating disorder." We smiled as we heard this because we knew what was coming next. Glasser is notorious for his passionate attacks against traditional psychiatric labeling. He did not disappoint us.

"I don't label any kind of disorder. To me the only human disorder is unhappiness, and when you are unhappy, goodness knows what you will do." Then, with a dramatic pause, he added, "Her problem was eating from garbage cans."

"Eating from garbage cans?"

"She would walk down the street and dip into garbage cans."

This didn't seem that unusual to us. Many homeless people scrounge for food wherever they can.

"Yes, but this was in West Los Angeles in a very good neighborhood."

Slowly it was dawning on us that this was elective eating behavior. Apparently this young woman was treating the garbage cans on her street as a smorgasbord.

Glasser wanted to tell us how he treated the case, but we interrupted him to get a clearer picture of what he was dealing with.

"She would go out and dig through garbage until she found something that seemed good to her."

"Did she have particular favorite things that she would eat?"

"Yeah," Glasser said. "Sweets."

He goes on to explain that although she had rather strange eating patterns, she was somewhat attractive. Her main problem was that she felt totally worthless. She felt lost and unsure about where she was going in the future.

Before he could continue the narrative about her underlying feelings of inadequacy, Jeffrey interrupted once again. There was something about the story so far that didn't quite fit.

"Bill, what was her explanation for why when she craved sweets she just didn't go out and buy a Snickers bar?"

From what he could gather, Glasser figured out that the young woman liked to eat from garbage cans because it drove her mother crazy.

Aha.

FROM THE OFFICE TO THE STREETS

It was during this time in the 1970s that Glasser had written a new best-seller that was having quite an impact on mental health. *Positive Addiction* proposed that people could rid themselves of bad habits by substituting more healthy alternatives.

Glasser saw this young woman in the office a few times and learned a bit about how unhappy she was and how miserable life was in her family.

"I can't do anything about your family," Glasser told her. "But I can help you do something about yourself. What are you going to do about this problem?"

The mother was a meticulous, perfectionistic person. Cleanliness was certainly next to godliness to her. So the prospect of her daughter eating garbage was just about the worst thing she could imagine. This was obviously a daughter who knew exactly how to strike back at her mother.

Whereas some therapists might seek to promote some degree of insight into this inappropriate expression of resentment, or help the patient examine her underlying negative beliefs or understand the context of the past in shaping this pattern, Glasser has always been a firm believer in action. He isn't interested so much in helping people gain insight into why they are messed up as he is in simply helping them change the disruptive behavior.

Glasser sympathized with his patient's predicament and readily admitted to her that she lived in a pretty dysfunctional family. Nevertheless, he didn't consider this a sufficient reason for her to be messing up her life eating from garbage cans.

"You don't feel good about yourself," Glasser told her. "You look at yourself and you realize that you aren't doing anything with your life—that is, except aggravating your mother." Glasser paused a beat, then added, "That is hardly a vocation for a grown woman."

The woman readily agreed with this assessment but then wondered what she could do about the predicament.

Her therapist pondered the situation for a minute. "I just don't see how I can do any good for you sitting in the office talking about this stuff."

Glasser, you see, was (and always has been) skeptical about how talk therapy alone can have any enduring effect.

"OK then," the woman pressed him, "what *will* work?" Somehow Glasser had convinced her that it was time to move on to another stage of life beyond garbage cans.

After explaining the nature of positive addiction, Glasser presented regular exercise, such as running, as a legitimate alternative to her previous maladaptive dining habits. "As long as you are going to be addicted to something," Glasser told her, "you might as well pick something that is good for you."

Glasser explained that he has gotten a great many letters over the years from people who started running and regular exercise programs as a direct result of this theory of positive addiction. We readily agreed to the power of his influence. We never dreamed twenty years ago that we would befriend the man who got us both so addicted to running.

THERAPY ON THE RUN

In those days, when Glasser was in his fifties, he used to run on a regular basis, practicing what he preached to others. He believed strongly in the power of healthy habits, so much so that he was passionate in prescribing exercise to his patients. But in this case his treatment became a bit unconventional, certainly by the standards of his day.

"Instead of seeing you in my office," Glasser told his patient, "I will see you twice a week, but I'm meet you at the corner of San Maceni and Brentwood. That's the running street. Everybody runs there and I live near that street.

"You park in the supermarket parking lot, and I'll meet you there. We can run together, and we will talk while we run. The only difference is that you will run seven days a week, and I'll run two days with you. I can't make you run, but I think that this could really help you."

Glasser and his patient ran for thirty minutes, twice per week, and this went on for many months. After they completed their circuit, they would sit in the car and talk about her plans for the future. She talked about her interest in working with children and her desire to get a degree in early childhood education. Soon she talked about moving out of her parents' home and supporting herself, which she was soon able to do. And—perhaps it is no surprise—she stopped eating from garbage cans.

"Did you ever take her running on garbage day?" Jon asked.

"No. She was never tempted as we ran. Once she started running, the garbage thing disappeared totally."

"And how do you account for that?" Jeffrey asked him.

"She was doing something worthwhile with her life, something that she could control. Just like she could control eating from the garbage can, she could control her running."

Glasser stops for a minute, thinking about this patient for whom he cared so much that he became her personal trainer.

"Until recently, I used to hear from her every Christmas. First I heard she got married, and then she sent me pictures of her first child, then a picture of her second child with her husband.

"The next time I saw that pediatrician, even he admitted that I had really helped her."

By this time, Glasser had closed his office so he could devote more of his time to teaching and writing. In part, he remembers this case because she was the last patient he saw before abandoning his psychiatric practice.

THE GIRLS OF VENTURA

It didn't surprise us that physicians and other professionals would send Glasser their strangest, most difficult patients. By this time, he had managed to offend many of his colleagues by challenging the traditional ways that they did therapy. Glasser refused to use traditional diagnosis. He didn't delve into the past and didn't care much for insight. And he wasn't shy about telling folks that they were misguided in their efforts to continue using their favored methods. He thinks this is one reason why referrals were so hard for him to come by, and why he ended up working in nontraditional settings. We think it's because he has always genuinely enjoyed his rebellious role.

After so many years, it is hard for Glasser to remember many of his cases, even the so-called peculiar ones. But he does have the fondest memories about his years working in a juvenile prison for girls in Ventura, California.

"You must have had a few bizarre ones in there," we prompted him.

"Yeah. I'd say that Ventura was the last holdout for delinquent girls."

"So, tell us about some of those stories." Glasser seemed to need a bit of prompting.

"What's to say? They were locked up. It was a juvenile prison. I was the psychiatrist, and we had about six counselors. It was a good situation. All I remember is loving to go to work there. Those girls would have killed for me."

He was being literal.

"They loved me so much. I never had so much love in my life. They succeeded at our school."

Glasser's experiences in Ventura formed the foundation for his ideas about "schools without failure" in which children would be treated with respect and required to act responsibly.

"But some of those girls had committed some serious crimes."

"Murder, a few of them."

We agreed that this was rather serious.

"These were Indian girls from Northern California. They had killed, but only after they had been abused since the age of six or seven."

Glasser told the girls that he understood why they did what they did. Some of those people needed killing. It was the only way the girls could escape what was being done to them.

"We didn't let those girls go back to the reservation. They had to stay with us for three years. They were the best girls we ever had at that school. We arranged for them to stay in the community and go to work, and they did real well. They weren't delinquent at all. They just killed someone, that's all, sometimes a person who deserved to be killed, in my opinion."

We couldn't tell if Glasser was kidding or not, but we suspected that he was such an advocate for his patients that he really did understand why they did what they did. He didn't consider these kids he saw as being particularly unusual at all; their behavior was perfectly sensible given the circumstances in which they had lived. This discussion reminded him of one other patient he had seen earlier in his career.

THE ADOPTION

Although the man is now in his sixties, Glasser first saw him when he was a university student. Glasser laughed at this realization because the guy is now retired and Glasser is still working.

At that time, Glasser's book *Reality Therapy* had come out, a book that was a best-seller not only for professionals but also for the public. People would track him down just as they might journey to Lourdes— as a last chance before giving up.

"The young man had heard about me. He said that he had made up his mind, and he was going to kill himself. He was going down to the end of the street and heave himself off the cliff. He couldn't take it anymore. But he said if I would see him, convince him not to kill myself, then he might not do it."

Glasser could tell that as depressed and despondent as the guy was, he didn't really want to kill himself. He really wanted help.

"He lived with a dingbat mother and a stepfather. His father disavowed him when he was small and never saw him again. He had a stepbrother that the stepfather doted on. There were all the standard rejection kinds of things."

Glasser was very sad about the young man's situation, because he found him to be such a good person and yet his life was such a waste.

So, what did he do? Well, most psychiatrists would prescribe medication for the depression, and most therapists at the time would address the boy's feelings of self-worth or delve into the past to find the reasons for his suffering. Glasser instead went home to talk to his wife about the boy.

"Look," he told her, "this kid needs a mother and father. He's a nice boy, and I think we have to become his mother and father. I'm worried he is going to kill himself."

After living with Glasser for so many years, his wife was little surprised about his rather unorthodox treatment methods. She agreed to this arrangement.

"So we adopted him," Glasser says simply. "He became a member of our family. He became my kid's older brother and everything else. Now he is sixty-some years of age and retired. He has made a lot of money and been very successful."

Glasser says this proudly, just as if this *were* his real son.

"I know you are not supposed to do this sort of thing if you are a psychiatrist. But I don't have any rules or regulations. I do what I think is the right thing to do. So I continued to see him as a psychiatrist. He never moved into our house. He had his own place."

Although we were indeed surprised that Glasser would go so far as to symbolically "adopt" a patient who needed loving parents, we were reminded of the ways people do therapy in other parts of the world. In certain parts of Africa, for instance, the mentally afflicted move into the home of the healer until such time as he or she is cured. (Now *that* would motivate a professional to work pretty hard to help people, or they'd be living with you forever.)

The client/son eventually got married and started a family of his own. "But they always came to us for Thanksgiving because he said he had thanks to give at this house."

Glasser mentioned this casually, but we could tell that this meant a lot to him. After all, here was a case that he cared so deeply about that he devoted years of effort, even recruiting his own family in the enterprise. He had decided that what this boy needed most was stable parents and a healthy family, so this was exactly what he would provide.

"So, what's most strange about this case," we said to Glasser, "was not the boy's behavior but your own atypical response to the situation."

"Yeah, it was kind of bizarre, wasn't it?"

We realized that Glasser had adopted the boy symbolically rather than legally, but we wondered how he presented this idea. How do you tell someone something like this?

"I just told him that you need a mother and father so you come over. He met my wife. He met my kids. He came over for dinner. Not every night or anything. We became his family."

It seems incredibly ironic that Glasser is known primarily for a method that is specific, behaviorally oriented, and goal-driven. Teachers, counselors, therapists, and leaders from all over the world apply his Reality Therapy techniques in a few easy steps. Yet in all of the cases Glasser discussed with us—the woman who ate garbage, the girls of Ventura, and the man who wanted to throw himself off a cliff—it was his essential love and devotion that mattered most. Glasser was willing to go far beyond the call of duty to show these people how much he cared for them.

MAKING RELATIONSHIPS

Glasser readily agreed that involvement is everything in a helping relationship. He cited a chapter in one of his books in which he talked about Rebecca, a patient who had been diagnosed as schizophrenic. He could see her in the hospital only as a visitor because they refused to give him medical privileges. Even though UCLA Hospital had changed administrations a half-dozen times since his residency days, Glasser's presence was still not much appreciated on the grounds.

"What on earth did you do to these people that they didn't want you ever again to set foot on the property?" We wondered if he set fire to the place or physically attacked someone.

"When I was a resident," Glasser explained simply, "I told them psychoanalysis doesn't help anyone."

Glasser was being modest. Of course he would have told them that their prevailing form of treatment at the time was worthless, but it was the *way* he would have done so that left little room for him to retreat.

"I don't believe in insight, I told my supervisors. Everybody has insight; insight is worth a dime a dozen. People know what to do with their lives. They just choose not to follow through for a variety of reasons. The main one is because they are disconnected and nobody much cares about them."

So this is the clue as to why he has put so much of himself into showing people that he cares about them. He may be famous for his simple steps of asking people what they want, finding out what they are doing, and evaluating whether it is working, but the essence of his approach has always been embedded in his essential caring for others.

Speaking again of Rebecca, Glasser says that she got over her schizophrenia after they talked for a little while and related well to one another.

"I've never had too much trouble with these cases, even as a resident. We had a lot of people get over schizophrenia and became functional again."

Since Glasser has never believed that conditions like schizophrenia actually exist, he has rarely resorted to prescribing medications for these problems. He mentioned John Nash from *A Beautiful Mind* as a good example of someone who still has delusions and hallucinations, but he understands where they are coming from and chooses not to surrender to them. It is choice that is the center of Glasser's theory.

Going back to the case at hand, we asked what happened with Rebecca during his visit with her. How had he managed to talk her out of being, or at least *acting*, like a schizophrenic?

"We just talked together and I made a relationship with her."

"That's it? That's your secret?"

"Well, I don't believe that schizophrenia exists. Of course, there are psychotic symptoms. But in many cases, this is the result of trying to live up to your own, or other people's, excessive expectations.

"Rebecca was a brilliant student. Then, at a certain time in her life, she didn't want to be a brilliant student anymore. She just wanted to play bridge, and chess, and tutor students just to make a living. The family was all highly academic."

Glasser picked up immediately that her main problem seemed to be related to disappointing her family because of the choices she was making.

"So, what is happening with her now?"

"She's a college professor and doing well."

Glasser makes this all sound so simple. He takes people who don't respond to medication or shock treatment or therapy by the best the profession has to offer, and he "makes relationships with them." That, of course, is what he *says* he does with them. In fact, he does so much more. He challenges them. He encourages them to make different choices that are more in keeping with their true desires. And he demonstrates his total caring and commitment to their welfare.

There was one real turning point in Rebecca's case that Glasser remembered as particularly significant.

"Dr. Glasser," she asked him, "can you hear voices and not be crazy?"

"Absolutely," he reassured her. "You can create anything in your mind as long as you know where it's coming from. There is nothing crazy about this at all. They told Beethoven he was crazy when he was deaf because he heard music. Einstein, if he had been born a little earlier, would have ended up in the mental hospital because of his delusions that the physical world worked differently from the way Newton said it did. The same with Galileo—they put him on the barbecue. They said they were going to toast him until he said that the earth was the center of the universe. He said OK. Crazy is when you hear things that are so detached from reality that they start to screw up your life."

Glasser concluded his remarks by admitting that there are plenty of people out there who think that *he* is crazy. "Delusions are very common. It is just when they get a little bit out of the norm that people get upset. Psychoanalysis is a major delusion as far as I am concerned. People think I am deluded to say it, so there you are."

CHAPTER SIX

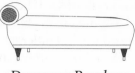

Domeena Renshaw

The Penis That Needed Permission from the Church

Prior to coming to the United States in the 1960s, Domeena Renshaw worked as a surgeon and physician in a small mission hospital in South Africa's Zululand. She had been trained in urology and gynecology as well as neuropsychiatry, a solid medical education that prepared her well for understanding the connections between psychological and physical factors involved in psychiatric disorders. After completing her psychiatric residency at Loyola University in Chicago, she joined the faculty and then started a premier sex therapy clinic.

For the past thirty years, Renshaw has seen thousands of couples for various sexual dysfunctions and has trained thousands of mental health professionals in methods of brief sex therapy. Her unique program consists of seven sessions that combine sex education and conjoint and individual therapy.

Renshaw published her ideas in a best-selling book, Seven Weeks to Better Sex, *that garnered worldwide notoriety for her systematic, integrative, and efficient approach. Earlier in her career, before settling on sex therapy as her specialty, she had also written books about hyperactive children and treating incest victims.*

To meet Domeena Renshaw is to encounter a bundle of energy. With her distinctive South African accent, diminutive size, and casual manner in which she talks calmly about the most explicit aspects of sexual behavior, there is little doubt in our minds that she is a unique presence in the fields of mental health and couples therapy.

—m—

Considering the number of years Renshaw has been in practice and that her chosen specialty is in sex therapy, an area where there seems to be more than its fair share of bizarre behavior, it's not surprising that she would have a large group from which to select an interesting case. Yet the patient she remembers most vividly is significant to her not because of any strange sexual preferences but because of how he taught her an important lesson about respecting the power of each patient's value system.

Speaking in the concise manner in which she would address a group of medical residents, she summarized the main features of the case.

THE PENIS WAS TIRED AND NEEDED SLEEP

"He happened to be an insulin-dependent diabetic," Renshaw began, pointing out that there were physical as well as psychological factors related to his presenting problem of impotence.

"He came to us about ten years ago. The time frame is important because it was way before Viagra. This was a second marriage for him, and this was a marriage of three years' duration. He had been previously married and had grown children."

His second wife, the one who brought him into treatment, was becoming increasingly frustrated and impatient because they had not as yet consummated their marriage due to his problems in having an erection. Originally he had made excuses for not having premarital sex with her because, as a practicing Catholic, he wanted to wait until they were married.

It had now been a few years since then, and he was still proving uncooperative, or at least his penis was. Other than their sexual problems—or, rather, their lack of sexual activity whatsoever—they appeared to have a loving marriage. The only thing they ever fought about was their sex life. When they were in bed, the wife would show strong interest in the husband, but he would withdraw and fall asleep.

THE PENIS NEEDED INJECTIONS

Renshaw began by assessing the medical dimensions of the husband's case, including conducting a thorough physical exam. She discovered that he awoke with morning erections, which meant it was likely that his problems were psychologically based. Nevertheless, because of his history of diabetes and insulin dependence, she referred him to a urologist to assess penile blood flow, which can be affected by his disease.

The examining urologist found that that there had indeed been some restriction of the small blood vessels. The good news was that there were injections available that the husband could use to chemically induce his own erections. He could easily be taught to do this procedure during those times when he wished to have sex.

As Renshaw was telling this part of the story, we were having a difficult time getting the image out of our heads of this huge needle poised over this poor little tired, uncooperative penis. We were wondering where one inserts the needle and how much it must hurt. She reassured us that the needle is actually quite small and that the procedure, though not exactly pleasurable foreplay, did produce consistent results. We can now appreciate just how great a miracle Viagra must be for those couples who need it to function.

A week later, the husband came back for his trial injection, and the results in the doctor's office were rather spectacular. Yet rather than rushing home to his eager wife, who has been waiting years for this moment, the husband inexplicably decided to stop at a restaurant on the way home to have dinner. Hearing this, we pictured the husband sitting at a table, his throbbing penis bouncing in his pants, yet he is ignoring it in favor of a shrimp cocktail.

"By the time he got home," Renshaw said, "the erection was descended. The wife was furious with her husband and insisted that he make another appointment to see the doctor. This time she would go with him to learn how to do this injection herself."

We were just about to ask Domeena how one teaches someone to do this sort of thing. Do they have a mock penis to practice with, or must the woman experiment on her husband? Again, an uninvited image came to mind. We pictured the guy's penis splayed out on an operating table, perhaps draped in one of those surgical gowns with just the head exposed. The doctor and wife are poised over the little patient with that huge needle. Her hand is shaking, so the doctor steadies her and directs the tip to the target.

THE PENIS IS AMBUSHED

Renshaw interrupted the fantasy. "He was still delaying and delaying. Our program is only seven weeks, and it was now in the seventh and last week of the clinic. The husband came in terribly upset, and his wife was even angrier than he was."

Renshaw persuaded the couple to calm down and then asked them what had happened. It was obvious there had been a major setback between them. Even during all these years of conflict over the lack of sex they had still managed to remain respectful and caring toward one another.

"What had happened," Renshaw explained, "was that the husband awakened at two in the morning and found his wife kneeling over him with his penis in her left hand and a loaded syringe in her right. In between her teeth, she held a flashlight to illuminate the area of operation."

Needless to say, the husband was rather startled to find his wife about to inject his penis in the middle in the night. Apparently, she had planned to induce a chemical erection without his consent and then have sex with him while he was sleeping.

The husband was horrified by his wife's behavior. She was equally indignant that he was sabotaging their attempts to have a normal sex life—to have *any* sex life.

When she heard this story, "It was difficult not to laugh," Renshaw admitted. But she was determined to find out what was going on.

THE PENIS DEFENDS ITSELF

This critical incident provided an opportunity to explore more deeply what was going on with the husband and why he proved so determined to prevent sex from taking place in spite of his stated intentions. With Renshaw's gentle prodding, the situation became clear.

The husband was a practicing Catholic. Although he had been legally divorced years earlier, the Church had still not yet granted him an annulment from his first wife.

"The process was taking a long time because they had to investigate the wife as well as the husband. He felt that only when the Church excused him from this first marriage, and annulled it, would he be free in his mind to even think about having sex. He went through all the motions of going through the sex clinic. He applied to the program. He came with his wife. He did the touching and the foreplay, but when it came to intercourse, there was no way that this man was going to go through with it."

So really, this was a case of moral self-defense. The penis refused to cooperate with the program because it had not yet received Church permission to consummate the new marriage.

Renshaw explained, "It was only during follow-up, perhaps eight or nine weeks later, that the husband's annulment came through. He soon thereafter consummated the marriage."

Without our having to prompt her in the least, Renshaw immediately started to talk about what this case taught her about doing therapy and working with couples.

"It has so many lessons to teach us about being pushed, being coerced, saying with your mouth that, yes, you want sex therapy, but the penis, with its own language, says 'No way! I'm just not ready.'"

Renshaw paused for a moment, thinking about how futile it is to push someone to do something that he or she is not yet ready to do.

"It was a vain and fruitless effort on the part of the wife to try and coerce her husband, inject this poor penis, hoping that he wouldn't awaken."

THE PENIS PREFERS SAILING

In spite of how far we have come in being able to chemically induce erections, Renshaw says there are still limits on how far we can go without addressing people's actual needs and feelings.

"If you have injections, if you have the Viagra pill, it is not going to work unless you are cooperative. The pill came out on April 16, 1998, and I got a call from a couple—a woman actually—who had been to the sex clinic nine years earlier. She was a real noisy lady. She talked nonstop. The husband loved her, had no plans to divorce, but he had no sexual desire whatsoever. She would push and nag him to have intercourse. He was always too tired. He'd say that he was going sailing the next day so he had to be up early. So she dragged him to the clinic.

"The husband was a relatively young-looking sixty-two-year-old. He had normal erections and met his needs by masturbation, which was a secret he couldn't divulge to her. The biggest help that we gave to that couple was to teach her to masturbate, to encourage her to get a vibrator and meet her own needs. I hadn't even thought about her for years till she phoned and asked if I remembered her."

"How could I forget you?" Renshaw said to the wife. Actually, what she remembered most was how the husband used sailing on Lake Michigan as a means to get away from his wife's constant nagging and complaints.

"Will you give Viagra to him?" the wife asked Renshaw, finally getting to the point of the phone call.

"Certainly," she told her patient, "if he comes to get it."

"Well, I was kind of wondering if you could give it to me."

"Sorry," Renshaw said, understanding now what the wife had in mind. "I have to take his blood pressure and see if he is OK medically."

"I see," the woman answered, plotting another way to go about this. "Well, if I got the pills would I be able to slip one into his hot chocolate at night?"

"No, you can't do that. It's unethical and besides no one will give it to you. You have to give it to the patient."

What Renshaw didn't know then was that people could get Viagra over the Internet. You just answer a few questions, pay $50, and the company sends a prescription.

The woman was silent for a moment, then asked, "Will Medicare pay for it because my husband is now sixty-nine?"

Renshaw said that she didn't know the answer to that question.

"I never heard from her again," she says, "but I'm sure the husband is still sailing instead of using Viagra."

VARIATIONS ON A THEME

"I think the case that surprised me the most was a couple in their forties. She was a schoolteacher, forty-four, and he was an engineer, forty-seven. They were in an unconsummated marriage of twenty-three years."

We know that this whole phenomenon of couples who marry but never have sex is underreported. We also know that Renshaw and her staff have seen hundreds of these folks over the years, although it did seem unusual that this couple could manage to last over two decades.

When the couple came into the clinic, Renshaw was curious about one thing more than any other dimension of their situation.

"Why now?" she asked the couple. "Why after twenty-three years do you want help? Why not just accommodate to this?"

The wife looked down and then said very quietly, "We didn't know that there was a place like this where we could get help."

Renshaw sounded sad when she told this story. There are so many couples who need help, many of whom are truly unaware that there is help available. The treatment she offers works with well over 80 percent of the couples she sees. Even those who don't completely cure their symptoms still see significant improvement in their relationship. Yet her budget is so meager that she can barely operate her clinic. Managed care and most insurance companies will not pay for treatment. Her waiting lists are long, but most people can only afford minimal costs.

"This couple had seen many physicians and had been in couples therapy before, but nobody helped them because they were not dealing with the sexual problem. Nobody had even asked why they had not had sex. In this case, what prevented the couple from having intercourse was the wife's longstanding fear of pain that might accompany penetration."

With reassurance, a few weeks of tranquilizers, and a local anesthetic cream for the vaginal opening, the couple finally consummated their marriage. Both expressed regret for all those years of enjoyment they had missed.

CONFESSIONS

Hearing about some of these cases, we were reminded once again about why so many of the stories we have heard so far reflect variations in sexual behavior. In Jeffrey's earlier case, for instance, we have the guy who developed a rather strong attachment to a cow. Another therapist we know, upon hearing about this book we were doing, related the story of his own client who liked to have sex with cats. When the guy was asked whether he preferred male or female cats, he responded indignantly, "What do you take me for, a queer?!"

Renshaw thinks that one reason why so many unusual cases come up, besides the obvious taboos associated with sex, are the variety of ways that humans seek release. The evening before our conversation with her, she had been consulted by another therapist, who was treating a couple in which the husband had sadomasochistic fantasies that were upsetting to his wife. They had not acted out any of his spanking fantasies; the problem came from the guilt associated with even thinking about them.

"So many times therapists serve the need of someone going to confession. I often kid people and say I have a priest's collar in the bottom drawer of my desk so that when they start the confession I put it on.

"It breeds anxiety to keep secrets inside. People need to tell someone about them, and the therapist can serve that purpose."

Renshaw illustrated this point by talking about a case she worked with twenty-five years ago. "We had two parents come in with a tall sixteen-year-old girl who was as sociopathic as God made anybody. She was in high school and was working in a part-time job. She was getting bored by this job, so one day she hopped on a bus to O'Hare Airport in the middle of winter. She walked to a United Airlines gate and picked up a throw-away boarding pass. This was during a time when security was not what it is today."

Renshaw continued the story with relish, indicating that although she was appalled by the immorality of the girl's behavior, there was something about her cheekiness that was almost admirable. So the girl arrived in Honolulu and took a bus to the beach with her last few dollars, stole wallets from beneath towels on the beach, and then went on a shopping spree using stolen credit cards.

Finally, the girl tired of Hawaii, so she planned to head to California next. She was caught and jailed by authorities at the airport trying to use the stolen credit cards to purchase a plane ticket. It was at this point that her father flew to Hawaii, got his daughter out of jail, and brought her home to the Loyola Clinic to fix the situation.

"The mother was about a foot taller than the father. He was a sweet, passive little man, and the wife was a real controlling, domineering, and angry lady. They came in to see us at the clinic, and I was supervising the resident who was seeing her. He happened to actually be a priest who was training in psychiatry. He was in civilian clothes while he evaluated the girl. It was his assessment that the girl was sociopathic. He told the parents that she didn't need hospitalization. She needed therapy. And most of all, she needed limits.

"At this point, the mother got very angry and stood up and said, 'She doesn't need a psychiatrist. She needs a Catholic priest!' And the three of them stormed out of the office."

Renshaw supervised the therapist afterwards and asked why he didn't simply lean down, put his collar on, and tell the family that he really *was* a priest. It was the kind of situation he could have waited a lifetime to have happen again. He explained that he was so startled by the mother's sweeping departure that he forgot who he had been and what he had done in his other life.

CHAPTER SEVEN

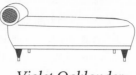

Violet Oaklander

Therapy with a Gopher Snake and a Horned Lizard

As one of the premier child therapists in the field, Violet Oaklander is known for her creative uses of play, puppetry, art, music, and storytelling to help troubled kids. Her book, Windows to Our Children, *is considered one of the standard resources for working with children and adolescents, especially for those who follow an experientially based Gestalt approach. Throughout her career, Oaklander has developed and described methods particularly well suited for dealing with issues such as hyperactivity, childhood trauma, withdrawal, autism, and aggression.*

Violet trains many therapists to work with children and adolescents all over the world and is an adjunct faculty member at Pacifica Graduate Institute near Santa Barbara, California, where she makes her home.

—⁓—

All Oaklander knew about the boy was that he was dangerous. His mother had called the night before, frantic, because her fourteen-year-old son had chased her around the house with a knife. She had been afraid he was going to kill her.

"Has he done anything like this before?" Violet asked, concerned for her own safety and wondering if she was the right person to work with this boy.

"No, he's somewhat different," the mother admitted, "but nothing like this has ever happened before. He just gets so angry sometimes at my husband, his stepfather. So when can you see him?"

FIRST IMPRESSION

They scheduled an appointment for the very next day. Oaklander went out to greet the young man and his mother, a bit apprehensive about this potentially violent, knife-wielding adolescent. She let out an inadvertent scream when she saw, standing in the waiting room, a slight, smiling boy with a huge snake wrapped around his neck.

"On my gosh," she cried out, "what on earth is that?"

"It's a snake," the boy said proudly, and then held out its head in her direction, its long, snaky tongue flicking out then moving from side to side before it withdrew into the serpent's head. "You wanna hold him?"

"Uh, no thanks." The snake was huge—at least four feet long, muddy brown, with blotches all over its body. Surely it couldn't be poisonous? Would this mother really let her son carry around a poisonous snake? But then again, he *had* threatened her with a knife. Oaklander suddenly remembered that the mother was there; she introduced herself, and they shook hands. The boy's mother seemed unperturbed by the snake and smiled pleasantly.

Oaklander did her best to appear composed, and escorted them both into the office. Once they were settled comfortably, or as comfortably as could be expected considering there was a dangerous-looking reptile crawling around her client's shoulders, she asked the boy what his name was.

"Gregory," he replied cheerfully.

"And your friend there," she said, pointing to the brown thing encircling his thin body, "what's his name?"

"Oh, he's just Snake. He doesn't have a name."

"I see."

"You wanna hold him?" he asked again.

"No, no, that's OK." The damn thing's tongue was enormous. It looked long enough to reach out and touch her if the snake were so inclined. "Besides," she added, "I don't know how to hold a snake."

"Oh," Gregory reassured her, "you don't have to worry. He won't hurt you. He's just a gopher snake."

"Does that mean he isn't poisonous?" she asked him, then glanced over at his mother for reassurance. Gregory's mom nodded and smiled.

"Nah, he just eats rabbits and lizards and stuff like that. He squeezes them to death."

Somehow Violet did not feel greatly reassured by that last remark. Yet she prided herself on her ability—and her willingness—to make contact with children on whatever level they offered. This boy hardly seemed violent—if anything he appeared completely harmless and rather helpless—but you never know with these things. Although she was not exactly snake phobic, she wasn't a snake lover either. Against her better judgment, she reached out and tentatively touched the thing, as far away from its mouth as she could get. It felt smoother than she thought it would. Gregory was pleased. "He likes to be touched," he said.

SILENT TREATMENT

Oaklander tried to engage Gregory, but he would not respond to questions and didn't seem to be very interested in talking. He just sat there with a smile on his face, stroking the snake, occasionally repositioning it on his shoulders or across his lap.

"Gregory, do you know why you're here?" Oaklander asked.

He looked away.

Violet turned to the mother. "Could you tell me what prompted you to bring Gregory here so that he can know that I know what happened?"

"Well," she said tentatively, "he chased me with a knife yesterday and that scared me. But I don't think he meant to hurt me," she added vehemently.

Gregory looked at his mom and smiled.

"Gregory," Violet said, "do you mind if I ask you a few questions?"

Shrug.

"I wonder how you sleep at night? Do you have any nightmares about anything?"

Gregory just looked her and smiled, petting the snake.

"How about your appetite? What kinds of things do you like to eat?"

"Snake likes to eat mice. And some birds too."

"That's nice. But what about you? What do *you* like to eat?"

Shrug.

This was very peculiar. In some ways Gregory seemed almost autistic—immobile, unresponsive. The only thing that seemed to pique his interest was any conversation that had to do with the snake.

Oaklander examined her client carefully. Although he was fourteen, he was very slight looking, fragile, with curly blond hair. Although he wouldn't talk, only nod his head and shrug at times, he remained smiling throughout their time together. Because he was unresponsive to her questions, Oaklander turned to the mother to ask the usual kinds of intake questions. Besides questioning her about appetite and sleep behaviors and medical history, Violet asked about other siblings (none), school (he hated it), friends (he had none), his own father (he left when Gregory was about three and there was no contact with him), his relationship with his stepfather (he hated him), and early development (normal till about age four). Gregory's mom answered each question in short, crisp sentences, though she elaborated quite a bit about her husband's relationship with Gregory. She admitted that he was extremely intolerant and verbally abusive of the boy, and she sometimes had to restrain him from hitting Gregory. Throughout this conversation, Gregory did not react in any noticeable way; he just sat and stroked his snake. Oaklander wondered what it would be like to meet with him alone—well, alone if you didn't include Snake.

In the next session, alone with Gregory, he again arrived with his companion. Oaklander thought about asking him to leave the snake at home, but her instincts told her that doing so wasn't the way to begin a good relationship; rather, it would be cutting him off from the one person—er, reptile—he felt close to.

Gregory just sat in the chair, again caressing the snake but otherwise lost in his own world. He didn't look at Violet or pay attention to her in any way. It was as though he were alone.

"Your mom said you weren't too happy in school, and I'm wondering if you can tell me what it is like for you?"

No answer. No response. It was as if he didn't even hear her. Just the rhythmic stroking of the snake.

"I can see that you are really interested in your snake."

As soon as she mentioned Snake, Gregory came back from wherever he went. Oaklander soon caught on that the only subject that would engage him and bring him into contact with her was talk about the snake. He completely ignored any other topic or attempts to speak with him.

He showed no interest in anything in the room: games on the shelves, art supplies, a basket of percussion instruments, drums, puppets, the sand tray. At this point, he actually never even looked at anything.

"So where did you meet your friend?" she asked.

"In the desert, out behind our house."

"I see. And where do you keep Snake?"

"I got him a cage. That's where he stays."

As long as Oaklander kept the discussion centered on the snake, Gregory would answer, however briefly. Once she tried to move into discussion about anything else, he would just drift off. So Violet learned a lot during this second session—but it was all about Snake. She learned that he liked to eat mice best of all and that Gregory would work hard to catch them for him. Actually she was impressed with how much Gregory knew about snakes.

SAND PLAY

Just when Oaklander thought she might have been making some progress, Gregory showed up at their third meeting with a whole bag full of snakes. This was not going well at all.

That week, Gregory's mother had called to let her know that some kids had beaten him at school. He refused to go back because the teachers wouldn't let him bring his snakes. So Oaklander realized how important it was that she had allowed him to bring them to sessions, even that whole bag of squiggly creatures rustling on the floor.

Oaklander took out a Polaroid camera and offered to take pictures of Gregory and his snakes. She mounted them on tag board, then taped the board to the wall before each session. Each time he came in, he would go immediately to the wall and examine the pictures from their previous meetings.

"Here's Lady," he would point. "She's my king snake. And this here is Tyrone, the other gopher snake. I think he's a cousin to Snake." He insisted that Violet write all this down next to each picture, and then underneath he carefully wrote the words, "Owned by Gregory."

Gregory loved the picture taking and was very involved. When Oaklander mentioned the beating incident, his energy faded, and he "disappeared." She brought the subject back quickly to the snake pictures, and he came alive once more. At their fourth session, Gregory came in with a new snake that Oaklander had never seen before. "Can

I put him in the sandbox?" he asked her. "He likes sand 'cause he comes from the desert."

"No, Gregory, you really can't do that. It's not really a sandbox. It's called a sand tray." This was a wooden box, about two feet by three feet, waist high, resting on a small table. It was filled with pure white sand, and on a shelf above it were many miniature objects—trees, houses, people, symbolic things like stars and crosses, monsters, animals, figures, shells, rocks—all kinds of things.

"What's it for?"

"Well, children, and adults too, make scenes in the sand using any of the objects on the shelves. They tell stories about the scene, or sometimes I'll ask them to pretend to be some of the figures and talk about what it feels like, or they make a scene about a dream they had, or about a safe place they wish they had, things like that."

For the first time, Gregory showed real interest in something other than his snakes. He sat on the chair in front of the tray and arranged a bunch of soldiers and a tank and big rock. He had brought a little toad, Myra, with him that day, along with the new snake, and he asked permission if he could at least put his toad on top of the rock. "I won't put the snake in, but the toad won't move off the rock. I'll make sure he doesn't," he said. It looked rather harmless, so Oaklander relented and let him do so. It seemed so important to him. There were also a few toy snakes on the shelf, so of course he incorporated them into the scene. Throughout the whole enactment, he didn't speak at all, but he was very involved and seemed to enjoy what he was doing very much. The toad watched carefully but, as promised, never left his perch.

"Do you want to tell me about your sand scene?"

Gregory ignored her, continuing to arrange things to his liking. He placed a few of the soldiers, dead, lying on their backs. Violet couldn't even imagine what any of it meant, although she was struck by the war scene and the toad sitting on the rock. "Your toad is sitting so safe on the rock away from all the violence. I wonder if Myra feels safe from being hurt."

"Uh huh."

"I bet you wish you could feel safe sometimes."

That was all he was going to say about it. When time was up, he picked up his snake, put Myra in his pocket, and walked out without saying goodbye.

SNAKE THERAPY

It was the next week that Oaklander met a new friend, Bert. He was a horned lizard, a frightening-looking creature that had horns growing out of his head, right above his eyes. He looked menacing with rows of spines along his back like armor and a look that seemed quite suspicious, as if he wasn't sure he wanted to be there.

Oaklander dutifully took Bert and Gregory's picture together, just as she had before, and the boy carefully wrote along the bottom of it, "Bert, Owned by Gregory."

After all this time, Gregory still would not talk to Oaklander about any of his problems at school or home. They could only converse about the snakes or about Bert, in which case he would give brief answers about where he found them or what they ate. At least Violet was making progress with her own reptile aversion, as she could now hold the snakes herself without getting the willies. In fact, during one session they built an obstacle course around the room with blocks and toys and then each took a snake and had them race from one end to the other. She wasn't sure if Gregory was getting any better, but she was certainly enjoying their rather unusual interactions. Sometimes they would both lie on the floor, watching the snakes crawl across the room through tunnels that Gregory would make out of blocks.

Then one day an idea came into her head. Rather than speaking to Gregory, she felt she had developed a good enough relationship with Snake and Lady and Tyrone that she could talk to them directly. She looked at Gregory first and said, "I'd like you to imagine that you can speak for your friends, and that they can talk and say some of the things that you would like to say. Can you do that? I want very much to talk to them!"

Gregory nodded his head cautiously, not sure what he was committing himself to.

"Good," she said in a way to indicate that they had made some kind of agreement. Then she looked at the gopher snake crawling on the floor; his name was One. "Hey One snake, how are you doing today?"

"Fine," answered Gregory for his friend, and getting into the game.

"Do you have any friends, Mr. Snake?"

"Sure. Lots of them," Gregory answered, concentrating seriously.

"What you guys do together?"

"Oh, we catch mice and lay in the sun and stuff like that."

And so the sessions took a new turn.

"Hey, Snake," Violet would say. "Do you feel lonely sometimes? I bet it's pretty lonely being in cage all by yourself."

"Yes," Gregory answered on behalf of the snake. "I do feel lonely. When Greg goes to school during the day there's nothing to do. And I really don't have any friends I can play with."

"And what about you, Gregory? Do you feel lonely too?"

A nod. A small nod, but it was there nevertheless.

"So Snake, do you get mad sometimes?"

"Yeah, lots of things make me mad."

It was very slow going, just a little progress at a time. Eventually, through patience and endless conversations with snakes and lizards, and sometime even a toad, Gregory became interested in things other than his reptiles. He began to notice things in the office other than his photos on the wall. Oaklander brought in a bucket from home and filled it with sand; that way Gregory had a place to put his friends so that he and Oaklander could talk together. They played in the sand tray. They did some modeling in clay. They played some games. Sometimes he would become anxious and would shut down and go right to the snake bucket.

"I guess something happened that bothered you, and I know you don't want to talk about it. That's OK." Oaklander said soothingly, letting him know that she understood his reluctance. It was at such points that they would return to communications via the snakes.

"Do you have a family?" she asked the snake.

"Yes."

"How about brothers and sisters?"

"No."

"Do you have a mother?"

"Yes."

"A father?"

"No."

"How about a stepfather?" The man was not often mentioned in their conversations. She had yet to meet him.

Gregory hesitated for a moment, then nodded his head.

"So you have a stepfather?" she asked the snake.

Slight nod of the head.

"Well, what is your relationship like with him?"

"Hate him. Hate him."

"Gee, that must hard for you then to have to live with someone you don't like very much."

Eventually, Gregory began talking about his stepfather, and every time he did, he talked about how much he despised the man. Oaklander wondered why he hated the guy so much, so she invited the mother to come back to find out what was going on. Apparently her husband couldn't stand being around this weird kid who was always draped in snakes and lizards.

Once Gregory said to her, "You are always trying to get me to draw, so I'm going to draw a picture. But you can't look." Oaklander was delighted. He drew for a while and then said, "OK, you can look now." He held a sheet of paper half way over his drawing and asked her what she thought it was.

"Well, it looks like a shaggy dog with long ears."

He whipped the cover paper off, and it was obvious that the drawing was of a naked lady. He was totally delighted with this drawing and told Violet a neighbor boy had showed him how to do it. Since this was the first age-appropriate thing he had done in all the time she was with him, she felt it represented great progress. They talked about the "trick" for a while, and she casually asked him if he had a girlfriend.

"Well, there's a girl in school I like. She's nice to me. But I guess she's not really my girlfriend." He smiled shyly.

SUDDENLY GONE

About a year and a half passed, during which time they met on a weekly basis. Every four to six weeks, Mom would join them for a session, but each time she would come, Gregory refused to sit with them in the chairs. He would pile up pillows and hide behind them.

"So, how are things going?" Oaklander asked the mother at one of their joint sessions. The mother started to cry, then reached into her purse to grab a tissue.

"What's going on? What's wrong?" Oaklander was alarmed and imagined something terrible had happened—maybe more knife chasing.

"Nothing," the mother sniffed. Violet could see Gregory peeking out from behind the pillows, concerned about his mom.

"I notice you're crying," Oaklander said.

"It's just . . . It's . . . The most wonderful thing happened last night." She broke out into a most glorious smile and Violet grinned back, relieved.

"What's that?"

"Well, last night Greg came up to me and he hugged me. He told me he loved me. He's never done that before." Gregory's head popped up above the cushions, and Oaklander could see he was smiling broadly. He was trying to hold the smile back but it was just too big for him to contain.

This is the point in the story that is supposed to have this satisfying, complete ending in which everyone lives happily ever after. Gregory's mother decided to file for a divorce, and after that she was so broke she rather abruptly moved to another state to be with her family. All of a sudden she was gone, and Gregory with her.

Gregory and his therapist had a last meeting together—a session where Gregory concentrated mainly on the snake he brought with him, the one Oaklander recognized as the first one she had met. She said heartfelt good-byes to Gregory and to the snake and told them how much she liked them and would miss them. But this time there was no response from either of them.

"This was a bizarre experience for me," Oaklander related. "We had worked so hard together, for so long, and yet I never got to find out how the story ended. It was just over, just like that. I never even found out how his anger had gotten so out of control that he had chased his mother with a knife that one time. I assume that he was being physically and emotionally abused by his stepfather, but I never confirmed this. There was so much we never got to talk about, and so much I never learned."

If this seems frustrating to you, just imagine how difficult it was for Violet, who had invested so much time and energy into this relationship—and even learned to enjoy holding snakes.

Violet still has the series of Polaroid photos of Gregory, standing tall and proud with Snake, Lady, One, Tyrone, and all the others. She sees the words he inscribed in his neat script at the bottom of each one: "Owned by Gregory." Occasionally, she takes the photos out and studies them, wondering what he is doing today and how he is getting on. She would like to think that he eventually found his own voice, that he no longer had to communicate solely through his reptiles.

She had hoped that one day she might hear from them again, or at least receive a call from another therapist who wanted some information about the case, but the call never came. And Violet is left to wonder.

CHAPTER EIGHT

Harville Hendrix

Getting Rid of Old Junk

Harville Hendrix is the founder of Imago Relationship Therapy, an approach to couples work that combines his early spiritual-religious training with communication and relationship enhancement features. This unique method was published in a series of books: Getting the Love You Want: A Guide for Couples; Giving the Love That Heals: A Guide for Parents; Keeping the Love You Find: A Guide for Singles; *and* The Couples' Companion, *which contains a series of exercises and activities for following his program of "conscious marriage."*

Hendrix describes himself as a New Yorker who sleeps in New Jersey. He and his wife, Helen LaKelly Hunt, have not only collaborated on their books and the Imago Institute but also produced six children.

Several years ago, Hendrix and his wife produced a series for Public Television based on their best-selling books. It was called *Getting the Love You Want* and was introduced and endorsed by Oprah Winfrey, who also promoted the program on her show. This, of course, reached a wide audience, many of whom contacted Hendrix for help with their faltering marriages. Among them were Fred and Greta, who managed to track Harville down and request a consultation at his earliest convenience. This is the story of what happened.

THE OPRAH SHOW

Fred and his wife, Greta, are sitting in the living room watching *The Oprah Winfrey Show.*

"You see that guy?" Fred asked his wife.

"Yeah," she answered, "so what?"

Greta was from Hungary, the product of peasant stock, and spoke with a thick accent. She was also quite a feisty woman, especially when it came to her husband. They had met when Fred attended an education conference near her home. He was a teacher at an elite private school, and although an American, he had long ago adopted British mannerisms and speech patterns. Greta, also a teacher by profession, had met her future husband at the conference, and they had been married for thirty years.

"So," Fred responded to his wife's challenge. "I was thinking maybe that guy could help us."

"See him? *See* him? What the hell could he do? He's one of those quacks. We had guys like him in Hungary. Say what you will about the government, but they never would allow frauds like that to be on television. He'd end up in the prison. He'd . . ."

"Look, Greta, I was just saying that he's an expert on marriage. Look at him. He's on *Oprah,* for Christ's sake! She wouldn't have just anyone on her show. Maybe he could do something for us. Nothing else has worked."

"Hah!"

"What's that, Greta?"

"I said, hah!"

Fred just shook his head. He was a distinguished-looking gentleman, quite proper as befitting a teacher, and long accustomed to his wife's moods. They had been sitting silently for most of the two hours they had been watching the show. Hendrix had been demonstrating ways that couples could learn to communicate with one another more effectively and express themselves in more respectful, caring ways. They were especially thoughtful during the segment when Hendrix talked about anger, as that feeling was so pervasive in their relationship.

"Look," Fred tried again, "I was just saying that maybe we could see the guy." His voice trailed off at the end, as if he acknowledged that things were hopeless as well.

"Hah," Greta said a third time, but with less force than before.

Greta was a petite woman, but a bundle of energy. She had curly dark hair, worn in a tight bun. She wore thin, metal-rim glasses that framed her wrinkled face. She was rail thin, not at all fitting the stereotype of a Hungarian peasant.

"Well," Greta continued after a long pause, staring at Hendrix on the screen, watching him work with a couple. He did seem kind of nice, and he had a wonderful, resonant voice. "I don't know if anything could help us, especially help you. But I agree we have to do something. I don't think there is any help for this marriage."

This was the same conversation they had been having throughout their whole married life. If they both agreed on one thing, it was that their marriage was lousy and always had been. Yet something emotionally bonded them to one another. And then there was the mutual respect they held for one another in their professional capacities.

"Well then," Fred said, leaving the rest of his thought unfinished. He was not quite sure how to take this conversation any further without ending up in another argument. Fred had been a teacher throughout most of his career, and he valued proper comportment above all else. He even dressed the part in his rumpled tweed suits, white shirts, and striped ties.

Whereas Greta could be a bit shrill and aggressive at times, Fred's style was to be more passive-aggressive—he would resist his wife not by opposing her directly but by dragging his feet. After years of combat, they had each adapted to one another's style in such a way that they could sustain their conflict indefinitely.

THE GERMANS INVADE

Greta grew up in a small village in Hungary during World War II. She had vivid memories of German troops moving through the countryside and of having to hide in the cellar with her family to avoid contact. There had been weeks at a time when they had to go without much food and minimal water. It had been freezing cold as well, so frigid that they had to burn horse manure to stay warm. Then, when they had to eat the horse, they lost their only source of fuel for heat.

It was Greta's mother who had somehow kept the family together, kept them safe, and helped them survive. Each time enemy soldiers were spotted, she would gather the family together and hide underground, where they would gnaw on rotten potatoes and drink whatever water they could find from the rain gutters.

Once the troops moved on, the family could resume their hard life trying to eke out an existence on the war-ravaged land. When the Allied troops chased the Germans away, they were perceived as no less dangerous and unpredictable. This life in fear went on for years, and it helped explain, in part, why Greta was so intense and reactive.

BEGINNING THERAPY

Fred and Greta showed up at Hendrix's office with little hope for relief. Fred walked in first, genteel and proper as always. Greta straggled in behind him, looking defiant and angry.

"Where do you want me to sit?" she barked at Hendrix before he had a chance to introduce himself.

"I'll let the two of you decide where you want to sit," Hendrix answered, curious as to how and where they would arrange themselves. "I am going to sit in this chair, and you pick which chair you want to sit in."

"You sit over there," she directed her husband, "and I'll take this chair." They positioned themselves in exactly the same configuration they were accustomed to at home: Greta on the left, Fred on the right.

"So," Hendrix prompted the couple, "what can I do to help?"

Greta just crossed her arms and glanced at her husband, as if to say, "You dragged us into this mess, so you explain why we're here."

"We can't talk to each other," Fred answered simply but accurately. "We just can't seem to talk without getting in a fight."

"Whatdya mean?" Greta challenged him, demonstrating exactly what he had just said. "I talk just fine. You're the one who never talks."

Hendrix looked at Fred, waiting for a response.

"That's true," he agreed. "I don't talk much."

"OK," Hendrix acknowledged. "What would you like me to do to help?"

"We saw you on TV," Fred said shyly.

"Yes."

"We saw what you did with that couple, the way you helped them talk better."

"Hah," Greta mumbled under her breath, but clearly audible.

"Did you say something?" Hendrix asked her.

Greta just scowled and crossed her arms. This was a very angry lady.

"So," Hendrix responded, looking carefully at each of them, "you're both hoping that I might do something to help you talk to one another better. You haven't had much success working on this on your own, so you came to me for help."

Greta stared at Hendrix over the rims of her wire glasses. "Whatever," she said with a shrug. Hendrix wasn't sure if that was an agreement or mere indifference.

"I wonder if each of you might say some more about what you'd like from these sessions. And I'd like you to talk to one another rather than to me."

Fred began first, an easy choice considering that Greta looked determined to remain mute and uncooperative. "I'd just like for us to be able to talk," he said, "without a lot of yelling and shouting."

"Look at your wife when you are saying that," Hendrix directed him.

Fred nodded his head, but still looked at the therapist rather than his wife.

"What about you, Greta?" Hendrix probed. "What do you want?"

"I don't know," she said. "I don't know what I want." For the first time, she looked a little vulnerable, as if she were not nearly as strong as she pretended.

"OK," Hendrix acknowledged. "Say that to your husband. Tell him that you don't know what you want from him."

Greta turned in her chair a few degrees in the direction of Fred, but stared at the space between their chairs rather than at him. "I don't know what Fred can get . . ."

"Fred is sitting right there," Hendrix interrupted. "Tell him, not me."

Ignoring the instructions, Greta continued to talk to Hendrix as if Fred wasn't in the room. "I just don't think he can get anything from this. He's not emotional. He doesn't talk. That's it." Then she crossed her arms again.

Throughout the rest of that first session, Hendrix continued to get them to talk about what they felt were their greatest difficulties. He noticed that whereas Greta had no trouble talking about her disappointments and dissatisfaction with her husband, she had nothing to say about herself. Fred, on the other hand, was self-deprecating, but he seemed to do this as a way to hide and avoid having to talk about anything meaningful.

A ROOM FULL OF BOXES

About the only thing Fred was willing be critical about when it came to his wife was that she was a lousy housekeeper. They had a very dirty house because Greta didn't like to clean. She refused to dust, mop, or scrub. By the standards of rural Hungary, their home was probably perfectly normal.

For Fred, who aspired to be the perfect English gentleman and kept his own appearance immaculate, Greta's poor housekeeping was frustrating.

"Tell her that, Fred," Hendrix instructed. "Tell your wife what you'd like to change."

"I did," Fred pleaded. "I do tell her. But it doesn't make any difference."

"Don't tell me, Fred. Tell your wife. And look at her when you speak."

"She knows. Believe me, she knows."

"Sure I know," Greta challenged him. "How could I not know? You tell me all the time. The house is fine with me. You're the one with the problem."

She had a point in a way. The messy house *was* his problem, but it still became an ongoing flare point in their conflicts. It was particularly annoying to Fred that Greta had filled up a whole room with stacks of boxes containing nothing but junk—old magazines, worn-out clothes, and other useless stuff. The boxes were stacked to the ceiling.

"She never throws anything out," Fred accused her. "She's got so many damn boxes in there you can't even walk in the room."

That wasn't quite true, as Greta had left a narrow pathway in the room that allowed her to browse through the boxes and add more things to the collection.

"These boxes," Fred said, for the first time showing real emotion, "they are all full of junk. There is nothing valuable in them. They are like our relationship. Our relationship is full of junk and accumulated stuff. Nothing ever moves through our lives. Nothing ever gets cleaned up. Nothing ever changes."

Hendrix was impressed with this observation but also incredibly frustrated with the way things were going. It seemed impossible for him to hold these two angry, resentful people in dialogue. It felt as though he were trying to contain two wild animals. Greta was like a bucking bronco. Fred resembled a gentle lamb, except that he would lash out unexpectedly, just when his wife calmed down.

When pressed to explain why she kept the boxes, Greta said they were full of memories. "I had nothing growing up. Any little thing we had was used for something. Nothing was wasted. Nothing was ever thrown away. I just thought that someday, we might need something that's in one of those boxes. If I threw the stuff out, we might regret it."

This was only one ongoing source of conflict between them, but the most dramatic one. Hendrix tried to get them to look at the symbolic meaning of the boxes and at their conflicted interactions over them. After a period of time, they finally reached an agreement: Greta would sort through one box each week and throw out the stuff that was never going to be needed. This wasn't the most interesting therapy, or the most dramatic progress, but it was all they could do for now.

DIALOGUE

It soon became apparent that both Fred and Greta lived in a survivor mentality. They had little money and lived on the edge of poverty. He was paid very little as a teacher in a private school, and they lived in a very expensive area. Greta lived in constant fear that they would lose everything, that at any moment Fred could lose his job and then they'd be sunk. This wasn't a rational fear, considering that he'd held the position most of his working life, but fear had always been a part of her life.

Meanwhile, they worked on the boxes, one at a time, making steady but slow progress unloading the junk in their lives. The one high point besides this was their mutual love of classical music. Attending concerts together or listening to records provided the one safe haven where they shared pleasure rather than mutual pain. There was actually an expression of rapture on Greta's face when she described a recent symphony they had heard together.

A thought struck Harville as she talked about the experience. "Tell me," he asked her, "when the two of you listen to music, do you hold hands?"

"Hold his hand? Why would I ever do that?"

So even the most basic intimacies were denied them. This gave Hendrix an idea.

"I wonder if you might talk to one another about any feelings you have about being closer to one another."

Greta thought about this for a moment, but declined to answer. She glanced shyly in the direction of her husband.

"Sure," Fred said without hesitation. "I'd like to be closer. I think it's been five, maybe six years since we had sex."

"You were lucky to get it then!" Greta chirped in.

Fred looked at Hendrix pleadingly, as if to say, please talk some sense in this woman.

"Besides," Greta added, "why would I want to have sex with you?"

"Well," Fred stuttered, "well, it's just something that husbands and wives do." He was very uncomfortable with the direction the conversation had taken.

What emerged next was a picture of their sex life, as best as they could remember. Their sexual relationship had been unsatisfactory for both of them. Ever since they were married they had always had sex in the dark, and always with Greta fully clothed. There had never been any foreplay or passion, just awkward fumbling in the dark, fully clothed. That they had managed even to consummate their marriage was a miracle.

Hendrix was struck by how emotionally primitive they were even though they were so sophisticated intellectually. This seemed like a perfect opportunity to initiate an exercise in which they might engage one another on a more intimate level.

HOMEWORK

Hendrix structured situations in which the couple could engage in dialogue with one another about the feelings they had toward one another. Throughout their interactions he noticed a strange phenomenon he had never seen before: they never made direct eye contact with one another. They had been living together for over thirty years. They slept in the same bed. They ate their meals at the same table. They talked to one another about their days, about their dreams, about their fears, but they never looked at one another as they did so.

Once he noticed this pattern, Hendrix asked the couple to look at one another as they spoke. "When you say that to him," he directed Greta, "I want you to look your husband in the eye. And Fred, when your respond to your wife, I want you to make eye contact with her."

Each time he would repeat these instructions, both husband and wife would stare in the general direction of each other, but never look directly at one another's eyes. The task seemed so difficult for them that they seemed to have devised a way to stare at one another's fore-head or mouth or, more often, the center of the chest, but never in the eyes.

"I notice that when you speak to one another," Hendrix reflected back to them, "you don't make eye contact."

"I can look at him," Greta insisted, "but I don't want to."

"Maybe you could try that now," Hendrix gently suggested.

Yet try as she might, the closest she could get was his nose, never directly in his eyes.

"What about you, Fred?" Hendrix tried next.

"It's just hard for me to look at her," he admitted. "She always looks so angry that I don't like to see that."

Hendrix reassured them both and said that it was obvious that they couldn't do what he was asking. The sort of intimacy that accompanied eye contact was just more than they could handle.

"What I'd like you to try, and you can stop any time you wish, is to experiment with something. Let's just see what happens. I want you to concentrate on your breathing. Just relax. Good. Now, I want you to look at one another. Look directly in one another's eyes, just for a few seconds. Then I want you to talk about what that was like."

As they stared at one another's eyes, Hendrix counted off the seconds, reaching five before they broke contact.

"I just can't stand that!" Greta sighed.

Fred nodded his head in agreement. "That was very, very uncomfortable for me too."

"That is perfectly understandable," Hendrix told them. "This is something you are going to need to practice. What I'd like you to do as a homework assignment is to spend some time, working up from five seconds, to reach the point where you can make eye contact with one another for two minutes."

They both looked aghast at that prospect. It was as if Harville had asked them to do the absolutely most distasteful thing imaginable. Nevertheless, they agreed to try.

Fred and Greta returned the next week and reported that they had had the worst fight of their marriage. It was vicious. It was sustained. And it was ugly. First, Greta had exploded. Then, uncharacteristically, Fred gave it right back to her. He started screaming at her, stood up, and locked himself in the study. Greta then started banging on the door, but he wouldn't let her in. Finally, this little woman became so enraged she took a chair and smashed it to pieces. This eye contact thing seemed to be far more than they could handle.

REVELATIONS

Hendrix invited Greta to talk about what happened for her. Something had been triggered by the exercise, and he wondered what that might be. The fear, the terror, seemed to go so deep that it was something she had never talked about before, perhaps not even admitted to herself.

She revisited the memories of her childhood when her village had been occupied by the Germans. It turned out that she hadn't actually escaped their notice after all. Greta and her family had been found by the soldiers. This was the end of the war, when they were on the run. They were desperate and had nothing to lose, since the outcome of the war was all but decided. As they retreated back to their own country, the soldiers wreaked havoc on the civilians they found. Greta, her sister, and her mother were brutally raped by the soldiers, more times than she could possibly count.

Greta tearfully told the story of why she so mistrusted men, why the very idea of intimacy with a man, any man, was so terrifying to her she could barely speak about it.

When Hendrix saw tears in Fred's eyes, he assumed he was crying as an empathic response to his wife's anguish. Yet when he asked him what was happening, the husband confessed his own secret, which he had kept all his life. Just about the time of puberty, Fred was molested by his mother, a sexual relationship that continued throughout his adolescence. His guilt and shame were so terrible that he had never told anyone about this experience, nor did he let himself even think about it. Like his wife, he had buried the past and married someone who would not intrude on his privacy, someone who would be content to live together with minimal emotional involvement.

Greta and Fred began to feel empathy for one another. They were indeed survivors of abuse that left them raw and vulnerable. Yet now that their secrets were out, they felt closer to one another than they ever had before. Remarkably, they even looked at one another's eyes as they spoke—not for long, but their eyes did meet.

As the session ended, the couple agreed to try the eye contact exercise again as a homework assignment. They wanted to see how long they could look at one another as they spoke.

This was not a fictional movie where there is an instant cure after a moment's revelation. It took many weeks before they worked up to the point that they could sustain fifteen seconds of eye contact before they had to break away. Then another month before they could last a half minute. Progress was slow but steady.

THEY DID IT!

One day Fred and Greta arrived at their appointment with a strange look on their faces. This was to be the last session for about six weeks during the summer break.

"So," Harville began the session, "what's going on with you two? Something looks different."

Greta smirked, suppressing a giggle, then glanced over to her husband, who was grinning.

"We did it!" Greta announced.

"That's fantastic!" Hendrix said with genuine pride. They had both worked so hard to get to the point where they could now make eye contact for almost two minutes without looking away.

"No," Greta said, "you don't understand. We did it!"

"You did it?"

"Yes. Yes! We did it. We fucked! For the first time in six years!"

Stunned, Hendrix looked at Fred, who nodded his head. "That's right! We did. And it sure felt good to feel a warm body."

"A warm body?" Hendrix clarified. "You mean you actually took your clothes off?"

Ignoring the question, Greta looked at her husband, directly in the eyes, and said, "You're such a hunk."

CHRISTMAS CARD

Spring ended and summer vacation began. When Hendrix returned in the fall, he was informed that Greta and Fred didn't feel they needed to come in again. They had not had a fight all summer long. They were having sex about once per week, without clothes and with the lights on. They could now look at one another in the eyes. This was about as good as things could get. They'd call if they needed any more help.

Six months later, Hendrix received a Christmas card with a note of appreciation. Fred and Greta wanted him to know that they were doing well. They also told him that they had finally cleaned out the room and gotten rid of all the boxes with all the junk. They no longer needed to hold on to the past.

CHAPTER NINE

Scott Miller

The Terminator Finds Himself on a Mental Ward

Scott Miller represents an interesting blend of empirical researcher and relationship-oriented therapist. Together with colleagues Barry Duncan and Mark Hubble, he has analyzed the research on what leads to lasting changes in therapy, and concluded that the actual techniques practitioners use are relatively unimportant when compared to other factors. The latest research, for example, has shown that the method used contributes at most 8 percent to success. Far more important are clients' and therapists' positive expectations, the quality of the relationship, and the client's own resources and motivations—the last two accounting for the bulk of change in successful therapy. What this means, according to Miller, is that the best kind of therapy establishes a relationship that harnesses the client's own ideas, recuperative powers, support systems, and inner resources.

In a series of carefully researched books, Miller, together with Duncan and Hubble, have combined humanistic, relationship-oriented approaches with the efficiency of brief therapy. Their best-known works include The Handbook of Solution-Focused Brief Therapy; Escape from Babel; Psychotherapy with Impossible Cases; *and* The Heart and Soul of Change, *which reviews the latest research on what works best in clinical practice.*

In his most recent book, The Heroic Client, *Miller together with Duncan continue their research and theory building related to the client's self-recuperative powers.*

In addition to his work on the essential ingredients of therapeutic change, Miller has long been involved in work with disadvantaged populations (including the poor and homeless). The Institute for the Study of Therapeutic Change is the base from which he does therapy, conducts workshops, and continues his investigations.

—⁓—

Miller spent his early years working in a hospital setting with people considered psychotic. The clients he met were typically struggling with delusions, hallucinations, and behaviors annoying to others and often to society in general. It is from this population that he can think of dozens of stories that would qualify as extraordinary, although they didn't seem that way to him at the time.

"Hey, Scott," Miller's niece once joked with him one day, "what's it like to be talking to all these weird and sick people all day?"

He thought about it for a moment, puzzled by the question at first. "This is just my job," he explained to the girl. "There really isn't anything all that magical or mysterious about it. For the most part, the people aren't that strange. They look the same as most people. Their problems are similar."

Of course, to anyone else, the people Miller treated would have seemed *very* unusual. They were inclined to talk to themselves, but they also heard voices answering them inside their heads. Their behavior could be rather erratic and unpredictable, even with their systems all loaded up with medication.

As would be the case for anyone who spends a lot of time with mentally disturbed people, Miller became accustomed to the work and to the behavior he encountered. By the way, it should be mentioned that he doesn't like the people he works with referred to as *disturbed.* Though he can't remember where he heard it, he recalls an old story about a deaf man who, while out walking one evening, happened on a home in which a party was taking place. Music was playing, and the people were dancing. Spying the people moving in strange and exotic ways through the window but unable to hear the music, the man concluded the people were mad. He ran to warn the village. Miller said to us, "We call some people strange or—more politically correct—

disturbed. Maybe we just can't hear their music. I just try to dance to the music the client hears."

With that said, there are cases that stand out from the rest. One in particular was so unique that Miller can vividly remember the minutest details of his interactions with the client.

THE TERMINATOR IN BIBLE COUNTRY

At the very beginning of his professional career, Miller was working in a hospital in a conservative religious community. To people who did not understand their meaning and origins, the culture and customs of the dominant culture would seem strange. The same may be said of the practices and atmosphere in your average psychiatric unit.

"This was the heart of Bible country," Miller explained, "so in walks this nineteen-year-old kid who was about to leave on his religious mission to some distant land. He had been learning a language at a special language training center, preparing for his assignment. It was a fairly high-pressure atmosphere where the missionaries have to learn a foreign language in just eight weeks and then pass a proficiency exam."

The pressure seemed to have gotten the better of this young man, who was admitted to the hospital and given a diagnosis of brief reactive psychosis. In sum, he was delusional, paranoid, and seemed quite tortured. His tall, muscular build and disheveled appearance also made him a frightening figure to encounter on the unit. In order to make him more pliable and easy to control, he was immediately given powerful drugs.

When Miller first met his new client, the young man was stripped down to his underwear and locked in a seclusion room. This was a special place that had padded walls and rubber floors where those thought to be dangerous to themselves or others were kept in isolation. There was only one small window located high on the door.

As Miller approached the room, he could see the top of the lad's head appear at the window and then disappear again. Apparently, because the window was so high, the client was trying to see outside by bouncing on the rubber floors as though on a trampoline. Miller figured that the young man was also experiencing akathaisia, side effects from the neuroleptic drugs that lead to intense restlessness, rocking, and lifting of one's feet.

By the time the attendant opened the door, the young man was sitting on the floor Indian-style, with his legs crossed and his outside foot moving restlessly.

"Hello," Miller said, introducing himself, "my name is Scott. What can I call you?" He then positioned himself on the floor, mirroring the posture of his client.

"I'm the Terminator," the young chap said matter-of-factly, as if he were tired of having to tell people the obvious. "You know, I have to save John Connor."

"Wow, that's amazing. Pleased to meet you."

Miller waited a moment to see if the nineteen-year-old would explain more about how he had ended up captured in this facility. He had already been briefed on the case by the staff. They had said the boy had insisted he was the Terminator, the Arnold Schwarzenegger character from the two famous films by James Cameron, from the moment he had arrived. What's more, he now believed that his enemies were holding him in a prison. It was for this reason that he had managed to escape the ward several times, in each case bringing a few other "prisoners" along with him. Several times, the staff nurse would receive a phone call from someone on the obstetrics floor who noticed a group of patients doing the "Thorazine shuffle" toward the exit. (When you are overloaded on these potent medications, it is hard to move any faster than at a shuffle pace.)

Needless to say, the staff on the mental ward was embarrassed and increasingly frustrated by "the Terminator's" getaways. No matter how close an eye they kept on him, he always managed to figure out new ways to get off the floor. At the same time, the series of escapes and recaptures only served to reinforce the young man's belief that he really was a fearless fighter working against the unjust enemies keeping him against his will.

THE TERMINATOR IS INTERROGATED

Miller noticed that rather than talking in the heavy Austrian accent that would be expected of the Terminator, the boy spoke in a staccato, rapid-fire speech that was difficult to understand. Miller figured he was talking like that because he couldn't find anyone to listen to him. Before he could get the words out to people, they would lock him in a room or medicate him more.

"May I call you Terminator?" Miller asked the boy in his skivvies.

"Sure," he quickly replied, reaching out to shake hands.

"Call me Scott," Miller said, pointing to himself, and then continued, "They've called me a lot worse."

"Me too," the young man quickly replied, "They've also been interrogating me off and on."

"How often?"

"Never can tell how often or when."

"Same person?"

"Well, one guy. I think he's the commandant or something. But the rest come and go as near as I can tell."

"Brilliant strategy," Miller said. "Always keeping you guessing."

"Yeah, huh. They're poisoning me, too. Trying to corrupt my software with a virus."

A good point, Miller thought privately. Actually, the missionary was not far off in believing that his captors were poisoning him. After all, they had given him drugs that were making him feel disoriented and agitated and causing his body to act strangely.

"So they're pulling out all of the stops, sounds like," Miller said after a moment's reflection.

"Yeah," the young man said, looking down at the floor and slowly nodding his head.

A DISGUISE

Miller knew that his job was to convince the boy that he was *not* the Terminator. At the very least, he was supposed to follow the traditional psychiatric approach that stipulates not doing anything that might feed into the "delusion." One needn't have been Sigmund Freud to see, however, that the confront-and-drug-the-delusions approach employed on the unit was not working. If anything, *it* was stoking the young man's beliefs.

Drawing on his limited experience at the time, Miller began looking for some way of joining with his client. He remembered the case of a famous hypnotist named Milton Erickson who had once met with a man who insisted he was Jesus Christ. The unorthodox psychiatrist, as Miller recalled, did not oppose but rather simply accepted his client's assertions at face value.

Before thinking about where the conversation might lead or the possible censure he would get from his supervisors, Miller took a deep breath and pressed onward. The pair spent some time discussing the Terminator's exploits and adventures up until this point. This included not only the recent hospital escapes but also selected scenes from the Terminator movies. Although Miller was hardly an expert on this subject, he recalled enough from the films to both prompt and follow the young man in talking about one fight or chase or another. At least they were talking.

At some point along the way, the glimmer of an idea began to occur to Scott. Once again, this was based on the case of Milton Erickson. In that instance, Erickson had not only accepted his client's reality but also put it to work in a way that would ultimately be of service to the man. "Are you Jesus?" he'd asked, "the carpenter?" And when the man responded that he was, Erickson put him to work at the hospital building bookshelves.

Putting the missionary's idea into play, Miller then asked the crossed-legged teenager, "I've been wondering if you really are the Terminator?"

The boy gave him a look of great suspicion and anger. Here it was again, the same thing: another one of the evil captors was going to tell him he was not who he claimed to be. He wondered why these people were so stubborn and stupid. Couldn't they see who he was? How many times did he have to explain himself?

"Wait, wait," Miller quickly interjected, aware that he was about to lose his client. He continued, "It's just that, as I've been listening to you talk, I've had the sneaking suspicion that you really aren't the Terminator after all." Then, after pausing a full beat, he added, "Aren't you really Arnold Schwarzenegger?"

The statement seemed to catch the young man off guard. Gradually, the look of surprise on his face transformed into what seemed like amusement.

"How did you know?!" the boy said in true astonishment. "How did you know who I really am?"

Sitting opposite this huge, underwear-clad, grinning guy, Miller thought to himself, "Just damn lucky," and then wondered how he'd guessed this might be a good thing to try.

"So," he said, "what should I call you? Do you prefer to be called the Terminator or Arnold Schwarzenegger?"

"My friends call me Arnold," the boy grinned again, then licked his lips. Dry mouth, Scott thought, another side effect from the drugs.

"Well, OK Arnold, thanks. So, aren't you married to Maria Shriver?"

"Yeah, isn't she great?"

Right before Scott's eyes, a major transformation had occurred. Now he was talking to Arnold Schwarzenegger, trying to remember as much as he could about the actor's various movies. While they were

reviewing what it was like to make the Terminator films, Miller was trying to figure out where to take this next. It had seemed like a good idea
at the time, but he wasn't sure if things were any better off with the guy
believing he was Arnold Schwarzenegger rather than the Terminator.

A DIFFERENT ROLE

Somehow Miller had to use the leverage he had found to help the boy
take a step closer to a different reality, one that more closely paralleled
the world that most of us live in.

"You're obviously a great, great actor, Arnold."

"Thanks."

Although this might very well have been what Schwarzenegger
would have said, the boy didn't use anything remotely like the real
Schwarzenegger's slow voice and distinctive Austrian accent. Instead
his words came out rapid-fire, as if his voice were a machine gun.

"I am wondering if you are up for kind of a very different role for
yourself?"

"What do you mean?" the boy asked, now curious where this was
leading.

"I had in mind a role for you that is very different from ones that
you've played before. This wouldn't involve being a warrior like the
Terminator. It would be something far more, well, *challenging*."

"I can play any role. It's just that these Hollywood hacks, well, I've
been stereo-whatdoyoucallit."

"Stereotyped?"

"Dat's it. But I could do a lot more."

"I *believe* you," Miller responded. "That's why I think you'd be perfect for this part."

"OK, OK, sowhatofyougot?" He was so excited, his words ran together and both his feet were tapping on the rubber floor. He looked
as though he was going to lift right off the floor. Miller remembered
again his first glimpse of the young man, the top of his head bouncing into view in the high window.

"This isn't a quiet, strong person like the Terminator," Miller prepared him.

"IknowIknowthat'sOKthat'sOK."

"It isn't an action hero at all."

The boy's head nodded up and down.

"OKalready, so whatisit?"

"I want you to play the role of a mental patient."

"What does that mean?" He genuinely looked confused, expecting something altogether different.

"It means that I want you to take on the role of a patient in a mental ward. This means that you participate in all the activities of the other patients. You go to group and talk about your problems. You show up for therapy sessions."

"Does this mean I'd have to go to arts and crafts?"

He was referring to the ridiculous activities they scheduled where the patients were supposedly kept busy doing socially useful things like making clay pots and finger paintings.

"Yeah," Miller said, taking on the persona of a movie director. "This would be a very, very *challenging* role for you to play."

"Ah," said Arnold.

"But I think you're up for a challenge."

"Yes," the young man said thoughtfully, his voice now slowing.

"Nobody could know it was just an act. You'd have to really be convincing."

The boy nodded.

"And one more thing," Miller added.

"What's that?"

"No escapes."

BACK TO THE MISSION

Once they had agreed on the next steps, Miller assured his client he would have a talk with the staff about letting him out of the rubber room so he could begin his new role as a mental patient.

"When I told the staff what I'd done," Miller told us, "there were feelings of both shock and intrigue. Remember, this was a traditional psychiatric facility in a pretty conservative place, so folks were anxious to remain based in reality and not try anything too far out. But they were also pragmatists. What had been tried so far had not worked. Even so, the general opinion, as near as I could tell, was that my naive enthusiasm was inspiring but not likely to be effective in the long run."

"Anyway, over the next couple days, I continued to meet with this young man. I would seek him out or he would come tell me that he was doing this—that he was acting the role of a mental patient. And guess what? After three or four days, the boundaries began to blur. You couldn't tell if he was the Terminator or Arnold Schwarzenegger or this other guy—a missionary—who everybody said he was. More and more often, he ended up playing himself."

As he looks back on this case in the present, even Miller isn't sure if the guy recovered because of what Miller did, what the nurses and other staff were doing, or as the result of the medication the young man was given.

"It was probably a combination of all those things. But what struck me about this case was how plastic and how flexible reality was—not just for him but for everybody. Additionally, it really showed me how important it was to get along with rather than fight the people we try to help. I had to give this guy some way to participate in the process rather than try to convince him that he was deluded."

Soon after this, the boy was released from the hospital and once again began preparing for his mission—not a Terminator type of mission but the religious variety. When Miller followed up on the case, he learned that the church decided to keep him closer to home rather than sending him abroad. There was always the concern that this was not just a brief psychotic break but the beginnings of full-fledged, chronic schizophrenia.

DECODING INTENTIONS

Although by today's standards Miller's approach is more common, during those days his behavior would have been considered strange if not unprofessional. It was precisely because he was a beginner that he was willing to take risks that would not have occurred to his more conventional supervisors.

We wondered what others could learn from this case. Miller explained that so much about therapy, or relationships in general, involve figuring out what the other person's perception of reality is all about and then joining that viewpoint. This idea reminded him of another, more recent case.

The person was a man in his forties diagnosed as both schizophrenic and alcohol dependent. What this means is that in addition to taking antipsychotic drugs, he also medicated himself on alcohol binges that wreaked havoc on his body and already fragile mind. He was being treated at a community mental health center, and Scott was called in to consult on the case. The treatment team felt a bit stymied after seeing the man for four years. Their current work was based on helping their client "internalize what he had been taught in therapy."

Said Miller, "Anyway, so I go in to talk to this guy, and the more I talk to him, the more clear it becomes that his idea is that he cannot be sober for himself. The only reasons he will be sober are to make his therapist look good and to be a humble servant of God. My suggestion to the treatment team at the end of the session is that they focus *less* on helping the man internalize what he has been taught and instead find a way for this guy to serve others by being sober."

Miller said this so simply, but the concept is profound. In his work, one of his most important tasks is to figure out the intentions of his clients, to hear *their* music.

"It's easy to understand people who think or feel like us. We have to understand acts and behavior from the perspective of the people who do them in order to have any useful dialogue with them. Change is not possible without that."

CHAPTER TEN

Insoo Kim Berg

They Learned to Live with Ghosts

Combining Western scientific methods and brief therapy strategies with Eastern philosophy, Insoo Berg collaborated on a number of influential projects to advance the practice of solution-focused therapy. As codeveloper of a therapy model that emphasizes brief, directive, and creative solutions to problems that are presented, Berg has been instrumental in helping therapists work more efficiently and effectively. Rather than following traditional practices of bringing up the past, searching for underlying issues, and treating symptoms as mere signs of deeper issues, Berg emphasizes the importance of remaining in the present as much as possible and treating the presenting problem.

In addition to her work in clinical practice and her position as Executive Director of Brief Family Therapy in Milwaukee, Berg has authored a number of books, including Interviewing for Solutions; Tales of Solutions; The Miracle Method: A Radically New Approach to Problem Drinking; *and* Solutions Step by Step: A Substance Abuse Treatment Manual.

Berg thought of two clients who fit the bill as the most memorable of her career. Both could be considered schizophrenic with auditory and visual hallucinations. Because she does not ordinarily subscribe to traditional diagnostic labeling, Berg looked at both clients as holding some rather unusual perceptions of reality and began to think about how to utilize these, instead of correcting the clients' perceptions.

HE LIVED INSIDE HER HEAD

"I want to get a job," Tanya said, "like in a hardware store."

"OK," Berg agreed, "so what's the problem?"

"I've been divorced for about four years."

"I see," Berg said, not seeing at all what this had to do with a job in a hardware store. She did notice that the woman had some sort of nervous tic.

"They put me on all kinds of medicines," she added helpfully, "but I don't want to take that stuff anymore. It makes me feel funny and it doesn't work."

Now there were three threads Berg was trying to follow: something about the woman's medication, her divorce, and that job she wanted in a hardware store.

"So, what do you need to do to get a job in a hardware store?" Berg wanted to begin with something they could do something about.

"My ex-husband. He keeps bothering me. Won't leave me alone, and he is always there telling me I can't do this or that."

"Your husband keeps bothering you?"

"Uh huh."

Realizing that it was more useful to ask about when Tanya was doing well rather than when she was not, Berg inquired about those times when her husband left her alone.

"Well, sometimes he does leave me alone," she agreed.

"How does he decide to leave you alone?"

"I don't know, but I think he feels sorry for me sometimes. Then I get to vacuum my house, take my dog out for a walk, and things like that."

"OK," Berg said, trying to track carefully the nature of what was going on in this confusing beginning. "And when does your ex-husband bother you?"

"Right now."

"He's bothering you right now? As we speak?"

"That's right. He is always telling me what to do."

"How do you know that?" Berg asked. "How can you tell he bothers you?"

"Because I can hear him talking to me, like right now."

"You mean he is talking to you right now?"

Tanya nodded her head gravely.

"Well," Berg stalled for a moment, trying to figure out what was going on. "May I ask where he is?" She wondered for a minute whether he had entered the office while she wasn't looking. This was getting spooky.

"He's right here in my head," Tanya said, pointing a finger to her forehead. Berg also noticed that the more Tanya talked about her ex-husband, the more frequent her tic became. Now, every few seconds her face would twitch to the right side of her head, and her head would jerk back.

Tanya was insistent that her ex-husband lived inside her head and was always ordering her around, just as he used to do when they were married. He went with her everywhere, always telling her what she could do and what she couldn't do. Lately, he had been telling her that she should stay inside mostly.

"You're not supposed to vacuum the house?" Berg clarified.

"That's right. He doesn't like the noise."

"And you said he won't let you go outside much."

"Uh huh. He doesn't like for me to go for walks. Sometimes I think about going outside, but because he's in my head he knows what I'm thinking before I do because he is inside here. That's how he stops me."

Berg stopped for a moment to gather her thoughts and figure out where to go next. She felt there were so many options possible, one of which seemed especially creative and fitting.

A CHANNELED CONVERSATION

Because Tanya insisted that her ex-husband went everywhere and knew everything she did, Berg decided to follow her line of thought.

"Do you think he can hear me talking to you?" she asked.

"Oh, yes, he can hear everything you are saying, and he doesn't like it one bit."

"You mean he can hear what I'm saying and also understand it?"

Tanya nodded.

"Since you can hear what he says, but I can't hear him, do you mind telling me what he is saying?"

"I don't know," Tanya shrugged. "I can try."

"OK then, what's his name?"

"Michael."

"Michael it is," Berg confirmed. "OK, Michael, I'd like to have a word with you."

"He says he can hear you." Tanya answered on behalf of her husband.

"Good," Berg said, "Well, Michael, I am very curious about your situation here. Most men, after four years of divorce, move on with their lives. And I understand from Tanya that you are remarried and have a new baby."

"He says 'Yeah,'" Tanya answered.

"You obviously must still love Tanya very much to hang around her all the time and get her to do things that you think would be good for her and avoid other things that you think would be bad for her."

"Like vacuuming."

"Exactly."

"So Michael, I just wondered how come you haven't moved on with your own life? Why do you continue to live in Tanya's head when you've got your own life to lead?"

"He says it's none of your business."

Berg kept on talking to Michael, hoping to get a more polite conversation going this time. Berg also noticed that Tanya's tic was a bit less pronounced.

"Michael, I'm still confused about this situation you have here with Tanya. As I said, I can imagine you still must love Tanya very much, and you find it hard to let go of your past with her. What do you need her to do so that you can move on with your own life?"

"He says it's none of your business, and he ain't gonna talk to you anymore. Bitch!"

After a couple more attempts to talk to Michael without him responding, Berg became irritated. "How dare you speak to me that way! I don't appreciate your crude language. And what kind of man are you, anyway? Why don't you stand up for yourself instead of hiding inside this poor woman?"

Berg turned to Tanya and said to her, "He is not a very polite person, is he?"

"Michael," Berg tried again, "you are being very rude."

"I said I don't have to talk to you. Bitch." That last word was hurled out, leaving no question that he was not going to cooperate further.

With a gesture of disgust, Berg turned to Tanya. "He's not only rude, but he can't even stand up for himself."

"Yes," Tanya agreed, "he is like a little mouse, isn't he?"

IT'S NOT YOU, IT'S HIM

During the rest of the session, Tanya explained that the money from her divorce settlement was running out. She had to get a job, and she'd always wanted to work as a sales clerk at a hardware store in town. The problem was that every time she tried to leave the house to try to find a job, Michael in her head would stop her.

Berg couldn't imagine Tanya working as a salesperson anywhere. Her frequent tics would be so distracting they would make almost any customer uncomfortable.

After taking a few minutes to think about the interview and the gist of the conversation she had with Tanya, Berg composed a list of things to compliment Tanya on: the courage it took to stand up to Michael in her head and the wisdom of recognizing that she needed to get a job. Berg also complimented her on the strength it took to defy Michael by coming to the session. Berg further explained that Michael was a very mixed-up person, that he had lots of problems of his own. He was not the sort of person that anyone would want to listen to for very long.

"When you come back next time," Berg directed her, "I want you to make sure you bring Michael with you. He is obviously a very disturbed man, and I think he needs help."

By framing the problem in this way, Berg managed to deflect attention away from Tanya's own eccentricities and instead label the voice in her head as the problem. It was Michael who was crazy, not her.

IGNORING THE VOICE

When Tanya returned for the second meeting three days later, she looked much calmer and more relaxed, and she reported feeling much better. In fact, the tic had almost disappeared altogether.

"So," Berg asked, "what's better for you? You look so different."

"When I left last time, instead of going right home, I went to visit my brother and his wife. They live not too far from here, and they always tell me to come and visit with them, but I haven't done this in the longest time because Michael wouldn't let me. But I went there anyway instead of going home. I spent the weekend with them, and I played with my nephew, which was so much fun." Tanya smiled and laughed as she related what had happened. The tic was now almost unnoticeable.

"I wonder what you can do to make sure that Michael doesn't control you any more, so you can visit whomever you want and even vacuum the house without his interference."

"To tell you the truth," Tanya said, "he was always like this, so bossy and all. Even when we were married. I feel sorry for his new wife."

The treatment of Tanya was not speedy, nor without ups and downs. Berg eventually discovered that Tanya was consuming a great deal of alcohol, which had to be brought under control. But gradually her symptoms improved, and she eventually found a job where her nervous facial mannerisms might not be a problem. She found work as an in-home health care assistant, taking care of elderly people with their daily lives.

The most recent follow-up information Berg had after three years was that Tanya was self-supporting, and the elderly man she cared for and his family absolutely loved her. She stayed in contact with the mental health service clinic now and then, just to let them know that she was still doing fine.

It wasn't as if Michael ever left her head. He continued to pester her at times and give her orders. But she simply decided to ignore him. After all, they weren't even married any more. And Berg had persuaded Tanya that it was in fact he who was seriously disturbed.

THE SON COMES TO VISIT

Berg's other case, which bears a striking similarity to the previous one, involved a woman, Jackie, who said she was visited every day by the ghost of her dead son. Not only could she see him clearly, but he usually spoke to her. The young man had been killed in a car accident three years earlier. He had been on his way to school at the time of his death.

Jackie needed lots of time to walk from the waiting room to the therapist's office, leaning on her cane with one hand and holding a Styrofoam cup of coffee in the other. She declined a helping hand as she slowly navigated down the hallway. She slowly sank into the chair, as if it took all her energy just to make it to the office. She was an African American woman in her forties, but she looked much older, as if she had a very hard life. Her face betrayed little emotion, and her voice inflection was flat. It was as though she were dead inside.

Berg wondered if she was on any kind of medication, but Jackie insisted she was not. When asked how coming to see a therapist would be useful to her, Jackie explained that she was very afraid of her son who comes to visit her. Her voice was barely audible and Berg had to pull her chair closer and closer as time went on. Puzzled by this initial information, Berg asked Jackie to elaborate.

Apparently this kind of open-ended request was too much for Jackie to handle, so Berg had to formulate the question in a more pointed and detailed manner, asking a great deal of who, what, when, where, and how questions.

"When does he come by to see you?" Berg wondered.

"Just all the time," Jackie answered.

"What part of the house do you usually find him in?"

"He's standing at the end of my bed. But sometimes I see him in the living room, standing in the corner."

"What does he say when he visits you?" Berg asked.

"Don't know." She said this like she said everything—with no facial expression or changes in her voice intonation. She seemed barely alive.

"You don't know what he says to you? How come?"

"'Cause I turn up the TV real loud. That way I don't have to hear him. Scares me half to death."

More detailed question about her son only produced information that he "mumbles" when he visits her and that he comes and goes, with no predictable pattern to his visits.

WHAT THE GHOST IS SAYING

In order to unravel the mystery of this ghost, it seemed crucial to Berg that she find out what the son was trying to say to his mother. But Jackie insisted that she did not know. As the interview continued, Jackie's voice remained the same and at times became a soft whisper, so quiet in fact that Berg had to move her chair closer to hear anything. She took it as a very good sign that Jackie allowed her to close the distance between them.

Once she was practically sitting on top of Jackie, Berg noticed that her hands had long fingernails that were painted in multicolored hues. Berg tried to engage Jackie by admiring her beautifully painted nails, and asked questions about who had done the work and how she had decided on this particular pattern and this selection of colors. Allowing Berg to hold both of her hands, Jackie talked, slowly but in clear articulation.

Jackie related that her sister did the nails for her. This led to further conversation about other members of the family. Berg learned that in addition to her ghostly son, who had been nineteen when he was killed, she also had a seventeen-year-old daughter, Angela, who was attending high school. Jackie said proudly that Angela was a very good student.

Did her daughter know that her brother comes to visit her mother?

"No, because I don't tell nobody about him."

"Does your son visit his sister as well as you?" Berg asked.

"I don't think so," Jackie answered, so softly that Berg had to lean in to hear the words. "At least she hasn't said nothing about it."

"So you're the only one your son visits right now?"

"Well, he used to see his girlfriend. That's what she told me. But he don't come around there no more."

"So he only comes to see you because he likes to talk to you. You're the one he trusts the most."

"Maybe so," she admitted. "We was very close, him and me. He was a good boy."

"I wonder what your son is trying to tell you?" Berg asked, then answered the question herself. "It seems to me that he must love and miss you very much."

"I expect so," Jackie agreed, nodding her head.

Jackie still had no expression on her face, but tears started streaming down her cheeks.

"I was just wondering," Berg said, "whether your son visits you anywhere else besides the bedroom and living room?" She was thinking that maybe they could confine the visit from the ghost to just designated places, a confined space in the house so that Jackie might find sanctuary elsewhere.

"Just those places," Jackie answered.

"What about his own bedroom? Does he ever go in there?"

"Don't know. I never go in there."

"How come?" Berg wondered.

"I'm too scared." Jackie explained in a whisper that ever since her son had died, she had not reentered his room. She left it exactly the way it was, never touching a thing.

Thinking perhaps some sort of good-bye ritual might be useful, Berg asked further: "How about the cemetery? Do you ever visit your son there?"

"No, I'm too scared to go there. I don't like going there neither."

So Jackie lived in terror that her son's ghost would haunt her wherever she went. Yet what most confused Berg about the story was that the son was such a good boy and that they enjoyed such a close, loving relationship. Why on earth would she be afraid of her own son? Berg was really confused about where to go with this.

SPEAKING THROUGH TEARS

After taking some time to think about what she had learned during this interview, and to collect her thoughts and formulate the kind of feedback that Jackie might find useful, Berg made the following observation.

"Jackie, I'm really glad that you decided to come and talk to me today so that you can somehow figure out what to do with your son's unwanted visits. It shows what a strong woman you are and how you want to be in charge of your life. The more I learn about you and your son, the more I realize what pain you have been coping with these past three years. I can't imagine how awful that must be for you to lose your child in that way."

"That's true," Jackie said in quiet voice. Tears were still leaking out of her eyes.

"The more I listen to you, the more I am beginning to think that maybe your son is trying to say something to you that is important. I guess we will need to figure out what he is trying to say."

"That sounds all right."

"I think it would be a good idea," Berg suggested, "if you meet with your son only in his room. Nowhere else. If he shows up in your bedroom or in the living room, just tell him that you will meet with him in his bedroom. He belongs only in his own room, so that's where you should meet him."

Jackie thought this might be a good idea and decided she'd give it a try. The following week she returned to say that she was still afraid of her son wanting to talk, and she was quite clear that she did not want her son to visit her no matter what.

Conversation was quite the same; the only difference was that Jackie's tears flowed more freely, every time her son's visit was mentioned. Berg explained that the son's unwanted visits might be his way of expressing how much he missed his mother and that he wished to say something personal and intimate to her.

"I never got to say good-bye to my boy," Jackie said, for the first time showing real emotion in her face. She was now crying freely. "I never got to tell him how proud I was of him. I just miss him so much, but I wish he'd stop coming around."

Whenever there was an opening, Berg offered suggestions about how much her son must want her to be happy and have a good life for herself. Sometimes Berg added that knowing what a thoughtful and loving young man he was, she was sure that he must be looking down at his mother from heaven every day and wishing her a good life.

Jackie nodded her head in agreement but couldn't speak through her tears. When Berg handed her tissues to wipe her face, Jackie just held them in her hand, as if she were reluctant to touch the tears.

Over the course of six sessions, Jackie continued to grieve over the loss of her son, crying continuously throughout the conversations, even using the tissues to dab at her cheeks. She finally reached the conclusion that her son really did mean her no harm, that he was just trying to say good-bye because Jackie needed this closure. Yet she was reluctant to hear him speak, because she thought that then he might go away and she'd lose him forever. At the end of six sessions, Jackie said that she did not need to come anymore because she felt that even though he comes to visit her now and then, she is not as scared of him and will learn to live with his visits.

It has been almost two years since Berg last saw Jackie, and there has been no further contact.

CHAPTER ELEVEN

Michael Yapko

The Woman Who Should Have Been Depressed

Michael Yapko has written a dozen books about treating depression using a combination of methods that include clinical hypnosis as well as cognitive and strategic therapies. Three of his recent books, Breaking the Patterns of Depression; Hand Me Down Blues: How to Stop Depression in Families; *and* Psychological 911: Depression, *are practical sources of information and guidance for depression sufferers. His other works, including* When Living Hurts *and* Treating Depression with Hypnosis, *provide therapists with guidelines for using brief interventions when working with depressed patients. In addition, he has written several training texts, such as his classic book* Trancework, *on clinical hypnotic methods.*

———∿∿∿———

Yapko is a psychologist, based near San Diego, who has specialized in working with troubled individuals, couples, and families. His unique emphasis on studying how people do things well has led to some innovative applications of his work; for example, he worked as a consultant to the San Diego Wild Animal Park in their captive elephant breeding project. His job had been to teach trainers more effective ways of relating and communicating with elephants in the hope that these skills would increase the elephants' breeding success.

As someone who had spent three years working closely with elephants and their trainers, we expected that Yapko would have a fairly large caseload of unusual cases from which to choose the one that is most memorable. Yet the case he selected is considerably different from the others in this book. He didn't focus on the strange features of the case or on the unusual symptoms his patient exhibited; rather, what struck him as most memorable about this particular case was the courage and resilience of the woman he helped in the face of the health profession's shortcomings she was forced to endure.

Like those of many of our contributors, Yapko's case occurred during the early stage of his career. He received the referral from another therapist at a time in his life when he was overscheduled. He was in the middle of teaching an intensive hypnosis training program to health professionals, after which he was headed out of the country to teach abroad. The only way he would have the time to see the new urgent patient was if she agreed to work with him in a live clinical demonstration as part of the workshop. That meant she would be talking about her problems in front of an audience of strangers, a situation that might usually dissuade someone from opening up during a very first session. It turned out that this was the least of her problems.

BLACK AND BLUE INSIDE

Vicki had been referred to Yapko for instruction in pain control with hypnosis. Just a few weeks earlier she had been diagnosed with cancer that had metastasized throughout her body—it had spread into her adrenal glands, her bones, her lungs, and her brain. She not only had little time left to live but also was often in excruciating pain that she hoped could be managed with hypnosis.

Yapko met Vicki for the first time when she showed up at the appointed time for her consultation. He knew next to nothing about what he would be facing, except that he had only one chance to help her deal with her pain. Although he had been warned to expect a woman in her early forties, he could see that the disease that was ravaging her body had taken its toll on her appearance as well. She was of slight build, with long brown hair down the middle of her back.

She moved awkwardly and was in obvious discomfort. Her bright green eyes were her most riveting feature.

"My greatest concern at the moment," Vicki began the conversation, "is that I know I have a very short time to live. And I don't want to spend it being zonked out on drugs."

Yapko was both surprised and delighted by her bluntness. He knew this was a difficult situation for his patient, confessing that she was dying in front of a room full of strangers. For him to be helpful, he would somehow have to put her at ease and earn her trust.

"I'm OK with dying," Vicki continued. "That's not the hard part. The hard part is being able to get done all that I want to get done in the time I have left."

As she spoke, Vicki rearranged herself in the chair trying to find a comfortable position. The tumors that had spread throughout her body caused pain in her feet and nearly immobilized one of her arms to the point where she could no longer rest very peacefully. When Michael asked Vicki about the nature of her pain, collecting information so he could better concentrate his hypnotic efforts, she spoke matter-of-factly about the adversity she was facing.

"There's a lot of pain in my shoulder," Vicki admitted. "It feels like there's something huge inside the joint, which is exactly what it is. And it's pressing, pressing, pressing—so hard that the bone feels like it's ready to explode. And it's just growing, growing—there's no room for it to grow so that's the kind of pain it is. Not only that, but it makes me unable to move my arm in certain ways. I can't lift my arm."

Vicki showed what she was talking about by trying unsuccessfully to move her left shoulder. When she spoke, she gestured only with her right hand.

"It feels like somebody hit me in the shoulder with a baseball bat," she said, "and I have this horrible bruise. Only there's no bruise, but if you looked inside, it would be black and blue everywhere."

FALSELY IMPRISONED

Yapko noticed immediately that although Vicki was taking inventory of her aches and pains, she was doing so in a way that invited no pity. She was straightforward and casual about the challenges she faced. Not so, however, when it came to the anger she felt toward the many doctors she had seen over the years.

Vicki had suspected there was something wrong for a very long time. Yet every doctor she consulted refused to listen to her because they thought she was crazy and a hypochondriac. As a result, her cancer was not diagnosed early enough to treat it effectively. She was going to die because nobody had believed that she was sick or in pain.

Yapko asked Vicki to say more about her history. She described how after the birth of her daughter more than twenty years ago, her estranged husband had her hospitalized in a mental institution for what Yapko suspected was probably postpartum depression but at the time was misdiagnosed as something altogether different.

"My husband put me in a psychiatric hospital," she said, "and I was diagnosed with catatonic schizophrenia, a back ward patient that would never be out of the hospital again. And that's an awfully hard label to overcome."

Indeed, the label of being crazy followed Vicki ever since she was falsely imprisoned, so to speak, even when just a few months earlier she had consulted a therapist about joining a support group.

"I hit this woman with some of my background," Vicki said, still angry about the way she had been consistently mistreated by doctors. "I've been in and out of hospitals a good part of my life. She told me that I was too sick to be in her group—after one hour of talking to me, and then charging me for the session, which I thought was kind of crummy."

Yapko explained to us that there was almost nothing that Vicki could do to shake her label or convince people she wasn't crazy. Once people jump to a conclusion, it is difficult at best to get them to change it.

"In the hospital," Vicki said, "they gave me so many psychotropic drugs. And I had such horrible side effects from them. I would try to tell people . . . but nobody would listen to me. They would say, 'You need more Thorazine.' The more they gave me, the sicker I got. I kept trying to tell people, but nobody listened."

This was to be the refrain of Vicki's life: neither her doctors nor her husband nor even many of her family and friends ever believed or understood much about what she was really going through. Once she had been labeled "crazy" by the doctors, despite her recent accomplishments in life, nobody took her seriously, even when she tried to tell them about what was happening to her body.

TO KNOW THAT I COULD

Yapko spoke with such pain and anger himself when he told Vicki's story. He was indignant that she has been treated so shabbily. And he was in awe of her strength and inner resources.

"Her relationship with her husband was painful. It had been a very violent marriage," Yapko explained, reviewing some more of her background. "She finally ended up leaving her husband, but with nowhere to go became a homeless person living in doorways and on the streets for quite a while. She somehow finally decided to get her life together. She ended up going into therapy with a very competent therapist who really helped her a lot. She also went to school to get her bachelor's degree. Now she was working on her master's degree. There were so many aspects of her turnaround that were simply amazing."

Yapko said this in a hushed voice, apparently still haunted by the power of this woman.

"If you were to say to the average person, 'I'm really sorry but you have three or four months to live,' that would almost instantly depress most people. Here was a woman who had reason to be depressed and probably should have been depressed, but she refused to give up."

Yapko found himself intensely curious as to how Vicki had managed to keep her dignity, her optimism, her hope, in the face of so many, many obstacles. He told us this was a turning point for him in understanding the nature of depression and the power one has to deal with it. He was simply astonished by her attitude toward her life and her forthcoming death.

"At first," Vicki told Yapko, "I was really bummed out that I'm not going to get to graduate. I've been carrying a perfect 4.0 grade-point average. But then I guess the lesson is that I don't have to graduate. It's just as important to know that that I could."

MORE THAN YOUR HISTORY

Yapko and the audience of therapists were intensely moved by Vicki's story.

"I don't think there was a dry eye in the group," Yapko recalled. She was wanting to take charge of her life and of her body. That's the reason why she was there—to learn hypnosis for pain management. It was something very special to see this amazing transition in somebody with a history of hospitalization in a state psychiatric facility, with a diagnosis of catatonic schizophrenia, from a violent marriage to being a street person to ending up a 4.0 graduate student. Vicki powerfully highlights some of the most important lessons I think there are to learn in life."

Yapko wishes that other therapists would get over their misguided belief that a person's future is so automatically predicted by his or her history.

"It has been such a critical piece of my work to be able to communicate to any patient I see, particularly the severely depressed patients, that they are more than their history. Your history is not your destiny. You can change almost any aspect of your life if you approach it in a way that has some merit, sensibility, and appropriateness, and has some well-focused drive to it."

Vicki lived this lesson the hardest way possible. She proved, beyond a shadow of a doubt, that she could still overcome all the labels she had been assigned: homeless, schizophrenic, catatonic, hypochondriac, and personality disordered.

"Vicki described so eloquently how once you get the label of crazy, people treat you like you are crazy. And you start to believe you are crazy. And then you start to act crazy. You live down to people's lowest expectations."

This case, perhaps more than any other, taught Yapko how important it is to strive to use therapy to expand people's strengths rather than merely to shrink their pathology.

FINALLY BEING HEARD

"It turned out," Yapko explained, "to have been a very valuable thing that our session was being done in front of a room full of therapists. As Vicki said, she was a woman who had a pretty extensive psychiatric history. She had whole sections of her memory that were unavailable to her as a result of overmedication and other things that were done in the name of 'treatment.' This led her to be very suspicious of mental health professionals."

Yet here Vicki was getting therapy in front of an audience comprising all those same types of people who had always ignored and mistreated her before. Now they were listening. Now she was being heard. For more than two uninterrupted hours, she could directly tell them many of the things she wished they would have heard years ago.

"Her injunction to me was a very clear one," Yapko said. "In essence, she was saying to me, 'Unless you want to be like those other doctors, you had better listen to me.'"

It took Yapko exactly two minutes after she first hobbled in and sat down to figure out what was going on. "As soon as she said she had a short time to live and didn't want to spend that time drugged and foggy, I was pretty much done with the interview just knowing that was what she wanted. She used language like 'part of me this . . .' and 'part of me that . . . ,' and it was very clear that she thought in dissociative or compartmentalized terms. So I knew the goal was hypnotic anesthesia. And I knew the mechanism would be some sort of dissociation."

Yapko was speaking about his hypnotic method in which he customizes the hypnosis session to the individual language, metaphors, thinking, personality, and needs of each patient.

"I could have done the session literally five minutes after meeting her, but clearly she needed to talk. So I let her talk. I empathized with her and commiserated with her and reinforced her strengths. In spite of having been mistreated by professionals, she was still able to transcend their behavior and build a life for herself. How strong she must be to be able to do that. How clear of vision she must be to be able to do that. I just basically validated and appreciated her throughout the interview."

TRANCEWORK

After the first hour of allowing Vicki to tell her story, Yapko collected all the information he needed about her background, her style, her favored images, and her language patterns so that he could construct a hypnosis session that was ideally suited to her situation.

"Begin by taking a few relaxing breaths," he guided her. "When you feel like you're ready, Vicki, just let your eyes close. Just let yourself go inside for a little while."

Yapko was initially being as permissive as he could possibly be, gently inviting her to relax, to be comfortable in listening to him, and to trust the learning process as well as her own internal resources.

"Just allow yourself the exquisite luxury of letting your mind travel or relax. . . . It can do a lot or it can do nothing. . . . It can listen and it can not listen."

Rather than using traditional hypnosis that gives direct instructions that are simply to be obeyed, Yapko worked to give her choices, to empower her, to keep her in control of her own discovery process. He also did something unique to this sort of gentle hypnosis in that he emphasized certain words as a way to include embedded suggestions. These are the kinds of hypnotic suggestions that are generally beyond awareness but, because they bypass the conscious mind, also lessen resistance.

"Because the mind is so complex," Yapko continued in a soft, soothing, mellow voice, "it's really convenient, really a *comfort* to know that while the conscious mind tends to notice whatever captures its attention for the moment, there's a *deeper* part of you that can really experience *a surprising level of relaxation and comfort*."

Yapko was marking the words *comfort, deeper,* and *relaxation* in order to draw on them later as he attempted to deepen Vicki's absorption in the experience.

"I did a pretty lengthy hypnosis session with her," Yapko told us. "It lasted about forty-five minutes or so, which is a little on the long side. I knew it was going to be a one-session intervention. I wasn't her therapist. I was in the role of a consultant to teach her a specific skill. There were so many issues that I wanted to be able to address both directly and indirectly in order to help her in my role as a consultant."

Yapko clarified that hypnosis is one way of helping people alter their subjective experience, their perceptions of reality, by giving them particular focal points on which to concentrate. "Depending on what you focus people on," he explains, "and how you focus them on it, this will foster different kinds of experiences."

He used as an example how if you listen to a piece of music while watching a sunset, as opposed to while you are trying to read, you will tend to focus on and hear different things.

"In this particular case, I was wanting to get Vicki absorbed in her internal experience. I focused her on ways that she could experience her body differently."

Yapko cited an impressive array of research that supports hypnosis as one of the best ways to control pain, especially when people are taught to dissociate themselves from what is going on in their bodies.

"By dissociation I mean when people are able to take global experiences and break them into their component parts. Then you can amplify one element of a person's experience simply by focusing on it while you deamplify another. In other words, while I get someone totally focused on identifying their thoughts, I am indirectly moving them away from focusing on what is going on at that time in their bodies. When you focus on one aspect of experience, you simultaneously defocus on another one."

In Vicki's case, Yapko was helping her distance herself from her body to the point where she could experience it as a more comfortable place to live. He helped her experience numbness in the parts of her body that had been the most painful, especially in her feet and shoulder. The most important part, however, was that she could learn to do this on her own and use the skill as she chose after the session was over.

OPEN YOUR EYES

"Without disturbing your relaxation," Yapko said to Vicki as he began to ask her about the quality of her hypnotic experience while still in it, "you might find it a particularly interesting experience to have your throat and voice so comfortable and relaxed that you could describe to me what you're experiencing."

"Heartburn is gone."

"Good. Your body is comfortable."

"It feels soft."

Yapko now had feedback from Vicki that her pain symptoms, even her superficial one of heartburn, had dissipated.

"It is an interesting experience, isn't it? To have your body in trance. . . . To have your mind comfortable. . . . And how far away is your body from where you are?"

"Not far."

"Just close enough for when you need it. And just far enough to be really comfortable."

Yapko continued to get reports on how she was feeling, what sensations she was experiencing, and to what extent her pain had diminished. He reinforced what she had been able to do and offered further suggestions that she would be able to repeat this experience whenever she needed it. Then he guided her awareness slowly back to the room.

"Whenever you feel like it . . . whenever you are ready . . . you can let your eyes open."

Vicki's eyelids fluttered, as if they were glued shut. She was trying to open her eyes but the light was bright, and she still felt so comfortable, so at peace. She was reluctant to break the spell and closed her eyes again.

"Take a moment," Yapko reassured her. "No need to reorient fully . . . just yet."

Vicki waited several seconds, squinted into the light, then opened her eyes and adjusted her position.

"How are you feeling?" Yapko asked her with a smile.

"I liked that a lot! I got very much in touch with being over there. I hope I don't forget."

Yapko reassured her that she would have a tape of the session that she could review whenever she wants.

"Well," Vicki said, "it *was* a very nice experience."

"That's good," Yapko replied. "Would you be willing to . . ."

"Yes!" Vicki answered before he could even finish the sentence. Yapko was surprised that someone who had been so mistrustful of professionals would be so willing to agree to whatever he asked of her, even before she knew what it was. He felt great that he had established such solid rapport with her, and in such a relatively short period of time.

"What I was going to ask you, Vicki, was whether you would be willing to respond to questions from the audience?"

Vicki quickly agreed, even enjoyed the chance to speak about her experience to professionals who were finally listening to her and who considered her the only true expert on her own experience. This was quite a reversal from what she had been used to.

EPILOGUE

A few days after the session, Yapko received a thank-you note from Vicki telling him how grateful she was for the experience. He was already out of the country when it arrived.

For the first few weeks after the consultation, Vicki was able to watch the videotape of the session and practice the pain management skills she had learned. As the radiation treatment, chemotherapy, and tumors continued to eat away at her body, however, she could no longer watch herself on film, especially after her beautiful long hair fell out. Instead, she used an audiotape of the session she had been given as a guide for her pain management sessions.

Once the cancer further spread within her brain, Vicki began having seizures, and her ability to concentrate for long periods diminished. She died less than eight weeks after her session with Michael.

LESSONS TO BE LEARNED

Yapko sees a number of important lessons in this case, not only for therapists but everyone.

"People get so intimidated by doctors that they passively accept the situation when doctors don't listen very well. Instead of demanding high-quality care, Vicki let herself be victimized. She took total responsibility for this. She certainly wanted to communicate the message to people that doctors aren't gods. Doctors make mistakes. Doctors get blinded by their own belief systems, prejudices, and expectations. If you are not going to trust yourself and stand up for what you believe, you can easily be victimized—with potentially fatal consequences, as was true for Vicki.

"Most people will never go through the kind of horrible experiences that this woman went through. Most people are not going to be thrown into a state psychiatric hospital, diagnosed catatonic schizophrenic, and drugged until they are nearly comatose. Most will not be victims of physical violence in their marriages, or end up living on the streets. But the fact that Vicki was able to turn her life around so dramatically should convince anybody who reads this that you are not your history."

There was such sadness and frustration—and considerable anger as well—in Yapko's voice when he discussed this case. This happened twelve years ago, yet he still thinks about Vicki a lot, still uses this case to teach therapists about the importance of listening without prejudice, the importance of finding and amplifying each individual's strengths instead of focusing on his or her pathological labels. Yapko considers these perspectives to be far more helpful to people than any single technique employed.

"I still see the same thing come up over and over again," Yapko said. "Even to this day, I see what is going on in our field. This country is so enamored with medications that fully 75 percent of the world's Prozac gets consumed here, 90 percent of the world's Ritalin. Drug companies use their incredible influence to make it seem reasonable to think that anything that goes wrong in your life is entirely the result of some neurochemical imbalance instead of your circumstances."

Yapko's voice rises in passion as he warms to this subject. "And psychologists," he says with disgust, "who should have the best arguments against the overselling of medication as sole solutions, instead want drug prescription privileges themselves! And they are slowly getting it. So instead of emphasizing what psychologists can do better than medical doctors in treating psychological disorders with drugs alone, they have jumped on that drug solution bandwagon."

Vicki's legacy—to Yapko, and he hopes to many others whom he has trained—is that listening to people is far more important than labeling them, and is at least as important as anything else that is offered in the way of treatment.

Here was a woman who had every reason to be depressed. She was dying. She was often in excruciating pain. She had finally gotten her life together, precisely at the point when she had run out of time. She had endless reasons to feel embittered, to be angry—and certainly to be depressed—but to her last breath she refused to surrender to despair or to pain.

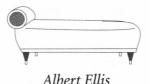

CHAPTER TWELVE

Albert Ellis

The Woman Who Hated Everyone and Everything

As the founder of Rational-Emotive Behavior Therapy (REBT), Albert Ellis is among the most influential theorists in the history of psychotherapy. In the 1950s, when the field was dominated primarily by the psychoanalysts, Ellis developed a comprehensive form of therapy that helped people examine the ways their internal thoughts and beliefs shaped their subsequent feelings and behaviors. This was among the first brief therapies, and certainly remains as one of the most popular approaches among practitioners today.

Throughout the last decades, Al has been based at the Albert Ellis Institute in New York, from which he has traveled the world promoting cognitive methods. His scholarly output has been staggering, having written more than six hundred articles and close to sixty books. His first book, How to Live with a Neurotic, *was written fifty years ago. Since that time he has authored books for professionals, including his seminal works,* Reason and Emotion in Psychotherapy, *and* Growth Through Reason— *books that launched the cognitive therapy revolution. He has also written dozens of books for the public about how to apply rational-emotive behavior strategies to counteract irrational and self-defeating thought patterns. Some of his most popular works include* A Guide to Rational

Living; Sex Without Guilt; How to Control Your Anger Before It Controls You; *and* How to Stubbornly Refuse to Make Yourself Miserable About Anything—Yes, Anything.

Now approaching ninety years old, Ellis has still not lost much of his acerbic wit and strong desire to get to the essence of dysfunctional behavior as fast as possible.

—⁓—

We have tried particularly hard in this chapter to preserve the theorist's voice as much as possible, as Ellis speaks his own language, frequently peppered with abbreviations he invented to describe phenomena he observes. He is also known for speaking his mind as bluntly and directly as possible. It is indeed rare in his sixty-odd years of practice that he ever encountered anyone—colleague, student, or client—who tried so hard as the one described in this case to get under his skin. It took every bit of his resolve and characteristic self-talk to keep himself calm in the face of the one person who taught him the most about being patient.

USA, UOA, AND ULA

In describing his most memorable case, one that occurred in a therapy group he was leading, Ellis introduced us quickly to the unique diagnostic language he uses to assess the ways that people upset themselves.

"Dorothy had practically everything under the sun that I aim to change in therapy. First of all, she was low in USA—that's unconditional self-acceptance. She put herself down immensely and beat herself up continuously. Second, she was very hostile to many other people and had practically no UOA (unconditional other acceptance)."

What Ellis is telling us is that Dorothy was not only critical of herself but also especially critical of others. She made life extremely difficult for others in her therapy group and in her outside life, because she was so accusatory and consistently blamed everyone and everything for not meeting her expectations. She reserved some of her most angry outbursts for Ellis himself.

As if that were not challenging enough, Dorothy also had an almost complete absence of what Ellis calls ULA—unconditional life acceptance. Rather than taking things in stride, she was easily frustrated by almost everything that happened in her life. By showing steady rage and low tolerance of frustration, she managed to chase away almost everyone with whom she came into contact.

"Most of her hostility," Ellis said, "was reserved for her mother. She called her the worst bitch under the sun! At work, everybody was 'thoroughly reprehensible.' In the therapy group, she was constantly fighting with others. She often bawled me out personally and accused me of all kinds of skullduggery."

Ellis saw Dorothy for two years, in both group and individual therapy. Even so, she didn't have enough outlets for her wrath, so she began seeing another therapist at the same time just so she could lash out at two targets at once.

"I've never seen anybody so consistently hostile all over the place to various kinds of people. You name it and she could easily—very easily!—make herself enraged at them. You could say she was a genius in this respect!"

RAGE CONTROLLED AND UNLEASHED

During one group session, Ellis said something to set Dorothy off. He pointed out to her that by being so angry and ornery all the time, she was not getting what she wanted. Quite the reverse!

"I have never seen anything like the tirade that followed," Ellis recalled. "She went off against me, against our institute, against the world, against everything she could think of. She just bawled me out and said she was going to prosecute me and persecute me. She told me that I was no damn good and I wasn't helping her at all."

The other group members were shocked into silence. They had already learned that if they spoke up when Dorothy was in one of these moods, she would turn her anger toward them. Hiding from her like this rarely helped, however, as she would say that they all should drop dead because they were completely failing her.

The really strange thing about Dorothy's interpersonal style was that she managed to operate effectively in her job as an administrative assistant. Somehow she found a way to muzzle herself during work hours so as to avoid alienating coworkers. That is not to say that she liked anyone at work—in fact, she felt universal disdain for them—but somehow, she found a way to keep her critical voice under control, at least until she got outside her office.

HOW SHE GOT THIS WAY

We asked Ellis his opinion about how someone becomes so hateful and critical of others. For those familiar with his theory about the power of internal thinking to shape behavior, his answer represented an exception to the usual rule.

"Dorothy's case is similar to many other severe personality disorders," Ellis explained. "Almost always both heredity and environment lead to these disorders. Her mother, and her whole family on her mother's side, had severe personality disorders as far as I could determine. I think Dorothy could have been diagnosed with a borderline disorder. But it was more complicated than that since she had multiple disturbances. She was severely depressed since the age of two or three and often had suicidal thoughts and wishes. Of course, there were also serious environmental factors involved because her mother was very negative and criticized her severely.

"Dorothy only accepted herself temporarily when she performed exceedingly well at something. But if she made the slightest mistake or misjudgment—or if anyone else slipped up in small ways—she would launch herself on an all-out blaming war. And I mean war, with a capital W!"

Ellis did his considerable best to explain the concept of unconditional self-acceptance to Dorothy. This means that no matter what you do or how you dismally you behave, you still accept and value yourself as a person. "You accept the sinner," he pointed out, "but not the sin. You simply acknowledge that you did less than you preferred to do, and then you move on. You learn from your mistakes without spending undue time obsessing about them and blaming your entire self or being for them."

No matter how many times Ellis drove home this point or cued other group members to reinforce these ideas or suggested homework assignments for her to complete, she refused to comply and continued her negative criticism. Ellis continuously pointed out that Dorothy, as a person, was not the same as what she *did* or did not *do*. "You can't possibly be what you do," Ellis said to her, "because if you acted well and therefore were a good person, you would always have to act well in the future. If for some reason you acted badly, then you would once again become a bad person. Moreover if you became a bad person, then that means you *always* act badly."

This logic of self-forgiveness sometimes made sense to Dorothy in-tellectually, but she never got it solidly. Every time she screwed up in some way, or noticed someone else acting less than perfectly, she treated it as a horrible, unforgivable sin that could never be rectified.

ABYSMALLY LOW TOLERANCE OF FRUSTRATION

Although Ellis specializes in treating clients with low frustration tol-erance, he says that he has never met someone who had it as seriously as Dorothy. As a typical example, she always took the bus when she went to work from her apartment in Brooklyn because the subway was too crowded and she might not get a seat. She would get up an hour earlier than required so that she could be absolutely sure that she got a seat all the way to her stop.

Returning home at the height of rush hour, it was impossible for Dorothy to find a seat of her choice, so she was forced to stand. What did she do? She started crying because she was enraged at all the seated people who "absolutely had no right to deprive me of a seat that I was thoroughly entitled to have!" So almost every weekday night Dorothy broke into loud wails and a cascade of tears as soon as she entered a crowded subway train. The other riders were quite startled, assuming that she was physically ill, so someone inevitably would give up a seat to the distraught woman. Even that did not appease her: for twenty minutes more she cried and wailed, completely hating all the people in the train, including the person who had given her the seat.

When Ellis and the other group members suggested that the "hor-ror" of standing for a while in a subway train hardly justified her ex-treme rage, Dorothy refused to entertain the possibility that she might be overreacting a bit. In fact, she believed everyone in the group was a bastard just as inconsiderate as those on the train.

THE GIRL WHO CHEWED GUM

One of the most satisfying experiences for any therapist occurs dur-ing those times when we encounter a clinical situation that is so chal-lenging, so far beyond what we have dealt with before, that we are forced to create a new way to deal with it. Ellis faced just such a situa-tion when his most foolproof, time-honored, empirically tested techniques failed to put a dent in Dorothy's defensive armor and interrupt her raging.

One evening she arrived to the group therapy session in a state of wild fury. (When Dorothy was upset about something, the whole world knew about it.) At 7:30 that morning, on the subway ride to work, she found herself (seated!) on a very crowded train with no room to breathe. There was a little girl in the car, about ten years old, who was chewing and cracking her bubble gum, and there was no way Dorothy could get away from her. As she told the group about this incident twelve hours later, Dorothy was still incensed about the little girl's "incredible inconsiderateness and terrible selfishness." Dorothy screamed out in group, "I felt the overwhelming urge to kill the gum-chewing girl! I would kill her right now, cut her into a million pieces and completely destroy her! No! Cut her into *two* million pieces and show her what a great louse she is for cruelly trapping me, as she did, in a crowded train. I would so enjoy ripping her to pieces! She deserves it!" Ellis had seen a lot in his life, but this outburst shocked him to his core. Was Dorothy exaggerating about desperately wanting to kill this ten-year-old girl?

Dorothy confirmed the group's worst fears by continuing, "Even if I were arrested and convicted of killing the girl, it would be worth it! Selfish vermin like her *should* be murdered—and I would be extremely happy to go to the electric chair for ripping her into little pieces and then spitting on them!"

"Why is it so terrible," one group member challenged her cautiously, "that you had to put up with a little loud gum-chewing on the subway. I've seen things . . ."

"You weren't there!" Dorothy screamed at her. "You didn't hear how loud it was. It was one of the most obnoxious things I've ever heard. Not only should that impolite, horrible kid be sent away to a concentration camp, but her parents should be severely jailed and punished for raising her to be like that! Yes, jailed and punished!"

"Hold on there," Ellis interrupted. "Listen to yourself and the things that you are saying." Turning to members of the group he asked, "Can anyone help Dorothy notice all the irrational, crazy things she is spouting? As you've heard in this group over and over again, it isn't the kid who is driving Dorothy crazy. She's doing it to herself, and you can show her how to stop doing it."

"Dorothy has a bad case of the shoulds," one woman in the group called out, then ducked.

Another offered: "She's telling herself that the little girl should not be the way she is—that she must be more considerate."

"That's right," Ellis agreed. "Dorothy, you are 'shoulding' all over the place. You are demanding and commanding that this little kid be different from the way she is just because you are annoyed with her chewing gum." Ellis looked around the group and asked again, "What else did you hear Dorothy doing?"

"She's awfulizing," another group member, Dan, called out, and several other group members started laughing to support him. The group liked to confront Dorothy because she was so often on everyone else's case.

"Good," Ellis encouraged him. "Dan, tell Dorothy what you mean, because we've been over this many times before, and she has a difficult time seeing that things are uncomfortable but that defining them as awful won't help change them and will actually make them seem worse than they actually are."

"Just that she's telling herself that the little girl's clacking her bubble gum in Dorothy's ears was unbearable and catastrophic and made Dorothy suffer a horrendous form of torture. Dorothy is saying that this is almost the worst thing that ever happened to her, that nothing could possibly be worse."

"Tell that to Dorothy, Dan," Ellis directed when he noticed the group member was looking at him and not at her. "I already know this stuff pretty well."

The group laughed nervously, not so much because of the joke but because they were waiting to see when Dorothy would explode again.

Dan forced himself to look directly at Dorothy. He obviously was afraid to confront her. "I was saying that she . . . I mean, I was saying that you, Dorothy, are exaggerating this little incident and making a tremendous deal out of it. Instead, you could have told yourself, 'Yes, the girl's loud gum chewing is annoying, but it surely isn't terrible or horrifying.'"

There was complete silence in the group for a while after that. Partially, this was to see if Dan's confronting Dorothy had hit the mark and gotten through to her this time. It was also because the rest of the group members wanted to assess how well Dorothy was taking in Dan's remarks before they went any further.

Dorothy was stone quiet. She was either thinking or pouting, and Ellis couldn't tell which.

"We continued the dialogue for a while further," Ellis recalled, "and Dorothy surprised us all by remaining fairly calm. She nodded her head, like she understood what people had been saying to her. She realized that what happened on the subway was not really awful at all, but she was still considerably angry about it."

HOMEWORK

Ellis gave Dorothy a homework assignment—to vigorously and forcefully dispute her irrational belief that the little girl in the subway was completely wrong and should be drawn and quartered for being so "horribly selfish." Dorothy accepted this assignment and agreed to report back the next week.

"Did you do it?" Dorothy was asked as soon as the group reconvened a week later.

"Yeah," she said defiantly. "So what?"

"Well," Ellis encouraged her to elaborate, "so how do you feel now?"

"How do I feel now?" Dorothy screamed, "You want to know how I feel now?" Dorothy's voice was becoming shriller as she worked herself up. "I want to strangle that little girl until she chokes on that damn gum! She deserves to die for that rude behavior!"

Other members of the group became increasingly concerned and fearful, not because they actually believed that Dorothy would hunt down and murder the little girl but because they had never seen anyone so upset about something so trivial. Ellis persevered by asking her to complete the assignment again.

Dorothy returned the following week, still reporting that she was continuing to ruminate about the girl and the revenge she wanted to take against her. If Ellis is one thing, he is persistent, so he asked her to do the assignment a third time to vigorously dispute her irrational demands on others until she was no longer raging.

Three times was effective. Dorothy finally reported that she had let go of her anger toward the little girl. She accepted the fact (but didn't like it) that the girl could chew and clack her gum, and although this might be rude, it was not the end of the world. But before Ellis could congratulate Dorothy for giving up her rage, she went off on another rant, this time directing her anger toward him for taking so damn long to help her.

"Look," Ellis said to her, "right now, when you are very incensed with me, what are you telling yourself to make yourself so angry?"

"You're an asshole," Dorothy retorted. "How about that for a start?"

"OK," Ellis calmly responded. He had been seeing Dorothy long enough that he was, by now, almost amused by her unique style. "Is that the best you can do?"

"I was just wondering if you ever helped anyone with this shit? REBT certainly has its good points, but certainly *not* the way you do it. And this thing you call an institute, I can't believe anyone would work here long. What utter crap you teach here! You call this therapy?"

"Let's assume all that's true," Ellis agreed. "Let's assume that I did a terrible job with you, and that everybody would agree that I'm just no damn good as a therapist. Let's assume that our therapy at the institute is the worst therapy that ever existed. What good is it doing you to make yourself enraged at me? You're just making yourself unhealthily upset, and your fury is certainly not going to help you change me."

It may have seemed mysterious why Dorothy kept returning for therapy if it was really doing so little to help her. In truth, she had little choice. At age thirty-five she had been in therapy most of her life. As strange as it seemed, during the times when she stopped coming for help, she was even more depressed and anxious.

Dorothy eventually developed a number of serious medical conditions. She consulted doctors for her illnesses, but because she was so difficult to deal with and so noncompliant to her doctor's recommended treatments, she did not care for her health in a way that was any more rational than the way she managed the rest of her life. She was told that unless she received surgery for a serious form of cancer, she would likely die. By the time she got around to scheduling the procedure, the cancer had advanced to the point where it could not be controlled. Dorothy died friendless and alone. But in her final days she accepted her dying and used what she had learned to make peace with herself and the world.

WHAT ELLIS LEARNED

As was true of many of the memorable cases reviewed in this book, this unusual patient had significant impact on what Ellis learned about therapy, as well as about himself and the limits of his own method. He remembers that when he first started developing REBT in the 1950s, people who would today be considered as having personality disorders were diagnosed at that time as borderline psychotics.

"Actually, they are still borderline psychotics," Ellis says, "because in addition to having destructive beliefs and feelings, they have severe cognitive, emotional, and behavioral deficiencies or biosocial handicaps. Both genetic and environmental factors play a role in shaping these toxic personalities and make them exceptionally difficult for anyone, including the best therapists, to deal with."

In some ways, Ellis believes these individuals are often even harder to handle than psychotics, because they have great difficulty in unconditionally accepting themselves and others with their dysfunctions. Ellis went on to say, "Where 'normal neurotics' can fairly easily learn unconditional acceptance in the course of therapy, clients with severe personality disorders are almost allergic to this kind of profound forgiveness, and often rigidly stick to self-damnation and to damning others. They are unfortunately born and raised to be prejudiced against humans, including against themselves. They like being in a long therapeutic relationship, but they often do not listen to and heed their therapist's communications."

Ellis went still further: "Therapists, too, often have difficulty achieving unconditional acceptance of their clients and themselves. This is especially true when they work with unusually difficult clients like Dorothy; they often tend to condemn them for their 'resistance'—and, of course, frequently condemn themselves for failing to achieve great results with these 'resistors.' Consequently, if one therapy technique doesn't work too well, they may try several other methods, hoping that one will miraculously succeed. They refuse to acknowledge that in many cases, there is no therapeutic technique that will work very well with people who are securely stuck in their personality-disordered behaviors."

When all was said and done, Ellis found Dorothy to be endlessly interesting. He was tested in ways that he had never been challenged before, and this only helped him develop new ways of reaching people who had previously been beyond the reach of traditional cognitive therapy.

"She was such a pain in the ass," Ellis remembered fondly, "but she helped me a great deal. If I could deal with her, I could deal with anyone."

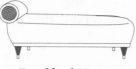

CHAPTER THIRTEEN

Bradford Keeney

The Medicine Man Who Never Had a Vision

Brad Keeney has to get the award for most eclectic collection of research interests and authored books. As an ex-academic, an ex-therapist, and now a cultural anthropologist and social critic, Keeney can divide his career into different stages, each of which integrated his previous work.

He has written classic books in therapy, including Improvisational Therapy, Aesthetics of Change, *and* Mind in Therapy. *He has written self-help books about cultural phenomena:* Crazy Wisdom Tales for Dead Heads: A Shamanic Companion to the Grateful Dead *and* The Lunatic Guide to the David Letterman Show. *He has also written several popular books, such as* Everyday Soul: Awakening the Spirit in Everyday Life *and* The Energy Break. *In* Shaking Out the Spirits, *Keeney tells the story of his transformation from traditional academic scholar to field investigator of shamanic and indigenous healing practices.*

More recently Keeney has been involved in projects in which he has studied and written about healing practices in Japan (Ikuko Osumi, Japanese Master of Seiki Jutsu), *Africa* (Kalahari Bushmen Healers), *North America* (Gary Holy Bull, Lakota Yuwipi Man), *the Caribbean* (Shakers of St. Vincent), *and a dozen other places around the world.*

Brad is vice president of Ringing Rocks Foundation in Philadelphia, an organization formed to advance knowledge about alternative healing practices in diverse cultures. He is also an adjunct professor of counseling at California State University, Fullerton, and a cultural anthropologist for the Mental Research Institute in Palo Alto, California. He lives in Tucson, Arizona.

——*ᴠᴠᴠ*——

Before we delved into his case, Keeney wanted to be clear that from the very beginning of his career he has been quite skeptical of the various schools of psychotherapy. The best work he has witnessed and participated in has taken place independent of these formal therapeutic systems, when people simply encounter one another in a creative way.

"I was a radical cynic," Keeney says, "and very much moved by the whole antipsychiatry movement, as well as the more exotic approaches. I always kept that spirit, and it moved me to push the edge in my own work. I think my own evolution as an antipsychologist has less to do with conduct that has anything to do with any therapeutic technique or school of thought. Over time, I have become more and more focused on creating helpful suggestions for what people should do."

We urge you to keep Brad's introductory remarks in mind as the context for a very unusual case that was conducted by a very unusual therapist.

FIRST IMPRESSIONS

Nate was a striking man. He had the sort of face on which you could see all the hardships he had suffered carved into the various scars on his neck and forehead. Nate was an ex-con and looked the part: burly and muscular, a solid, immovable block. He had a long braid of hair that went all the way down his back.

Once Nate began to speak, it was hard to reconcile his intimidating presence with the soft, expressive voice. He didn't speak a lot, but when he did, his words were thoughtful and warm. He was a medicine man of the Sioux Nation, a healer who was now a leader of his people. But there was a time earlier in his life when he had done some bad things and some hard time.

"He had the walk," Keeney told us, "of a Native American who had gone through battles with the bottle, relationships, and the kind of stuff that lands you in federal prison." Now, Nate devoted his life to helping others of his people deal with substance abuse problems.

Nate had contacted Keeney at the suggestion of someone of the tribe who had heard about Brad's work with Native American and other indigenous peoples. He had been told that unlike other whites, Keeney was someone who could sit and listen.

Nate came to Keeney's house for the meeting. He showed up with a man and a woman. His wife, Melanie, was very serious and didn't smile much. She was a heavyset woman who looked to Brad like someone who was serious about native traditions. She had watchful eyes that very carefully observed everything that transpired.

The man who accompanied Nate was his friend Ken, who looked more like a businessman than an Indian. He had short-cropped hair and was wearing khaki pants and a blue oxford shirt. This was in striking contrast to Nate, who wore blue jeans, cowboy boots, and a T-shirt with a Native American activist slogan. Ken was the administrator of the treatment center on the reservation.

TRADITIONS

The three of them sat in Brad's living room, Nate in the middle; his wife, Melanie, on one side; his friend Ken on the other. They chatted a little while, talking about their mutual acquaintances and places they had been and seen together. Keeney waited patiently, never once bringing up the subject of why they had come. That was up to them to broach whenever they felt ready.

"This is very embarrassing to admit," Nate began his story, "but I am a teacher of traditional ways. I help my people do the things that are most important to do in our culture. I help them learn how to take care of themselves. I help them go into sweat lodges where we pray and commune with the Creator. I help them prepare themselves to go sit on a hill to fast and have a vision."

Throughout each of these statements, Melanie nodded solemnly, as if confirming that what her husband said was not only true but also the Way Things Were. Ken, in contrast, looked a little bored by the whole thing, as if he had pretty much come along for the ride.

"In my tradition," Nate said in his soft voice, "we find the definition of our life in the most significant way when we go sit, fast, and pray. We wait for a vision that will give our life greater meaning and point the direction toward what we should be doing."

"Yes," Keeney encouraged him. "This I know."

There was a pause for a few moments, as if Nate was deciding just how far to take this. He looked at his wife for support, but Keeney could see no response that he could read. Melanie just sat immobile, staring at her husband with utter devotion.

"So Nate," Keeney prompted, "what's going on?"

"Um," he hesitated, "I am ashamed to tell you why I have come because I would not want my people to know."

"I see."

"As you know, I help people find vision for their lives. I go through all the ceremonies. I work in my culture, and people know me as a spiritual person. But . . ."

Nate stopped again, thinking, waiting, perhaps making a decision. It was highly unusual that a medicine man of his stature would ever choose to confide in a white man like this, much less talk about things related to his people's most sacred ceremonies.

"But," Nate said again, with his head down, "I have never had a vision. . . . I have never personally had a vision. . . . I don't know why. I have talked to several elders. They have put me out on the hill to fast and pray. I have done all these things, and have done them sincerely, but I have never had a vision." Nate then looked up at Keeney, looked him directly in the eyes, and said, "I want you to help me have a vision."

THE DARK ROOM

It is important to know that this was a time in Keeney's career when he was just on the edge of throwing away everything he had ever learned about psychotherapy. He had been spending the previous few years traveling to remote parts of the world—with Bushmen in Africa, Aborigines in Australia—and working with Native American tribes, learning as much as he could about indigenous healing. These experiences provided a background that had little to do with what we think of as traditional therapy. If he had treated Nate's case as a therapist would, he never would have considered what he did next.

"Nate," Keeney said, "let's go downstairs and do what you know should be done in situations like this: let's pray together."

Brad and Nate left Melanie and Ken to occupy themselves while they descended the stairs into the basement. Keeney had a tiny little room down there that the previous owner had used to store wine. It was solidly built, relatively soundproof, and completely dark.

They went into the tiny room, turned off the light, and sat cross-legged on the floor, facing one another. It is important to keep in mind that in Native American ceremonies, some of the most important rituals are conducted in the dark. Keeney intended to honor Nate's culture in a way that he knew would address such a serious issue by going into a special space that was separated from everyday discourse. The old wine cellar was perfect for this purpose.

"Nate," Keeney began once they were settled, "just put your mind at ease. Let yourself go to whatever you would like to have happen. Let us be still."

"Ho," Nate answered, the Sioux word for affirmation.

"You may feel so moved to talk or sing or chant or whatever comes to you."

They sat in complete silence for several minutes. Then Nate began to sing a traditional Sioux song, one that was unfamiliar to Keeney. He started softly and then began to sing louder, with more passion and feeling. Once Brad picked up the rhythm and the sounds, he joined Nate in a chorus, and they both sang together. They sang deeply. They sang with absolute devotion to the sounds. Keeney had no idea what they were saying, but he joined Nate nevertheless.

After several minutes of this, Keeney could feel himself go into an altered state. Here they were sitting in complete darkness, in a small space, singing their hearts out. In his own mind, Keeney got the first seedling of an idea. He didn't know where it came from, or why it occurred to him, but the idea began to grow and take shape.

THE TREATMENT OF THE TWELVE BRANCHES

"Nate, an idea came to me that I want to share with you."

"Yes," he answered, trying to keep the excitement out of his voice. But he was desperate for a solution to this most embarrassing of problems. There was nothing more shameful, more humiliating, for a medicine man to admit than that he had never had a vision. He felt like a fraud, as though he were guiding people on a spiritual journey that he had never been on himself. This was the most monstrous existential crisis imaginable for someone in his position.

"I am seeing you go off into the woods," Keeney continued. "This is near where you live on the Reservation. And this is what I want you to do. Go into the woods and gather twelve branches. These twigs should be no longer than a foot long. Cut off a branch that is facing south, one to which the Spirit leads you. The next one should come from the north. Then harvest one from the east and one from the west. The remaining branches should come from all the points in between."

Keeney thought he could see Nate nodding in the dark, but he wasn't sure.

"Mark each of the branches carefully so you can tell which direction it came from."

"What do I do with them?" Nate asked.

"I want you to be mindful as you gather these branches that you are seeking a vision. You are showing Mother Nature your pure intent, that you mean business. Show her that you are not holding back in any way."

"How shall I do this?" Nate wondered.

"You will go into the woods and ask permission to be led to each of the branches. Each one must be special."

"I understand."

"Then you are to take the branches home and place them underneath your bed in a circle. Each branch should face its original direction, with the south facing south, and so on. Do you understand?"

"Ho."

"I want the branches located so that the heart of the circle is located right underneath where your heart will be when you sleep. Then right in the center of this circle I'd like you to put an offering, some tobacco."

The two men stood and embraced and started back up the stairs.

"Before we return," Keeney instructed, "I want you to keep this just between us. Do not share with anyone what you are doing and why."

"Not even Melanie?"

"No, this is just between you and the Creator."

This made perfect sense to Nate because this was the way that things were done among his people.

When they returned upstairs, Melanie and Ken were talking about their favorite quarries for gathering stone to make pipes for young people. They had been apprehensive about what had taken place downstairs, but they knew better than to ask. They all gathered their things and left. Keeney stood on the porch, wondering how Nate would do. Even more curious, he was wondering where his own vision came from to suggest the treatment of the twelve branches.

The last thing he heard as they climbed into their car was Nate saying to his wife, "It was good down there."

ONE WEEK LATER

"Brad, this is Nate."

"Nate! How are you doing?" In truth, Keeney had been concerned that he had not heard from Nate sooner, but he figured that things were proceeding according to what was needed. If he had learned one thing over the years, it was patience.

"Man, I'm just blown away. I don't know what you did or what it was about, but I went out and did what you said."

"Uh huh."

"I went into the woods just like you said. I found the branches that the Spirit showed me. I put them under the bed like you told me."

"With the tobacco as an offering?"

"Sure. And then I went to sleep. I had this dream. But when I woke up I was still in the dream."

Keeney recognized that what Nate was talking about was what we call a lucid or waking dream. But to Nate it was a vision, a real honest-to-God vision.

"I was flying out of my body," Nate said, the excitement and awe in his voice. "I flew back to a time when I was a little boy, and I looked at my dad and my family and then I realized that I was flying and was wide awake and it freaked me out. Then I woke up."

"Well, I guess you had yourself a vision."

"Brad, man, that was too much. I'm freaked. I'm not sure I want to put those branches under my bed again."

"Whoa there! How much tobacco did you put under there?"

They both laughed.

Keeney was surprised as he received the report, but he wasn't thinking like a therapist, trying to analyze or assign causes to the experience.

"Nate, when you are sincere, and you show the Creator that you mean business, it is amazing just how the goods are delivered."

"I think I know what I need to do now," Nate answered.

Whereas a therapist might ask what that might be, Keeney preferred not to intrude; it was enough that his client had the answers he was looking for.

We asked Keeney, "But aren't you curious?" Here he had put together this wonderful therapeutic ritual, but he isn't sure what happened or why.

"I would rather just throw another log on the fire," Keeney explained, "as opposed to pulling one out and examining it and watching it cool off."

A few months later, Keeney did learn what happened to Nate. Based on the vision of flying out of his body and looking at himself as a child, he went on a vision quest of sorts, seeking to resolve some issues from his own childhood that would make him a better medicine man. Both he and Melanie traveled to places throughout the continent where they could continue to work on their growth together. Keeney was delighted to hear the excitement in Nate's voice as he described what he'd learned and what he was working on. And it all started with his first vision.

CHAPTER TWO

Soon after they returned from their trip, Melanie called to make an appointment for herself. "We were just knocked out by what you did with Nate and how this has affected his life. I want to see you."

"That's fine," Keeney told her. "Come on down."

This time four of them arrived together: Melanie and Nate, plus Ken and his wife. They arrived from the reservation around lunchtime, so they all shared a meal together and caught up on their lives.

When she was ready, Melanie announced that she wanted to go down into the room with Keeney. She said that a friend of hers had died recently, and she had not been able to sleep ever since. She didn't understand what was going on, but she had also developed a bad skin rash. She showed it to Keeney for him to inspect.

Once they were settled in the dark room, chanting and singing together just as he had done before with her husband, Melanie started shrieking. Although they were in pitch blackness, she said she saw a gigantic, luminous spider in the room.

"That is good," Keeney responded mildly. "Spiders carry medicine."

Melanie calmed down immediately, as it was well known among her people that spiders were considered sacred sources of medicine.

"Let us continue being here in a good way."

Again, Keeney had a flash out of nowhere. There had been no other conversation between them except for the abrupt announcement that Melanie had seen a spider.

"Melanie, I don't know what this is all about, and I don't know if this means anything to you. But this guy you mentioned who died, your friend. I am seeing him trying to give you a ring."

Immediately, Keeney could hear her begin to cry.

"What is that about?" he asked gently.

"He was a jeweler," she said between sobs. "That ring you are talking about is something that he always said he wanted to give me. I always teased him that I wanted it, and he said that he would give it to me someday. It was a game between us."

"Does his family know about this? Do they know that the ring was meant for you?"

"No," she said, "I didn't want to bring it up."

"I don't know why this is coming to me, but maybe you should talk to them. Maybe they are waiting for you to say something."

Sure enough, Melanie went to talk to the family to tell them about the ring. They were thrilled, absolutely delighted, to pass on this ring that meant so much to her. Soon afterward, the rash cleared up, and she was able to sleep just fine.

BACKING UP

When Brad and Melanie first emerged from the basement, both of them were pretty freaked out by what had transpired there. This was not ordinarily the way Keeney worked. "Here I was," he told us, "in the dark, literally, and flying by the seat of my pants, and something that has nothing to do with psychotherapy is organizing this interaction, and it is changing me drastically. It was allowing me to throw the whole of what I had been taught out the window, knowing that if you sort of poke around in the dark you can access something in the imagination. It was an unbelievable metaphor."

After Melanie and Brad rejoined the others upstairs, they all rejoiced that something profound had occurred.

"I have something I want to say," Ken jumped in, caught up in the enthusiasm. "I have been struggling as to whether to go back into the traditional ways and join the lodge, but my Catholic upbringing still has a hook in me because that is how I was raised. I have been struggling with that. I heard about what happened with Nate, and now I see what you've done with Melanie."

Keeney just smiled modestly. He wanted to explain that he really hadn't done much, but he figured it was best to keep his mouth shut.

"After I heard about putting the sticks under the bed," Ken continued, "I had the weirdest experience of my life. I don't know how to make sense of it."

"Go on, man," Nate encouraged him. "Tell him."

Ken looked toward his wife, who was sitting on the edge of the couch. She was a quiet woman who did not speak much. But she nodded her head, giving him permission to continue the story.

"Well, I had a dream where I was sitting in the lodge. It was made out of saplings, branches bent over. There were medicine people and a big fire and hides covering the branches. It's a big wigwam. I was sitting in there, and I saw my grandfather. He came over to me carrying red paint and a shell. He took his right finger and dipped it in the paint, and he put a stripe right down my forehead. It freaked me out because I turned around, and all the men in there had animal heads. I don't know if they were masks, but they looked like real animals."

Ken stopped and stared at his audience, as if he wanted to see if they were ready for the next part. He again looked over toward his wife, who nodded again.

"I woke up real startled. I was sweating and screaming, and I woke up my wife." As Ken said this, his wife gasped involuntarily, as if taking in a quick breath before diving beneath the surface of water.

"She jumped out of bed and turned on the light. Then my wife screamed."

They all looked toward Ken's wife, who still looked frightened by whatever had transpired.

"What my wife had seen was that I had a red stripe on my forehead."

Keeney is quick to point out that these were not the sort of people who were prone to making things up. If they said this was how it happened, then that was so.

THE TURNING POINT

This was a turning point in Keeney's life and his work. He decided it was time to pay more attention to shamen. It was time to disconnect himself from therapy and make a choice to begin his own journey, a quest to learn about healing.

"Every tradition," Keeney said, "has the idea that deep within each of us is everything we have been looking for. Whether it is a particular answer to a problem, or the whole meaning of life, it is within each one of us. Sometimes this is not always clear, which is why we sometimes need someone else to help us become more clear.

"The kind of praying that I observe around the world is more than articulating a table manners request of saying grace. It is a pleading. It is a shouting. It is a moving past words into pure emotion. It is allowing sounds to come out and then turning itself into song and music that comes straight from the heart. The power is in the asking. That is something that I think our culture has lost. We have these meek requests for help."

As he now looks back on the experience, Keeney is convinced that this is exactly what happened in the dark room—Nate and Melanie, and indirectly Ken, too, were invited to ask for what they really wanted, but in a passionate voice that left no room for anything other than compliance.

Keeney says that every therapist has had the kinds of moments that he had in the dark. The only question is whether they pay attention to those visions and learn from them.

CHAPTER FOURTEEN

Susan Johnson

The Woman Who Hanged Herself to Check Her Husband's Response Time

Sue Johnson is a founder of Emotionally Focused Therapy (EFT), an attachment-oriented approach to couples work that is both scientifically based and humanistic in its emphasis on constructive emotional expression. Her goal is to help partners access their unacknowledged deep feelings and communicate them in ways that build greater intimacy and mutual understanding.

Among her books are the seminal works on EFT: Emotionally Focused Therapy for Couples; The Practice of Emotionally Focused Marital Therapy; Heart of the Matter: Perspectives on Emotion in Marital Therapy; *and* Emotionally Focused Couple Therapy for Trauma Survivors.

Johnson is Professor of Psychology at the University of Ottawa in Canada. She is also Director of the Ottawa Couple and Family Institute.

—∿∿—

Listening to Sue Johnson, you hear the remnants of her Cockney accent, no matter how hard her mother worked to help rid her of evidence of her working-class roots. Sue and her family grew up above a pub, just the sort of place where one could develop an interest in people and how they connect with each other.

As she considered the strange cases she has encountered in her career, Johnson immediately thought of fellow therapists as the most challenging clients she has seen. And among them, one therapist stood out from all the rest.

THERAPISTS MAKE THE STRANGEST CLIENTS

Florence walked into the office, trailed by her husband. She was carrying a rather large book in her arms, which Johnson noticed was *The Diagnostic and Statistical Manual of Mental Disorders,* or DSM, which is used by all mental health professionals as the standard reference and resource for the diagnosis of mental health problems.

"I've read all your books," Florence began, "so I know exactly what you're going to do and how you're going to do it. I just hope that you are as good as you pretend to be."

Before Johnson had the chance to respond to this rather unusual beginning to their relationship, Florence further stated her requirements of the work they would be doing together. She demanded absolute punctuality. She stated her specific billing requirements. Then she stated her own qualifications and specialties as a fellow therapist. All the while Florence recited this litany, her husband, Ted, looked at Johnson pleadingly as if through his eyes he was saying, "Help me, help me!"

"I see you've brought along a DSM," Johnson observed, Florence having proceeded to leaf through the pages as if she were trying to locate a particular entry.

"Uh huh," Florence added, but refused to be distracted from her task. "Aha, here it is!" She used her finger to mark the passage she had been searching for.

"May I ask what you are doing?" Sue said more directly.

"Well," Florence said, "how could we possibly discuss my husband's condition without the DSM as a reference?"

"You believe your husband has a 'condition'?"

"Yes, of course. He is definitely personality disordered, although I debate with myself about whether he is schizoid or more passive-dependent. There could also be some Axis I features as well."

Throughout this discussion, Ted looked back and forth between the two of them, as if he were watching a Ping-Pong game.

Johnson's chin dropped. "Uh," she ventured carefully, "maybe before we get into your husband's diagnosis, first we could talk about why the two of you are here and what I can do to help."

"My wife thinks . . ." Before he could finish his very first thought, Florence interrupted her husband, making it clear that she would be doing the talking for both of them.

"I already put him in therapy with an analyst," Florence said, gesturing toward her husband. "He isn't doing too badly."

Ted nodded his head up and down vigorously in agreement. Actually, he was not only deep in psychoanalysis with a therapist his wife found for him but also had been "required" to see a sex therapist.

Johnson looked around her office for a moment, wondering if someone was playing a joke on her. She felt as though she were in some kind of comedy skit and that at any moment someone was going to jump out from behind the couch with a camera. Nobody did. Florence's monologue continued, highlighting all the pathological features she had identified in her husband. She spoke to Johnson just as if they were two colleagues consulting on a patient they were both treating.

Sue took a deep breath. "You have talked quite a lot so far about how you see your husband and what he does that you find so disturbing. And he said one or two words about how he sees things. Now I wonder how you see your part in this relationship and how things have evolved between you."

"What on earth do you mean?"

"I was just wondering because you have thought about this a lot, and you have put a lot of energy into analyzing this situation. You are obviously an expert yourself, so I am wondering how you see your role in the problems that have evolved in your relationship."

"Oh," Florence said, "I am not here to talk about me. There is no need; we don't have to talk about me at all."

"We don't?"

"No. Of course not. After all, I'm not the problem here. I have been totally splendid in this marriage. I have been warm, charming, and sexy, soft but assertive, challenging but compassionate. And you can see how much I care about my husband."

At this point, Ted simply closed his eyes.

Johnson felt the urge to laugh but also felt her jaw begin to clench as Florence went on at length about all her best traits—which, of course, were mostly unappreciated.

After some time, Johnson finally interrupted. "I am awfully sorry, because I know that you feel you have worked hard and been almost perfect in this relationship, and maybe you have been, but I don't really know how to work in couples therapy when the process is focused entirely on one person and the other observes. If you've read my books, then you know how important I believe it is to talk about the roles that both partners play in the dance they do together."

"Are you saying this is in any way my fault, that I had anything to do with this mess of a marriage?"

"No, Florence, I'm saying no such thing—"

"And I had heard such good things about you. Obviously not all of them are true." She looked defiantly at Johnson, waiting to see what she'd do with that challenge.

"Look, Florence, I don't mean to upset you. I just don't know how to do therapy the way you want me to do it. You've already, as you say, 'put' your husband in analytic therapy, and, Ted, you have agreed to go to that therapy. And you both say it's going pretty well."

At this point, Ted opened his eyes and again nodded his head up and down, repeatedly. For a moment, he looked as if he were going to say something again, but he changed his mind and again closed his eyes. And when Johnson tried to support him to speak, he withdrew further.

"So," Johnson continued, "I don't quite see why you need me— especially if we are only talking about Ted's side of the relationship."

This only enraged Florence further. "What-I-had-hoped"—she said this in clipped cadence—"was that you might teach him some ways that he might smarten up. As you can see, he has a long way to go."

"Isn't his therapist already helping Ted with this?" Johnson asked. Turning to Ted she asked, "Do you feel the need to come to see me?"

He shook his head. It was clear that he was not going to speak again and risk another censure from his wife, even if this new therapist did seem to be sympathetic to his plight.

Since Florence insisted on another appointment, Johnson next decided to schedule individual appointments for them, hoping this would facilitate her developing relationships with each of them individually. At least that way, she could learn a little more about Ted's side of things.

This strategy was just as ineffective. Florence remained angry and resentful that Johnson was not following the treatment plan that she had prescribed, one that involved focusing exclusively on Ted.

In all her years of practice, this is the only client that Johnson actually refused to continue to see. She became so frustrated, and was making so little headway, that she told Florence, "I am very sorry but I cannot do therapy according to the terms that you require. I do not know how, and I feel uncomfortable talking about Ted as if he is somehow broken or needing to be fixed."

Florence reluctantly agreed to terminate therapy, while still insisting that she did not need to talk about her responses but that couple therapy might help Ted.

Months later, Johnson was doing a workshop on emotionally focused couples therapy, and she was shocked to see Florence sitting in the front row. During the break, Johnson asked her how she was doing. Florence whispered conspiratorially that she was now doing so much better. She had decided to leave her husband, who was a "lost cause," and she had great hopes for a new relationship that was developing.

Johnson asked herself whether she could have done anything else to help Florence and Ted. In the end she accepted that the therapy process has to feel like familiar territory for her, and Florence's terms and the DSM used in this negative way had made the therapy feel strange and foreign and so unworkable. It reminded her of how hard it is to be a therapist who "knows" and to take off that therapist hat and just be a person who sometimes gets "lost" in his or her own life.

OUT OF HIS DEPTH

This case of the controlling therapist who tried to treat her own husband reminded Johnson of a similar pattern that had an even more unusual relational configuration. As a policy, Johnson avoids using DSM terms to categorize people, but sometimes a case comes along that is so strange that she breaks her own rules. In this case, she couldn't help but think in terms of psychiatric labeling.

The woman who walked in was extremely dramatic—shouting and using flamboyant gestures and over-the-top descriptions. Helga practically exploded as she began her story. She cried and wept and shouted and screamed. At one point, she banged her fist hard on Johnson's table, knocking over the objects perched there.

Her husband, Adam, in contrast, was similar to the husband in the previously mentioned couple. He sat quietly except for occasionally wringing his hands. He looked distressed throughout the interview but did not speak unless he was called on to do so.

They were both in their late fifties and had met on a cruise ship. He had been a confirmed bachelor his whole life, an outdoorsman, and a stamp collector. He was apparently very much out of his depth with Helga.

"You're the eighth therapist we've seen," Helga announced, "and none of them have been worth a damn."

"You haven't been helped by therapy so far?" Johnson reflected carefully. She was feeling a little worried that if this woman exploded again, the photos on her desk might not survive.

"You can say that! All they want to do is put me on drugs."

Johnson appeared to be nodding her head in sympathy, but she also found herself beginning to agree with this assessment. She'd met this woman for only ten minutes and already found herself wondering what she could do to help such an apparently volatile person. Helga then told this story.

SIX MINUTES

Helga had lived in Eastern Europe, somewhere in the Balkans. After she met Adam on the cruise ship, she moved to North America so they could be married. She was certain things were not working out, claiming that her husband was not who she thought he was.

"What do you mean by that?" Johnson asked.

"I have sacrificed everything for this man," she whined theatrically. "I left my country, my family, my friends. I left everything behind just to be with him. And he gives me nothing in return. Nothing!" As she said this, she held the backside of her wrist against her forehead in a gesture straight out of an old movie.

"Could you tell him?" Johnson directed. "Help him understand." She was trying to get the couple to communicate more directly rather than just complaining to the therapist.

"I have told him these things a hundred times," Helga said, continuing to speak to Johnson. Then she turned her wrath toward Adam. "And you! You are not a husband. You are . . . you are . . . you are a wimp! You wouldn't even lift a hand to save me if I was dying."

Adam appeared in genuine anguish, but he just continued to wring his hands.

"You don't feel like he is there for you," Johnson again ventured carefully.

"He just doesn't care about me," Helga moaned. "He doesn't care if I live or die."

Considering that Helga had already demonstrated her propensity toward exaggeration, Johnson did not take this statement literally. This was a mistake.

It seemed that earlier in the week, Helga had decided to test her husband's devotion. She told Adam that because he didn't care anything about her, and she had given up everything for him, she was going to kill herself. In fact, right that minute she was going to go down into the basement and hang herself. Adam had remained still and speechless.

Helga then did just what she said she would do. She went into the garage and got a rope. She walked deliberately past her husband carrying it in her hand. She stopped right in front of him and accused him of being so totally spineless that he would do nothing to stop her. Then she descended into the basement and slammed the door.

Adam looked nervously at the door but was not certain what to do or even what his wife wanted him to do. But then he was never very good at knowing what women wanted, and especially this volcanic East European lady.

Meanwhile, Helga had managed to stand on a chair to wrap the rope over one of the supporting beams. She then carefully made all the noises of gurgling and the chair falling over, as if she were in fact hanging herself. Then she held her watch up to her face in the dim light and checked the time.

"Six minutes," Helga said. "Can you believe it? It took the son of a bitch six minutes to come down and check on me. I could have been dead, and he couldn't have cared less."

"I tried . . ." Adam began, but was quickly cut off.

"I've already heard enough from you," Helga said.

"Wait a minute," Johnson stopped them, acting as a referee. "Let me get this straight. Are you saying you went into the basement and pretended to hang yourself just so you could time how long it would take your husband to try to save you?"

"Exactly! I could have been dead," Helga repeated, "and he wouldn't even lift a finger to help me. How can I live with such a man?"

GIN AND A WARM BATH

At this point, Johnson felt completely at a loss as to what to do with this couple. She drove all the way home that day muttering to herself in traffic. She was trying to remember who referred them to her so she could plot revenge toward that person some day. This woman was going to drive her crazy, mostly because Johnson couldn't make sense of what was happening. In her head, she opened the DSM and began to try different labels on Helga.

"I went home," Johnson told us, "and then I did something that I don't include in my books or workshops. But I find it to be the very best thing for these sorts of situations. I sit in the bath and drink a shot or two of gin. And that's exactly what I did. It is amazing to me, but this always works. I don't know why it works, but it does. I think it is mostly because there is some other part of me that comes out, another part of me that I can access."

In the bath, Johnson asked herself, "What the hell are you doing? I thought you were an experiential therapist. Experiential therapists take people where they are. They assume that people have very good reasons for being where they are. They try not to label people, they use their imagination to put themselves in the other's shoes and stay empathic. And this was an attachment drama—which always feels like it's about life and death—so what does it all mean?"

Johnson lectured herself in the bath, between sips of gin, and sure enough she made progress.

"Things felt different. It felt like I had moved to a new place. I felt like I was getting my head straight and could go in and be with Helga again."

The next session, Johnson approached Helga with a very different attitude. "I am so sorry," she apologized to Helga. "I realized in the last session how very tired I was. You were very upset, and I realized afterwards that I wasn't able to listen to you very well."

Helga was quite surprised by this confession. She quieted down immediately and listened intently.

"If I understood you right," Johnson continued, "what I heard was a rather strange story that surprised me at the time. But as I think about it now, you actually did something that was quite amazing and courageous. You actually do believe that this man, your husband, isn't able to take care of you in the way you need. You believe that you cannot count on him—and the most poignant example of this would be that he wouldn't be there for you if you were dying—the way we need a spouse to be there. You are very unsure if he can be there when you need him the most. Would he be there to hold you if you were dying? I think we all have this kind of fantasy that the one we love will do that, whether we speak it or not. Then you actually tested out your belief. I would never have the courage to do that."

Helga burst into tears and wept quietly for about twenty minutes. All the while she cried, Johnson felt less elated by the breakthrough than ashamed of herself for having begun to judge this woman and label her. Rather than trying to understand Helga's experience, which is one of the most important principles of her method, Johnson had begun to pathologize her. She felt further humbled by the story Helga then told about the traumas of her early life and the recent terrible loss and stress of her immigration to Canada.

THE POWER OF UNDERSTANDING

"All the other people said I was crazy," Helga sobbed through her tears.

Johnson took a deep breath because she had been on the verge of doing basically the same thing.

"Those other doctors all thought I was nuts. I just needed someone to tell me that I wasn't crazy, that this isn't right. I know my husband is not a bad man. He just can't be there for me the way I want. A lot of it is my own fault for expecting things that he just can't do."

Johnson was completely taken by surprise by the insights Helga then expressed. Once she felt accepted and validated, it seemed that she could talk honestly and with great maturity about her situation. Gone were all the histrionic mannerisms and dramatic exaggerations. It was as if she was a different person.

In the next session, Helga grieved the end of her marriage, but without blaming her husband or herself. She just accepted that they had made a mistake. They decided to separate and declared their intention to remain dear friends as they moved on with their lives. When she tried to thank Johnson for all her help, she felt guilty accepting the gratitude.

"You did all the work," Johnson protested. What she didn't say was how close she felt she had come to letting this woman down in the beginning.

"No really," Helga insisted. "What you did was so important. You accepted what I was saying. You told me I wasn't crazy. You just let me figure things out. Nobody ever did that for me before."

This case, perhaps more than any other, reaffirmed for Johnson how important it is to meet people where they are when they first come in for help. At this first meeting, people are at their most desperate and vulnerable. It is often hard to see their potential for growth and change right away. When you validate their reality and help them feel understood, this potential emerges, as happened dramatically in this case.

"Can you just imagine what that was like for Helga," Johnson asks, "standing on the chair in the basement, waiting to see if her husband would come to save her? That's the image I had of her when I was sitting in the bath sipping gin. That's what came to mind when I turned off the therapist diagnostic voice in my head and imagined what it must feel like to be her. Here is this desperate little woman, standing shakily on a chair, making noises like she was dying, checking to see how long it will take for her husband to come for her. Sometimes we choose strange ways—desperate ways—to see if someone cares for us in that special way. And sometimes therapists learn to see our common fears and longings in those peculiar responses."

CHAPTER FIFTEEN

Ernest Rossi

The Hip-Nose Doctor Finds the Michael Jackson Tickets

In the early years of his career, Rossi devoted himself to writing a series of books about hypnosis, including casebooks, manuals, and collections of papers. He next began developing a therapeutic approach that was responsive to mind-body interactions in the healing process. Along these lines, he published The Psychobiology of Mind-Body Healing; Mind-Body Therapy; The February Man: Ideodynamic Healing in Hypnotherapy; Ultradian Rhythms in Life Processes; The Symptom Path to Enlightenment; Dreams, Consciousness, and Spirit; *and, most recently,* The Psychobiology of Gene Expression. *It is in his latest work that Rossi presents the theory and research related to optimizing creativity and brain growth through an integrative approach that combines hypnosis, alternative medicine, and psychoimmunology. This presentation of his ideas represents the culmination of his life's work devoted to treating the mind-body connection in people's experience.*

Rossi is based in Los Osos, California, where he maintains a private practice.

Before launching into a description of one of his earliest and most controversial cases, one that he has never written or talked about much, Rossi wished to make clear that this client may appear and speak in a stereotypical way, but this was actually the way she expressed herself. Because the client's particular dialect was central to the misunderstandings and challenges that took place, we have preserved her language as she used it.

CONTEXTUAL BACKGROUND

In order to understand the significance that this case had in Rossi's life and work, it is important first to understand the personal context for his experience. Rossi's father had immigrated from Italy to a lower-middle-class, blue-collar neighborhood in Bridgeport, Connecticut. None of Rossi's relatives, including his parents, had ever gone beyond eighth grade in their education.

Rossi grew up during a time when his largely Italian neighborhood was becoming integrated with African Americans and other ethnic groups. "Lower-class blue-collar people were very afraid of the blacks. In fact, parents in my neighborhood would scare their children with threats: 'You better be careful or the bogeyman is going to get you!' And what was a bogeyman? Blacks were called bogeys."

Rossi became the most educated person ever to emerge from his family. He was especially proud that he had managed to transcend the prejudices and racism that were part of the neighborhood and family culture into which he had been born. Yet most of his "revolutionary" beliefs—at least by the standards of his neighborhood—were largely theoretical, as he actually had little contact with others outside his own culture. As much as he hungered for contact with those who were different from people he encountered in his childhood, few opportunities presented themselves until he left his neighborhood and ventured out into the wider world.

THE HIP-NOSE DOCTOR

Rossi had not been in practice very long when the phone rang one day in his office.

"You hip-nose doctor?" the woman asked. It was obviously a black person, and from the sound of her voice, someone who was older.

"Excuse me?"

"I say, you hip-nose doctor? You memory doctor?"

Rossi thought for a moment, trying to figure out what the woman was saying. Then it hit him. "You're wondering if I do hypnosis?"

"Thas right. I need hip-nose doctor for my memory. You do dat?"

Rossi immediately became interested. He was extremely anxious to branch out beyond his own limited experience and work with people from as many diverse backgrounds as possible. This would be one of the first black people with whom he had ever worked—that is, if he could get her to come in.

Although Rossi had some difficulty understanding the woman, he managed to schedule an appointment and give her directions to the office. Her speech had sounded so slurred and incomprehensible, he was fairly certain that she might have organic brain damage. Maybe that would account for her memory loss, he reasoned.

Yet after he hung up the phone, he realized that because of her slurred speech he was not able to get her name or her phone number correctly. It probably wouldn't matter, he thought, since it was doubtful she would even show up.

Much to his surprise, Mary did arrive at the appointed time. She was well dressed and personable, and the only thing the least strange about her appearance was that her hair looked disheveled.

"So," Rossi began, "you mentioned something on the phone about wanting hypnosis for memory loss."

Mary nodded her head vigorously, and when she did, the hair on her head fell to the floor. It was a wig. Rossi could see a lengthy scar running from the side of her head all the way to the front. She picked up the wig and placed it back on her head, all without the least embarrassment. Mary explained that she had been in a car accident and her memory just wasn't the same any more. This also explained her slurred speech.

Rossi was both charmed and fascinated with this woman, although much of the time he had no clue as to what she was saying. This was due not only to her garbled speech caused by her accident but also to his lack of experience listening to the cadence and rhythm of black speech.

THE CONCERT TICKETS

This case took place during the 1970s when Michael Jackson was at the absolute height of his fame. His concerts were sold out all over the world, and getting tickets to his shows was almost impossible.

Nevertheless, about a month earlier, a man had come by Mary's house and given her a bunch of tickets for a Michael Jackson concert that was coming up. These were prime seats, very expensive and exclusive, and involved hundreds of dollars.

Rossi tried to find out why the man had given her the tickets and why he had asked her to hold them, but he couldn't understand her answers. He just had to accept on faith that the tickets were given to her for some reason and that she had the responsibility to keep them safe until the appointed date. Apparently, the whole family would be able to use the tickets to go to the concert—that is, if the tickets could be recovered.

Because so much about this woman and her situation struck Rossi as exotic and mysterious, he easily accepted the confused description of the situation. For his purposes, he understood clearly what her problem was: she had hidden the tickets somewhere safe, but now she could not remember where they were. She wanted Rossi to hypnotize her so she could remember where she put them.

As a first step, Rossi went through what happened after the man gave her the tickets.

"Was anyone in the house when the man came?"

"No suh. Jus me."

"And do you remember which room you were in the last time you saw the tickets?"

"No suh. Cain't remember."

They continued to try to retrace her steps, but it was clear that her memory really was sketchy about the whole thing. She was quite upset, because in her opinion, as well as in the opinion of everyone in her family, she had lost one of the most valuable commodities in existence. The whole family had already devoted hours and hours on a treasure hunt, practically taking the house apart to find the tickets. Going to a Michael Jackson concert would be one of the best things that happened all year, so everyone was more than a little upset about the situation.

Actually, Rossi had to agree with his client. He was a Michael Jackson fan himself and indeed thought it a terrible tragedy that those tickets were lost forever. He was determined to help her find them.

TIME FLIES

The most significant thing that emerged from this initial conversation about the situation was that Mary kept saying she knew she hid the tickets in a place where nobody could find them.

Rossi became so interested in her story and so delighted to be working with someone who was so different from anyone he had seen before, that time just flew by.

"I was very pleased with myself," Rossi remembered. "Here I am, a young therapist with all this education, working in a million-dollar office building. There weren't many blacks who came to this part of town, and I can't recall a single other one who ever showed up at my office. There were big countertransference issues going on with me— I was so glad to be working with someone like Mary, someone who was more like my own lower-class background. I very much identified with her."

Rossi was trying so hard to do a good job that he lost track of time. He kept asking her questions about her life and family, when abruptly she sat back and shook her head sadly.

"You not hip-nose doctor?" she asked, dubiously.

"Yes, of course. I do hypnosis," Rossi answered, puzzled by her worried expression all of a sudden.

Mary looked at him searchingly. "You not real hip-nose doctor?"

Rossi glanced at his watch and saw there were only ten minutes left in the session. He had become so engrossed in Mary's story that he had forgotten to follow through on the hypnosis she had wanted.

Rossi explained that before they could do hypnosis, they first had to get some background information cleared up. He then asked her if she was ready to begin.

MAGNETIC HANDS

At this time, even early in his career, Rossi had begun experimenting with alternative ways to induce therapeutic hypnosis. It is the challenge of almost any therapist who does hypnosis that not everyone can go into a deep trance. Some professionals say that only about 10 percent of the population are truly hypnotizable. But Rossi wanted to achieve success with the other 90 percent, too, which meant that he had to devise a way that would bypass their usual resistance.

A standard way to measure people's susceptibility to hypnosis is to ask them to hold their hands about eight inches apart from one another. The therapist then suggests that the hands are becoming magnetized, drawing closer together all by themselves. Almost everyone experiences some movement, so this test is not highly regarded by researchers because it doesn't discriminate very well between good and poor subjects. It occurred to Rossi, however, that this easy success with an unusual experience of having one's hands seem to move all by themselves could be used as a novel method of facilitating trance states. Because the technique works with almost everyone, it would encourage and empower people's personal belief in achieving their own success with whatever experience they actually had during hypnotic induction. Rossi developed many variations of this innovate approach as a kind of healing placebo to focus people's attention on discovering a creative resolution of their own problems in their own way by activating hidden inner strengths and resources they often did not realize they had.

Rossi asked Mary to hold her hands up with the palms facing each other. He suggested that she might notice that one of her hands would soon feel warmer or cooler than the other. Or one hand might feel heavier than the other to signal that some part of her knew where the tickets were hidden. Sure enough, one of her hands began slowly and hesitantly to move downward.

"Yes, Mary, as that hand continues moving down more or less all by itself, I want you to notice how much more you are starting to remember."

As Rossi continued with his supportive remarks, he noticed that she was really focused inside. Her eyes had closed spontaneously without any suggestion to do so. She had a wee smile on her face, as if she were delighted by the journey she was taking. As her hand very slowly moved downward, he saw little eye movements and shifts in her facial expression, all very good signs about how well things were proceeding in her memory search.

While this was going on, Rossi supported her search by letting Mary know that the further her hand fell, the more she would be able to remember. Just about the time her hand reached the halfway point to her lap, she suddenly stiffened. Her mouth started to open as if she wanted to speak, but she seemed to be in conflict, fighting to keep her lips closed as if she did not want to disturb her inner focus and concentration.

"You've got it already, haven't you?" Rossi asked her.

Mary barely nodded her head to signal yes, very carefully, as if she didn't want to upset anything that was going on within her.

"You are going to continue remembering it, aren't you?" Rossi prompted further.

Again Mary nodded her head yes.

"You can really see exactly where you put those tickets."

Head nod.

"OK, that's great. In a couple of minutes, when you are absolutely sure that you know where the tickets are and you can tell me where they are, what is going to happen?"

Rossi paused for a moment, letting the question sink in. His signature technique is not to order or direct anything in the process but always to let the client decide what she wants to do. He always gives options so that whatever the person does works equally well. That way there is never any resistance to the process.

"Are your eyes going to open first? Or will your eyes remain closed when you tell me?"

Mary slowly opened her eyes with a fixed expression. Her body didn't move. Her hand was still in midair. She was still deep in a trance state. She looked directly into Rossi's eyes with a fixed stare.

"Are you ready now to tell me where the tickets are?"

Mary nodded her head.

"OK," Rossi said, holding his breath, waiting for the moment of truth. "Where are those tickets?"

MYSTERY SOLVED

It was at this point that Rossi glanced at his watch and saw that their time was up. He had another client waiting, and he was always very punctual about time. He would have to stop the session now because he needed at least a few minutes to bring her out of the trance.

Just as Ernie began to reverse the process, he heard a single word whispered from Mary's lips.

"Closa," she said, mumbling the word indistinctly.

"What's that you said? What, Mary?" Rossi was trying hard to control his excitement. Here she had the answer, but he couldn't understand it. Even under optimal conditions, he had trouble understanding her, but under hypnosis, her soft speech was even more difficult to comprehend.

"Closa," she repeated again, this time louder. "Is in de lina closa."

"De lina closa?" All Rossi could think to do was repeat the sounds he thought he heard.

Head nod.

"You are saying that the tickets are in the lina closa?"

"Yes suh, deys in dat closa."

Closa, Rossi thought. Lina closa. Then the idea hit him. Everything became clear. All of a sudden he understood what she meant: the tickets were in the linen closet!

The reason that nobody in the family could find the tickets was because in this well-ordered household, the one place that was off-limits to everyone was the linen closet. This was where all the most cherished objects were stored, and only Granny Mary had access to it. Nobody else would dare go near this sacred place, even if they had had the key. The family had torn the house apart looking for the tickets, but it had never occurred to them to look in Granny's linen closet. It was as if this forbidden place were invisible.

Mary had a huge grin on her face when she realized where she had put the tickets.

As relieved as he was that they had finally resolved the mystery, Rossi was concerned that Mary might not remember what she had just recovered because of brain damage that had resulted from the car accident. At the time, it was believed that hypnosis for recovered memories was not effective in cases of organic brain damage. So Rossi carefully wrote on one of his small professional cards, "Look in the linen closet for the tickets!" He intended to give it to Mary, who could then show it to her family so they could find the tickets.

Rossi was so excited and rushed at the end of this session that they said their good-byes quickly. It was only after Mary left that he realized that he never did get her name, address, and telephone number.

The next day, Rossi heard a message on his answering machine from one of Mary's family members thanking him profusely for helping Grandma remember where she had hidden the tickets. But once again, there was no clear name, address, or telephone number where Rossi could send the bill. It didn't really matter, though, as it felt to him like reward enough just to have been part of such an unusual and successful treatment.

POSTSCRIPT

A few years later, Rossi was in the process of relocating to a new office. While taking apart his modular desk in preparation for the move, he noticed a small card wedged into the side of it. He picked it up and saw his own handwriting written on the back. It said, "Look in the linen closet for the tickets!"

With a sudden shock, Rossi realized that in his haste to end the session with Mary years before, the card had accidentally fallen into a hidden groove behind his modular desk. She had actually left his office without the reminder card! Somehow, even with the brain damage, she had managed to remember the memories she had retrieved.

Only now, thirty years later, is neuroscience research documenting how the brain can heal even in adulthood by growing new neurons with appropriate experiences of novelty, environmental enrichment, and exercise. Maybe that's how therapeutic hypnosis actually works— it is a highly novel and enriching life experience that exercises our most creative faculties to facilitate healing.

CHAPTER SIXTEEN

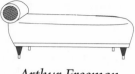

Arthur Freeman

The Lawyer from Hell

Art Freeman's work in cognitive therapy has had a significant impact on professional and general audiences. He has written a series of books for professionals that apply cognitive methods—those that seek to change a person's internal thinking processes in order to alter their perceptions and behavior—to severely disturbed populations. He has devoted much of his career to working with the sort of difficult patients whom other practitioners may dread—those with chronic, intractable personality disorders that lead them to be very manipulative and deceptive and to constantly test boundaries.

Some of Freeman's best-known books for professionals include Cognitive Therapy of Personality Disorders, Clinical Applications of Cognitive Therapy, *and* The Comprehensive Casebook of Cognitive Therapy. *He has also translated these concepts for a more popular audience in* Woulda, Coulda, Shoulda: Overcoming Mistakes and Missed Opportunities *and* The Ten Dumbest Mistakes That People Make and How to Overcome Them.

Freeman is Chair of the psychology department at the Philadelphia College of Osteopathic Medicine.

—*w*—

When Percival first walked into the office, Freeman squinted his eyes to make sure he was seeing correctly. A man with impeccable posture stood there wearing a bright tartan plaid red suit. The fabric was the sort you might see at a country club—if the pants had been accompanied with blue blazer. But this guy was wearing a three-piece suit that screamed for attention. It was hard to look at him without averting one's eyes.

Percival came with an excellent pedigree, and that was the first thing that he let Freeman know about. A graduate from Yale College. Harvard Law School. Then a year at Oxford. Although he had spent only a year studying in England, he had taken on the accent and expressions of a British barrister, which is exactly what he fancied himself.

"Well, my good man," he addressed his new therapist just as if he were holding court, "let us begin."

FAMILY HISTORY

Freeman soon discovered that although his patient with the fake British accent and red plaid suit had a first-rate education, he couldn't seem to hold a job. He had been bounced around from one position to the next, each one lasting several months.

Before exploring the nature of his client's current situation, Freeman first wanted to get some family history. What he learned was that Percival had been through his share of trauma. He had returned home from school one day, walked into his bedroom, and found his father lying in the closet. There was a pool of blood leaking out from underneath the door. His father had killed himself by slitting his carotid artery. For some reason, he had wanted his son to discover the scene.

Percival's mother died of an overdose of medication; it could not be determined whether this was an accident or also suicide.

One of Percival's younger brothers walked down to a frozen lake on a particularly cold day. He stripped off all his clothes and perched himself in the snow. He was found the next morning frozen to death.

Although these horrendous events didn't fully explain Percival's odd appearance and unstable employment history, they did provide some context for his eccentricity.

PERCIVAL GETS HIS FIRST CLIENT

Freeman next prompted Percival to say a bit more about the jobs that he had held and why he had lost them. Art was more than a little intrigued to find out how an Ivy League–educated attorney could fail so consistently in most things he tried.

Percival recited his job history by reviewing one series of mishaps after another. He then began telling the story of the incident that enraged him the most. He had been working as an attorney for the state and had managed to distinguish himself as one of the few such professionals who had ever been separated involuntarily from civil service.

Although it killed him to do so, Percival decided to apply for unemployment compensation. He went down to the inner-city benefits office, where he was not only the one white person present but also certainly the only one wearing a three-piece suit and carrying a leather attaché case. He got in line with hundreds of others, only to find after a several hour wait that he had filled out the wrong papers.

"Fill out Form 99-7," the clerk told him in a bored voice, "and then get back into line."

"How dare you treat someone of my stature like this!" Percival said in his most haughty British accent. "I'll have you know I'm a member of the bar in this state. I can have your job."

The clerk glanced up from the papers on his desk and stared hatefully at Percival. He didn't utter a word.

People behind Percival started heckling him, but he ignored the chiding and continued eye contact with the clerk. "I demand to see your superior," he said, looking at his watch as if he were far too busy to be bothered talking to such commoners.

"I have no superior," the clerk told him with real menace in his voice. "If you're some fancy lawyer fellow, how come you can't figure out which form to fill out? Now go back to the end of the line."

The people in line laughed appreciatively. Standing around for hours with nothing to do, they found this prime entertainment.

Percival maintained his position, unsure what to do next. He had already suffered enough humiliation for one day, but there was no way he was going to back down from this feeble idiot. He scanned around the area and noticed a door that was marked No Admittance, Employees Only. Aha. So this was where the supervisor was hiding.

Percival gathered up the forms, crumpled them up in his fist, grabbed his briefcase, and walked with perfect posture to the door. Because there had been an audience watching this interaction, the security guard was on alert and blocked Percival, who was trying to force his way into the restricted area.

"How dare you!" Percival screamed, to the delight of the audience. "Unhand me this minute. Police brutality! Did you people see the way this Neanderthal abused me?"

Eventually the police were called in to calm down the dispute. By this time, Percival had been charged with criminal trespassing and a number of other violations of laws about threatening state employees.

Percival had been trying private practice for some time but had been unable to find anyone to represent. The good news was that now he had his first case: defending himself against charges in court.

SUGGESTIONS FOR THE MANAGING PARTNER

Things settled down. The charges were dropped, although this was in no way the result of Percival's legal defense. A friend of his finally got him a job working for a large firm doing the sort of work that would be appropriate for a second-year law student. They put him in an office that was stacked high with mounds and mounds of unfinished cases that needed one final bit of paperwork or a follow-up phone call before they were to be filed away.

Once Percival found out what a low-level assignment he had been given, he became irate and indignant. How dare they treat him in such a disrespectful way! He decided to give the managing partner a piece of his mind. Storming past a secretary, he entered the inner sanctum, where he began screaming at a very astonished elder gentlemen.

"You are obviously not aware that these menial tasks that have been assigned to me are hardly commensurate with my education and status in the profession," Percival proclaimed. "Rather than doing this silly paperwork, I should be litigating your most difficult cases. At Harvard, they always used to say that unappreciated talent is one of the most common failings of places like this. As a matter of fact, I've prepared a list for you of ways that you might improve this shoddy organization."

Percival was immediately escorted from the office by a security guard. He was not even allowed to retrieve his attaché case, which was delivered to him once he was taken off the premises.

PERMISSION FROM THE CARDINAL

Freeman quickly figured out that Percival had lived through a consistent pattern throughout his life in which he went from one such crisis to another. It was always because he was unappreciated by others or because people did not realize the full extent of his capabilities. This was the case not only with the many jobs he had lost but also in other areas of his life.

"Let's set an agenda for today," Freeman would invite Percival at the beginning of a session. "Is there anything I need to know about from the last week?"

Freeman could not help but notice that Percival's face was swollen and his eye blackened. The frames of his eyeglasses were held together by tape.

"Well, I have been feeling a little down lately."

"I see. So, what happened to your face?"

Percival said that he had been walking down the street minding his own business when he was approached by a homeless person.

"Hey buddy," the man had said to him, "can you spare a cigarette?"

"First of all, you despicable creature," Percival had answered as he turned toward the man, "I am certainly not your buddy. Secondly, it seems to me that far more than a cigarette, you need to be gainfully employed."

Freeman marveled that Percival himself was no better employed than this homeless person but still had this talent for annoying people.

"So then what happened?" Freeman asked Percival.

"Well, the creature hit me. He punched me in the face for no reason! I tried to find a police officer but there was none handy."

"But Percival, why on earth didn't you just give the guy a cigarette, or even ignore him?"

"Why would I ever do such a thing?"

"To avoid getting punched in the face."

"Well, as long as such creatures inhabit our fair city, it is incumbent on me to let them know they will never find meaning in their lives until they find gainful employment."

Freeman tried his best to explain that there were far more practical, expedient ways to relate to people, but Percival insisted that he was just misunderstood. This reminded him of another story, or rather, another crisis that he had just muddled through.

He had been at the law library in a local university, doing research for his lawsuit against the state for the way he had been treated at the unemployment office. For a change, he had a bit of good fortune and met a librarian who was very helpful to him. They started dating and began a relationship, the first one he had enjoyed in a long time.

Percival's new love was a very religious Catholic. Because it had been longer than he could remember since he had had any sort of sexual relationship, he became rather amorous during their petting. As much as she liked Percival, the woman was insistent that she would not have intercourse until she was married. She would only allow him to fondle her through her clothes.

Percival pleaded his case to her—that they liked one another, that they both wanted to have sex—but she was firm in the limits she set. It was just against her religious convictions to have sex outside of wedlock and without the blessing of the Church.

That very week, Percival called the archdiocese to make an appointment with the cardinal. This was not just any cardinal but a very conservative old man who was three steps to the right of Attila the Hun. The monsignor invited him in and explained that the cardinal was very busy but that he would be happy to pass along any message that he had.

"Actually," Percival said, "what I had in mind was reasoned dialogue between two intelligent men. I have an issue with the Church, and I believe the cardinal can sort this out."

"Well," the monsignor said, "maybe you could tell me what this is about."

"Certainly, my good man. You see, I am seeing a young woman who is a member of your organization, or I should say, of your persuasion."

"I see."

"And we both care about one another."

"Very good."

"Well, that's just it," Percival blurted out, "we want to have sex but she keeps saying she can't because she is Catholic. I never heard of such a ridiculous thing!"

The monsignor paused for a moment, confused by the situation. "Are the two of you married?" he asked.

"Most certainly not!"

"Well, are you engaged?"

"No. But what does this have to do anything?"

"Then I'm sorry, but according to our customs, such behavior is not acceptable."

"So, you're saying that intercourse is out of the question?"

"Yes, Sir, that is exactly what I am saying. The cardinal cannot be bothered with such matters."

"Well then," Percival persisted, "what about her breasts?"

"Her what?"

"Her breasts. Her *breasts!* You know those things that ladies have on their chests."

"What about them?" the monsignor said, becoming increasingly flustered by the turn the conversation had taken.

"Well, I wanted to know if I'm allowed to touch them, or does the cardinal have to give me permission for that as well?"

"What I would suggest," the monsignor said in a tight voice, "is that you tell your friend to go to church as soon as possible and confess her sins."

"Then I take it that the answer is no?"

SPEAKING HIS OWN LANGUAGE

Prior to visiting Freeman, Percival had been in long-term therapy several years earlier, trying to come to terms with his traumatic past, trying to stabilize his job situation, and also recovering from his marriage to a woman lawyer who had attended a "lesser school" than he. They had a son together, but there was currently a restraining order against him to prevent his coming anywhere near his ex-wife and child. Apparently, he had been verbally abusive toward both of them in the past.

Knowing that previous attempts at therapy had proven unsuccessful, Freeman started out with a modest agenda. His main priority was to help Percival identify specific areas of his life where he might be more adaptive. This could include changing his interpersonal style in some ways, and certainly altering his unrealistic expectations for others. Because of his prior history of depression and family history of suicide, Freeman also administered an instrument to measure his current emotional stability. The test required Percival to rate each item on a 1–5 scale. Yet when Freeman looked at the results, he noticed that Percival had written in some items as 2.5 or even 3.65, unwilling to settle for the choices offered and wanting to be more precise in his responses.

Another time, Freeman asked Percival to fill out a questionnaire that required him to list his most dysfunctional thoughts, things like "The world will not end just because people don't act the way I would prefer them to," or "It is not realistic for me to expect that the cardinal would give me permission to have sex with one of his parishioners." Such homework assignments are critical to Freeman's method, in which people are helped to sort out the ways they tend to exaggerate and distort things that happen in their lives, thereby exacerbating their own suffering.

When the questionnaire was returned, Freeman noticed that the responses were not written in English.

"Percival, I couldn't help but notice that you did the homework assignment in French."

"*Mais oui!*" Percival said.

"And may I ask why?"

"Well of course! Because it is far more expressive."

"That's very fine. But how am I supposed to read this?"

"Do you mean to tell me that a man who is supposed to be as educated as you are cannot read French? *Quelle dommage!*"

"Look, Percival, I'm just a poor Jewish boy from the Bronx. In my neighborhood we never got around to learning French. And maybe your assumption that I would and should be able to speak your language is part of what happens to you in so many other of your relationships."

PERCIVAL THREATENS TO SUE

"Percival exhibited characteristics of both a narcissistic and histrionic style," Freeman explained. "He was frequently suicidal, and, given his family history, this was of great concern. He was taking medication for sleep because he said he had great difficulty relaxing in bed, where he spent most of his time ruminating."

During times of stress, or when he faced the latest in a series of crises, Percival would call Freeman for immediate help. During one late-night phone call, Art had reached his own limit. As concerned as he was about his patient, he had to enforce stricter boundaries in order to set appropriate limits.

"Percival, I told you many times before that we have an agreement."

"I am well aware of that, Doctor. I am, after all, a member of the bar, and an expert on contracts. You need not be condescending."

"If that's the case," Freeman said patiently, "then you'll recall that we agreed you would call only in the event of an emergency."

"Of course I remember that. But this *is* an emergency. I'm now smoking three packs of cigarettes a day. My stress level is so high I can barely get by."

"Percival, we can talk about this at our regularly scheduled appointment."

"But Doctor, what I'm saying is that you aren't helping me."

"Thank you for sharing this, Percival. And I promise we can talk about this next time, but now is not the time. I am going to hang up now."

"Doctor, if you hang up, I'm pretty sure I'm going to kill myself."

"If that's the case, then, we really need to get you to an emergency room. I'll call the police right now and they'll—"

Percival hung up.

Thirty minutes later, the phone rang again.

"Doctor, I just want you to know that I am now so upset by the way you spoke to me earlier that I was handling a very precious vase and I dropped it. It was a very valuable Chinese piece and now it is shattered on the floor. It broke because of your lack of caring. I do expect you to pay for this since this was your fault."

"Percival," Freeman said in a controlled voice, not willing to take the bait, "as I said, we can talk about this in our next session. Good-bye."

By the time they did get together for their next meeting, another crisis had emerged.

"You have rendered me suicidal," Percival began the conversation.

"I what?"

"You heard me. First you made me break the vase, and now you've got me so flustered that I've had another incident."

Freeman concentrated hard on not rolling his eyes. He had learned that with Percival and others like him who exhibit such manipulative, self-centered tendencies, it is critical to remain as calm as possible.

"So, what are you are feeling hopeless about this week?" In truth, Freeman could not recall a time when his patient had appeared so agitated.

"I thought everything was going to get better," Percival began. "I heard about this wonderful job."

"I see."

"They are looking for a senior partner in this big firm."

"Go on," Freeman prompted, focusing on not shaking his head in disbelief.

Freeman just knew there would be another amazing story to follow, and he was not disappointed. Percival went to the local copy place in his neighborhood to get his résumé printed so he could apply for the job as senior partner. The man who was operating the machine inadvertently bent one of the pages when he was running it through the machine.

"Look what you've done," Percival said to the guy. "You have absolutely ruined my document. This is completely unacceptable."

"Calm down," the man said, "it's only one page. I can easily run it through again if it bothers you."

"Bothers me? *Bothers me?* You've got to be kidding! You have now ruined any chance I have to get this important job. I'll have you know that I'm a lawyer. And now I'm so upset I won't even be able to go to the interview."

Percival then snatched up the papers, crumpling them even more. He put his attaché case on the counter and, with great flourish, opened the lid and placed the résumé inside. He then looked directly at the man and said, "I'll have you know that as an attorney, it will give me great pleasure to sue you and this shoddy institution."

"Oh yeah?" the counter guy said. "Well guess what? I'm a third-year law student. I've got a copy of your résumé. With your address and phone number on it. I know where you live. And I happen to know that you can't just threaten to sue people for frivolous things. That's against the law. And I intend to bring charges against you to the State Bar Association."

Percival now believed he was going to lose his license to practice law.

"So," Freeman asked him, "why is it that you find it so difficult to keep your mouth shut?"

Percival's only response was that he was misunderstood again, that none of this was his fault. The world was filled with cretins, idiots, and creatures. He'd just had another run of bad luck.

THE HOSPITAL

Eventually, Percival worsened to the point that he became seriously depressed and suicidal. Freeman suggested that it might be time for him to consider hospitalization for a time, and to his surprise, Percival readily agreed.

Percival's room had a phone, which was unfortunate. Somehow, he managed to convince a staff member to get him a copy of the medical school directory that administered the hospital he was in. With his trusty attaché case at his side and voluminous notes spread out over his bed, Percival began calling everyone he could think of in the directory. He called the dean of the medical school. He called the chair of psychiatry. He even called the president of the university and members of the board of trustees. In each case, he threatened them with malpractice lawsuits because of the incompetent treatment to which he believed he had been subjected.

Various committees were convened to investigate the allegations. Percival had constructed a huge brief that summarized all the inadequate care he had received, including a page or two devoted to how Freeman had treated him. Art noted that among the grievances listed in the suit, Percival wanted him to pay for the broken vase.

When called in to defend himself, Freeman came armed with his detailed case notes. It did not take the investigating committee very long to drop the charges against him and all the other staff listed in the allegations. Percival, after all, had a long history of threatening to sue people who did not live up to his expectations.

A few months later, Percival called Freeman again to resume their treatment. Art thought it best that they not continue and instead referred him to a psychiatrist who might better manage him on medication. He was then treated with various drugs, none of which put much of a dent in his continued self-destructive and interpersonally annoying behavior as the lawyer from hell.

WHAT FREEMAN LEARNED

Freeman is known primarily for his work with people with severe personality disorders. He is an expert on therapeutic narcissism, yet he still got himself in trouble with his patient because of his belief that he really could change the ongoing, chronic, intractable pattern that is most resistant to change.

"I think Percival was really untreatable, mostly because he never figured out what he needed. His grandiosity was incredible. His inability to self-monitor was the worst I've ever seen. His spent his life writing briefs and suing people who annoyed or disappointed him.

"I don't think our therapeutic technology is sophisticated enough to treat him. There are probably biogenetic factors that I can't even begin to address. I think the idea of being reasonable was not reasonable in his case. What Percival really responded to best was magic. He was attracted to the magic of psychoanalysis. He liked the magic of the medication. He might have responded to acupuncture or something similar. But the idea of a more directive, cognitive-behavioral approach really didn't work terribly well. He wanted magic, and I didn't provide it."

Although many of the cases profiled in this book show dramatic progress or even full-fledged cures, Percival is a particularly good example of the limits of psychotherapy. Medication is also not always helpful with the kind of severe personality disorder that Freeman describes. In cases such as this, the goal may not be so much to eliminate completely the self-defeating patterns as to help the person become a little more adaptive and effective in getting his needs met without becoming such a constant irritant to others.

CHAPTER SEVENTEEN

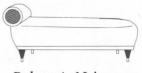

Robert A. Neimeyer

Reconstructing the Jigsaw Puzzle of a Meter Man's Memory

Robert Neimeyer is one of the foremost theorists in constructivist therapy, an approach that emphasizes the unique ways that people create meaning in problem situations and in the larger story of their lives. He has specialized in applying this approach to helping people deal with issues related to grief and loss. He has published seventeen books in this area, including Constructivism in Psychotherapy; Advances in Personal Construct Theory; Meaning Reconstruction and the Experience of Loss; *and* Lessons of Loss: A Guide to Coping. *He is also the editor of the journals* Death Studies *and* Journal of Constructivist Psychology.
   Neimeyer is Professor of Psychology at the University of Memphis.

―‿‿‿―

Because of the dramatic nature of this story, it is told a bit differently from the others in the book. The client, Bill, was referred to Neimeyer by a physician because the physicians and psychologists working with Bill were not having much success helping him make adjustments to life after a traumatic injury.

THE COWBOY BOOTS

Bill was behind schedule, so he walked briskly to the side of the house. Thankfully, this was a development in which the homes had all been built roughly at the same time, so he didn't have to waste time searching for the meters; the worst that he might have to do is push aside some overgrown shrubbery.

He was on autopilot, checking the meters just as he had a hundred times before. He carefully recorded the numbers and then rushed ahead to the next house. If he kept up this pace, he might even get back a little early.

"Hey man, lookit what we got here! We got us a meter man. Hey Mister Meterman. Whasup?"

Bill glanced up from the board that he used to record the readings and found himself facing four young men. Each was dressed in the uniform of a local gang—torn T-shirts, jeans, boots, and bandanas tied on their heads.

"I axed you, Mister Meterman, whadya doin'? You got any money?"

"What do you think I'm doing?" Bill said, and then brushed by them on his way to the next house. Damn, now he was falling further behind.

"I axed if you got any money. Now, put yo hands outta the way and give me yo wallet."

Bill just looked at the man quizzically, not sure why this was happening to him. All he wanted to do was finish his route and get home.

The next thing he knew he was on the ground with a pistol pressed painfully against his cheek, the front sight digging into his skin. All he could see through his one open eye was the worn cowboy boot of the guy holding the gun.

"You make one move, Motherfucker, and you're a dead man. You hear me Mister Motherfucking Meterman?"

Bill felt dizzy, disoriented, unsure what had happened. One second he was walking and the next he was on the ground. He started to raise himself up on one arm.

"I said," the guy with the boots screamed, "to stay the fuck down!" As he said those last words, he emphasized his point by kicking Bill in the stomach with his boot.

Bill felt the gun pressed to his head again, this time digging into his head and pressing his face against the pavement. "Now, when I tell you what the fuck I want you to do, you better fucking listen. You hear me?" Again, he emphasized the point by kicking him in the side. Bill could feel his ribs break.

With the sudden impact of the boot against his ribs, Bill couldn't draw a breath. He started to rise again, trying to get some air, when all four men began kicking him savagely. One concentrated on stomping on his hands, breaking the fingers. Another kept aiming blows at this stomach and ribs. By then, his lungs had been punctured by the broken bones and had started to fill with fluid. It was the guy with the cowboy boots who did the most damage, however: he'd back off, take a running start and then kick Bill's head as if it were a football.

Throughout the vicious assault, Bill kept trying to get up. He thought to himself if only he could get in one blow, just one, he'd feel like it had been worth it. It never occurred to him that with his mashed, useless hands and eyes flooded with blood, even if he had managed to get up he could not have landed a blow on his assailants. Yet still, as the men kept kicking and stomping him, Bill tried to get up—if only he could get up, he thought, everything would be OK.

As his companions worked on the extremities, Cowboy Boots kept going at Bill's face, breaking his nose, his jaw, knocking out all of his teeth except the back molars. He broke the facial bones around Bill's eyes. He fractured the bones in his cheek. He and his friends beat Bill until he was all but dead. The last thought that went through Bill's head before he passed out was that he'd never forget the close-up view of those cowboy boots as long as he lived.

ONE YEAR LATER

Neimeyer's first impression of his new client was that he had obviously had some sort of reconstructive surgery. Neimeyer later learned that it had taken seven surgeries to put Bill's face together. Yet the man still looked as though he had run into a wall. There were visible scars along his brow, cheek, and lips, and his teeth gleamed with unnatural whiteness. It wasn't that he was repulsive, but one couldn't help but wonder what had happened to him.

Bill was dressed as you might expect of someone from the blue-collar world: jeans and a flannel shirt. In spite of this rather ordinary style of dress, there was something distinctly odd about his behavior. As he first entered the office, he very deliberately and carefully skirted around the edge of the walls so he could take a seat against the far wall. He scooted the chair back still further so it was right up against the hard surface and so nothing would be between him and the wall. Neimeyer could tell instantly that this was a man who felt so vulnerable and hypervigilant that he was seeking safety in any way he could find it.

It took a while for Neimeyer to understand his client's story, as it was impaired by a flight of disconnected ideas and Bill's self-conscious mumbling as a result of the ill-fitting dentures he wore. When he later felt more comfortable with his therapist, he would eventually remove the false teeth. Although this would collapse the shape of his face, it let Bill speak in a way that he felt was more direct and somehow more real. And as it turned out, although Bill never graduated from high school, he was clearly bright and surprisingly eloquent in his speech. He had the kind of intelligence that was born from life experience rather than book learning.

Bill had been diagnosed with posttraumatic stress disorder, as well as a number of cognitive deficits that interfered with his memory and impulse control. Because Neimeyer was viewed as an authority on working with the aftermath of traumatic loss, he had been asked to evaluate and treat Bill, in the hope that this emotionally and physically broken man might be better able to function.

In addition to his fear that others were out to hurt him—and Neimeyer wondered if it could be called paranoia if his past experience had shown that people *were* out to get him—Bill was terribly depressed and suicidal. He was lonely and isolated, holed up in his house, jobless, apparently addicted to a constant stream of "reality programs" and police shows that seemed to constantly retraumatize him. Most of the time he felt helpless and desperate. Worst of all, he couldn't even remember what had happened to him in any coherent way; he had only disconnected snippets of images that continued to plague him. Most vivid was the recurring image of the cowboy boot continuing to crush his face.

CONSTRUCTING MEANING OUT OF CHAOS

Neimeyer realized that Bill needed help not only with his memory but also with finding some sort of livable meaning in the radically changed life he now had to live. In the sort of constructivist approach that he favored, Neimeyer strove to help people understand the context for their traumatic experiences and to find significance and mastery in the wake of a disrupted life story. In Bill's case, Neimeyer encountered a situation that had destroyed not only his client's face and body but also his sense of who he was. Certainly his appearance was profoundly altered, but so too was his sense of identity, his history, and his ability to reconstruct what he had previously lived. Sadly, Bill could not even tell a coherent story of what had happened to him because his memory was so disjointed and fragmented.

"Doc," he said in a despairing voice, "I don't even recognize who I am no more. It's like I look in the mirror in the morning and the man that looks back at me don't look nothing like how I used to look. And he sure don't act like nothing like how I used to act."

Indeed, although he had rarely before been given to aggression or rage, Bill had become volatile and unpredictable, so much so that his wife of seventeen years "couldn't take it," and left him. Recently he had been in a grocery store, shopping in his usual way—always with his back to a solid surface so that nobody could sneak up behind him. He could easily retrieve vegetables on one end of the store, and dairy products on the other, but any of the canned goods in the middle proved challenging for him. He might have to wait several minutes before an aisle was completely clear so that he would venture into it, quickly grab a few cans, and retreat to the safety of the back wall of frozen food. He lived life as if he were in the jungle, always hunted by the enemy.

As he made his way furtively toward the checkout line, Bill overhead a loud conversation.

"What do you mean you don't have any brie cheese?" a customer yelled at the cashier. "I need it and I need it now!"

"I'm sorry sir," the young boy said, "if you like we could call the manager and ask him when—"

"Forget it!" the customer snapped back. "I can't believe. . . ." The man never finished his rant, because by that time, Bill had him in a choke hold. It took three people to pull him off the guy.

"I just don't know what happens to me sometimes," Bill explained to his therapist. "I just don't have no control no more. It's like I've just got a fire burning inside, and I just explode sometimes. I don't even know why I jumped on the guy at the store but all I could feel was *danger.*"

It was Neimeyer's job to help Bill rebuild his memory and construct some sort of meaning out of an event that still gripped him. This was going to be a challenging task because it was so difficult for Bill to retrieve what had happened, much less order the narrative in a coherent story. From this concrete beginning, the goal would be to move from the past to the present and then to a more hopeful future.

JIGSAW MEMORIES

"I don't know why I'm so angry all the time," Bill said. "I was never like this before."

"You say, 'before,'" Neimeyer observed. "Tell me about the 'before,' about what happened to you that changed everything."

"I just don't know. I just can't remember! I just know these guys tried to rob me, and they beat me so hard I should have died. But I just can't remember much of it. It's all just kind of foggy in my head. I just can't deal with things no more." Then he started crying.

Because Bill couldn't tell the whole story of what had happened to him, Neimeyer decided to employ a technique that might be helpful. "Bill, I know you have told me some things about this terrible assault that you experienced, and I am wondering if it might be helpful for us just to be able to review that experience in a little more detail and maybe help you say some of the things to me that you carefully keep out of the story that you tell to other people."

"I told you I can't remember nothing. I just can't remember it."

"Sometimes what we find is that as we start to tell a story, more pieces come back to us. So what I would like us to do is start with the pieces that seem really vivid and clear to you right now, and then as other things come to mind, if they do, just to make a note of those."

"You mean like putting a puzzle together?"

"Exactly like putting a puzzle together. A lot of times the experiences in our lives that are hardest to wrap our minds and hearts around are like the pieces of a jigsaw puzzle that have kind of fallen to the floor. It seems like a bunch of the pieces are missing, and nothing makes sense. And so putting that puzzle together again is part of putting together the whole picture of our life."

"I used to like to put puzzles together when I was a kid."

"Then let's see if we can give that a try now. I'd like you to write down on these index cards anything and everything you can remember about the assault." He handed Bill a stack of three-by-five cards.

"You mean now?"

"Well, let's do a few of them now, if you feel ready, just to show you what I mean. Then you can do some more later, whenever an image or a memory comes back to you. Don't worry about the order of things—we'll put together the sequence of things later. So, start with one thing you can remember about what happened and then write it on the card." To help him get started, Neimeyer asked him to close his eyes for a moment and tune in to the earliest visual image that Bill could access that was associated with the assault.

After a minute, Bill opened his eyes, and in the jagged script of someone unaccustomed to much writing, printed: *On the job, approached by four men.* Then Bill crossed out "*men*" and substituted the word "*predators.*" Significantly, out of a cup of offered pens and pencils, he had chosen to write in bright red ink.

When Bill looked up and handed him the card, Neimeyer read it, checked to see if Bill felt he could continue, and then encouraged him to do another one.

Bill's tongue protruded from his toothless mouth as he thought for a moment. Then, with little prompting, he filled out another card and another and another, one vivid sensation, feeling, or image following another in no particular order—the flash of light as the boot slammed into his face, the glint of light on the gun, his own rage—all tumbling out in spasms of remembering. When Bill had a dozen or so of these, Neimeyer asked him, "I wonder if you could keep doing this, keep writing down everything you can remember about what happened to you, as any other memories come to you over the next few days until we meet again. Your memory of the assault is like a jigsaw puzzle, and right now you're coming up with the pieces so that we can work to put them together and see how they fit in with the bigger story of your life." Bill was intrigued but a bit shaken, and it was clear that he needed to take special safeguards as a time-out procedure to give him a break when things became too much for him. Working with him, Neimeyer found out that Bill could creatively deal with stress by listening to classical music, walking, and taking a long bath, so these became part of the therapeutic assignment as he engaged the traumatic past.

When Bill returned to the next session, with more cards, Neimeyer encouraged him to arrange them in sequential order and to construct links or bridges between the fragments. Continuing from the first part of the story described earlier, the finished narrative read:

> When I got to pole they came running toward me spread out where I couldn't run. They came up to me and put a 9 millimeter Ruger automatic to my head. Said What you got? Raised my hands. Said Take it. When they got what they wanted they hit me in the head with the gun

and I went to the ground. He said you motherfucker before he hit me on the ground.

Remember flashes of bright light. It was so bright. Couldn't see nothing. All these guys were kicking me in the head. One guy with cowboy boots was running and jumping on my face. I remember feeling intense rage mostly at the one jumping on me. I was thinking how could I hurt him easy if I could get up. I decided that it would be worth getting hit just to get one good shot at his nose with the palm of my hand with an upward thrust. I decide that I was going to do this no matter what. Every time I raised up I would get knocked back to the ground. I tried many times to do this—I would guess twenty times.

This "jigsaw memories" method had proved useful before with people who suffered disorientation and profound loss as a result of some trauma. Neimeyer hoped to help Bill recreate some order out of the chaos, to bind the trauma memories in a kind of structure that gave the dark incident some sort of meaning. Neimeyer's research and clinical experience with many other clients struggling with loss had taught him that doing so was often the first step toward making sense of the past, mastering it, and moving forward toward a more in-control present and more hopeful future.

RECONSTRUCTING THE PAST

"This makes me feel better somehow," Bill told Neimeyer in their third session together. "Figuring out things with somebody helps, and not just trying to keep me calm or give me sleeping pills. But I want to remember more than just what happened. I want to understand *why* this happened to me."

As it turned out, this was not the first time that Bill had been the victim of bullies or on the receiving end of violence. There was some recurrent pattern in his life that he wanted to understand.

Neimeyer recognized that it was time to expand the frame, to concentrate not just on the year-old trauma but also on the forty-two-year life story of which it was a part. Treating Bill's life as a biography, they identified several important chapters of his past life. Each one was anchored by very clear memories of those periods. For instance, when he was three years old he remembered riding his tricycle home from the neighborhood pool. His parents did not know where he had gone and they had been terrified, but Bill remembered feeling proud of his independence and competence.

When Bill was seven, he remembered his father being electrocuted in an industrial accident. Still alive, his father was taken somewhere far away for treatment, and his mother accompanied him. Because they were gone almost a year, Bill was placed in the custody of an uncle and aunt he barely knew. He remembered feeling lonely and confused all the time, uncertain why his parents had abandoned him. He was scared, too, not at all sure what would happen to him next.

Neimeyer and Bill moved forward in time, to his sixth-grade year, when Bill had been a wiry but gifted hitter in Little League. "Forwarding the tape" again, they considered his turbulent high school years, when Bill recalled being bullied a lot. He felt awkward and shy, developing a reputation as a crazy loner. "I'd fight back against anyone or anything," Bill said. "It didn't matter who was after me; I'd try to give as good as I got. After a while, people just sort of left me alone."

Bill was distinctly proud of his resistance, proud of the way he would stand up against all odds. Initially, he hadn't remembered the part of the recent beating when he had tried to rise repeatedly. It was only after writing on the cards that he recalled that, even as a victim, he had tried to fight back. This was an extremely important realization for him, that he had the courage and guts to fight back, even in hopeless situations.

As they reviewed the significant episodes of his life, Bill soon found a pattern in which many of the themes in his current life paralleled those that he had encountered before—being victimized and feeling abandoned.

Using the language of the constructivist, Neimeyer described it like this: "What I would say is that Bill incorporated the experience of the assault into a meaning system that he first began to construct at age seven. He elaborated further upon this with his high school experiences of victimization. This was the dominant script of his life, the 'dark side of the Force' that reemerged in the wake of his assault. But it was not the only story of who Bill was. We looked at the way he organized life episodes in light of his major life themes. What we found was that he tended to organize the plot of his life according to a very black-and-white dichotomy—everything was all good or all bad. This was associated with several other themes that emerged, such as liking himself as opposed to hating himself, being relaxed versus being mad, being out of control versus in control, being able to keep what was his versus being violated, being able to reason versus letting the fire blaze inside him, and trusting versus mistrusting others."

In the wake of the traumatic assault, Bill had in effect integrated the event and his sense of who he was now into the image of the frightened, angry, and abandoned little boy he had been at age seven. This recognition struck Bill forcibly, and he started to see that this was not the only way he could respond to the challenges the assault posed for him.

These reflective conversations resulted in Bill's moving from a general plot structure of his life in which he viewed himself as a victim, to an expanded view in which he saw the basic themes of his life as far more complex and varied. Eventually he was able to see the traumatic assault as reflective of only one recurrent theme, even if it represented the darkest one.

HOW THE STORY ENDS

"Doc, I feel kind of stiff today. I hurt all over."

"You do? What's that about?" Neimeyer asked curiously, noting Bill's subtle smile and the buoyancy in his voice.

"Well, I played my first game of pickup baseball in about fifteen years. I just joined a bunch of guys that were playing at the field nearby."

Neimeyer was stunned by this casual report. This experience represented a significant exception to Bill's previous dominant story; in the terms of narrative therapy, this was a "unique outcome." This was an empowering moment in his life, rekindling the days when he was a boy playing Little League baseball, about the only time he ever felt really competent. He had always been an exceptional player. Neimeyer made sure to draw attention to the significance of this step in reaching out to others and ending Bill's self-imposed exile from the human race. He did this not by interpreting the event for Bill but by asking him for details about how he found the courage to do something so public, to allow the catcher to stand behind him, and to place himself in a situation that again involved running, shouting, and physical exertion. He also wondered aloud with Bill about what this remarkable event signaled with regard to his possible future: now that he had gotten to "first base" in his match against paranoia, did he think he could "steal another base" and go still further? Who on his "team" most believed he was capable of making it "home"? Talking metaphorically in this way about the prospect of making further progress, Bill joined Neimeyer in a playful but serious consideration of displacing his dominant story of fear, isolation, and powerlessness with an alternative story of hope, reconnection, and choice.

Soon afterwards, Bill began meeting some local guys for coffee at a restaurant in town. Neimeyer also noticed another meaningful sign of his continued progress: while in session, Bill had gradually moved the chair away from the wall and closer to his therapist. He was not only closing the distance between them, demonstrating his trust in the relationship, but also saying that he no longer needed to watch his back.

Yet none of these improvements surprised Neimeyer more than what happened when Bill announced in their eleventh meeting that he wouldn't be returning for a while.

"You won't believe this, Doc, but I got together with my dad again. Haven't seen him in twenty years."

"Wow, that *is* something! Tell me more about it."

Bill smiled proudly, showing the dentures that he now wore unselfconsciously.

"Yeah," Bill said, "I've seen him a couple of times. We been working on my old Harley motorcycle, getting it in running shape. I probably haven't ridden the thing for twenty-five years. Maybe longer."

The metaphor of the motorcycle seemed profound. It didn't escape Neimeyer that Bill was rebuilding his life with his father, using the motorcycle as a way to venture out into the world again.

"I've been thinking," Bill continued. "I'm going to take that damn cycle and see as much of this country as I can."

Bill had never read the book *Zen and the Art of Motorcycle Maintenance,* but that was exactly the kind of spiritual journey that he began. He cruised the country, from coast to coast, facing many challenges and having many adventures before returning with a renewed sense of confidence and hope. He not only began to know himself but also found that he liked the person he was becoming.

In the few widely spaced sessions they had after his return, Bill talked with Neimeyer about how much pleasure he got working on his motorcycle and keeping it running. He had decided that he wanted to work as a mechanic. Although he continued to practice his skills with his father, he felt that the future he wanted for his life required more training, and he enrolled in a vocational program for diesel mechanics.

AFTERWORD

The outcome to Bill's case was mixed, as is so often the situation with severe trauma of this magnitude. The four men who attacked him were eventually brought to trial, and Bill was forced to testify. A lot of his rage was understandably reactivated once he had to face his assailants. The defense attorneys tried to attack him as well, reducing his credibility as a witness, but Bill mostly held up against the strain with the help of two friends who stayed at his side.

The leader of the gang, the guy with cowboy boots who was the only one who Bill got a clear look at, was sentenced to thirty years in prison, reduced to ten. The other guys got off with a "slap on the wrist."

Bill felt indignant at this outcome that only underscored the injustice in the world.

"I'm just so pissed off," Bill told Neimeyer in one of their last meetings, "at this whole crazy world. Nobody has any respect for human life anymore. And I just can't let go of the anger I feel."

To add more tragedy to an already troubled life narrative, Bill was soon thereafter diagnosed with malignant melanoma, the worst kind of skin cancer. Several surgeries were needed to remove the cancerous tissue, and that brought back all his worst memories about the pain and suffering he had experienced earlier with all the operations on his face and hands.

"I just know this melanoma will come back," Bill said. "I've lost three other friends and family members to this disease, and not one of them had a chance."

"And does that scare you?" Neimeyer asked him. "The prospect that you could die from the cancer?"

"Well, Doc, this wouldn't be the first time I've had to face something that scared me. Death isn't something that I look forward to, but it is not a fearful thing either."

"What do you think happens after death?"

"Your soul goes to one of two places. I once thought that I would go to heaven, but now I'm not so sure. I have this kind of hatred in me that has come back and won't go away. I'm trying to go to church when I can, and I have some hope that maybe this will make a difference, but . . ." Bill's voice trailed off.

"But you aren't sure if this is enough," Neimeyer finished the thought.

"Right. I mean, there are so many different religions. Who's to say which one is right and which one you should follow?"

"So," Neimeyer ventured tentatively, "you're feeling angry at God for subjecting you to so much pain in your life, and then just when you start to get some control back, you end up with cancer. It just doesn't seem fair."

"Well," Bill said, shaking his head. "The truth is I think I *deserved* the cancer for falling away from a good life. God didn't do this to me, but he *allowed* it to be done to me in order to get my attention. Just like when he let me get beat up in that robbery. And now the cancer. This is all a way of getting me back to church and paying attention to what is important. I feel like in some ways I brought the evil on myself, and getting cancer has really got me thinking about this. We are not here just to die, and the whole universe ain't put together just to be blowed up into a bunch of rocks. There has got to be some purpose in it, and I need to find that purpose."

Neimeyer sat in awe of this man who never finished high school, never read much, but somehow was forced to face the most painful existential questions and did so with such dignity. Bill could not change what happened to him, but with Neimeyer's assistance, he did rewrite the text of the story so that he became a struggling hero on a noble mission, rather than a passive victim whose fate was determined by others.

CHAPTER EIGHTEEN

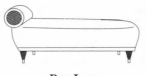

Pat Love

An Emergency Hypnosis to Solve the Crime at the Burger Joint

If there is anyone who fits her name, it's Pat Love. She calls herself a relationship consultant, having long ago lost the patience for ongoing therapy. She has authored and coauthored several popular books, including The Truth About Love, *a book that discusses the facts and fictions of happy, stable relationships;* Hot Monogamy, *a program for maintaining passion in long-term relationships;* Emotional Incest Syndrome: What to Do When a Parent's Love Rules Your Life, *a book that helps people alleviate enmeshment; and* How to Ruin a Perfectly Good Relationship, *whose title speaks for itself. Love is known as much for her charismatic presence on the media and lecture circuit as she is for her writing. She is irreverent, provocative, and inspirational.*

———

"Is this Dr. Love?"
"Yes."
"Dr. Pat Love?"
"Yes. What can I do for you?"

"I'm calling from the university counseling center. We have an emergency hypnosis case, and I was wondering if you could help us."

"Emergency hypnosis?" Love asked. Her imagination ran wild. Had someone been put in a trance and was now stuck? Perhaps a highly suggestible person had been told he was in a cool place and now was frozen like a solid block of ice. Did they expect Love to somehow thaw him out?

"Yes, we have a case that needs immediate attention. You do this sort of thing, don't you?" the frantic voice asked. "I was told you do hypnosis."

Pat was a faculty member in a counseling department, which offered several graduate courses in clinical hypnosis. She had recently undergone advanced training as a hypnotist to use in her practice as well as to teach students.

"Well heck yeah!" Love said with genuine enthusiasm. She was excited at the opportunity to apply her skills, but even more curious about the case. "When would the person like to schedule an appointment?"

"We were wondering if we could send him over right now."

"Now?" Love answered. "Well, since this is an emergency, sure, send him over."

"He's already on his way."

Love couldn't wait to see who walked into the office. A case of emergency hypnosis. What could that mean? What could be so pressing that someone needs an immediate trance?

She didn't have long to wait. Five minutes later a young man accompanied by two females came to her office door.

The young man was smallish with a slight build, and was dressed in what appeared to be some kind of uniform—khaki pants and a tan short-sleeved shirt. He was very anxious and fidgety, almost as if he was about to explode. The two women, in contrast, were quite calm, almost languid in their movements. One was full-figured, wearing a plaid blouse, full skirt, and tennis shoes. If not for her age, she looked like someone attending a parochial school. The other woman was plain looking and quite tall; she towered over the man. Neither one spoke a word, leaving it to the fellow to talk for all of them.

"You're wondering why I'm here," he started.

"Actually," Love said mildly, "I'm wondering why you are all here."

"Well see," he said nervously, "My name is Carl, and I work in a local restaurant. It's a good job. I like it. Or, I should say, I liked it."

"Oh," Love said, "you don't work there any more?"

He shook his head sadly. The two women examined him with real concern. Love wondered about their relationship. Were they his lovers, his sisters, or perhaps his bodyguards? They did seem protective. Each time he spoke, they nodded their heads in unison.

"See, I was working my usual shift, and some money got stolen."

"Some money was missing?" Love repeated.

"Yeah. But see, I didn't take it."

"OK, so how can I help?" Love was again wondering what this had to do with emergency hypnosis. And why were the women there?

"The company has a policy," he said, making it clear how stupid he thought this policy was, "that when any money is missing, they fire the whole crew working on that shift."

"Everyone?"

"That's right. Everyone. It doesn't matter who did it. If money is gone, then they hold everyone responsible. They don't even try to sort it out."

"So they fired you?"

"Yeah. And I know I didn't take the money." Carl looked as though he was going to cry. The full-figured woman reached out and stroked the back of his hand, but he didn't seem to notice.

"You didn't take the money, but they fired you anyway."

"Can you believe that? They didn't even give me a chance. They just told us all to leave." As he said this, he turned to look at his companions who frowned in sympathy.

"When the Counseling Center called," Love said, trying to get to the point, "they mentioned something about an emergency hypnosis. What is that about?"

"Well," he said, looking perfectly miserable, "it's probably too late to get my job back and all, but the three of us had an idea."

"Go on."

"Even if I don't go back there I still want to clear my name. I would never take money like that."

Even though Love had just met the young man, she believed him. His anguish was so real that there is no way he could be faking it. And there seemed to be no trace of guilt or remorse. There was a quality about him that appeared so innocent and vulnerable. No wonder these women followed him around as his custodians.

"You were about to tell me how you thought I might help you," Love reminded him.

"Like I told you, I didn't take the money. And if it wasn't me, then it had to be someone else that I work with because the employees are the only ones who can get into the register."

"Makes sense," Love agreed.

"The money was there. Then it was gone."

"Right."

"But the thing is that I was at the register the whole time. I'm the one who is in charge of the money on the shift, so there's no way that money could be missing. But I just can't remember what happened or who could have taken it."

"OK," Love said. "What do you think I can do to help you?" She left unasked her question as to what she could do to help all of them. She figured that if she waited long enough, someone would tell her.

"I was wondering if maybe you could hypnotize me—you know, take me back through every step of the shift from beginning to end. Maybe that way I could remember something, some clue, some incident, that might help me figure out who did this. It just really bothers me that someone would think I'd steal. I'd never do that."

The two women nodded solemnly in chorus. Were they his alibis, or perhaps they were there to vouch for his moral standards?

Yet in a strange way, this request made perfect sense to Love. Maybe she could put him in a trance that might help him remember some small detail or clue that could solve the mystery. Not too long before, she had used hypnosis to help someone remember where she had put a valuable family heirloom ring. Why couldn't she help this guy find out who might have taken the money?

"I might be able to help you with that," Love suggested.

Love was quite serious about the craft of clinical hypnosis and averse to treating it like a sideshow; without a clear rationale, it made no sense to have two observers simply watching. In addition, the presence of others might jeopardize the client's ability to focus and relax. Before she proceeded with the session, the issue of his companions needed to be addressed.

"So how can I be of help to the two of you?" Love asked, nodding at the two women.

"Oh, they're here to help me," Carl interjected. "It's like this," he explained, "whenever I go into a trance, I leave the earth."

"You leave the earth?" There she went again, so stunned that all she could do was repeat what he said.

"Uh huh. I leave the earth and go into astral projection. Do you know what that means?"

Pat nodded numbly. She had a flashback of a workshop she had conducted recently in this same part of deep east Texas where the Bible Belt buckles. She had used guided imagery and two people had gotten up and walked out saying, "Next thing you know she'll be smoking marijuana and having a séance." Pat could just imagine the local response if word got out she was taking part in astral projection. Folks in these parts didn't look kindly on outsiders bringing in their foreign ways. In fact, one of her doctoral interns was awakened one night recently by loud pounding on her front door. The angry man at the door was none other than the sheriff from the neighboring county warning her, "Don't you be doing none of that counseling my wife anymore if you know what's good for you!" Given what she knew about the local mores, Pat decided to slow down and proceed with caution.

"So when you go into trance, you leave the earth and go into astral projection. Right?" Love asked Carl.

"That's right," he concurred, "And Mary and Martha are here as my guides." He reached out and put an arm around each of them.

"They're your guides?" Love asked, even more curious.

"Exactly," he said, pleased that she seemed to understand. "They are here to bring me back to earth."

Love looked at the women and noticed that each was nodding her head in agreement. They were wide-eyed and appeared eager to be of service. It was as if they were saying, "Yep. That's what we do. Our job is to bring him back to earth."

OK, I can work with this, Love thought to herself. One of the principles of solid hypnotic technique is utilization—that is, to use whatever the client gives you. In this case, what the client was presenting was a very specific view of what would help him and what he needed to make this journey feel safe and secure to him. If he thought he needed two guides to bring him back to earth, who was she to argue?

"Fine," Love said. "Let's do it."

She asked all of them to relax and close their eyes even though she was concentrating and speaking mainly to Carl. She had decided to use a general induction that might work for all of them, since she was not completely sure how this would unfold.

Once Carl seemed deep in a trance, Love asked him to go back in time to the beginning of his shift. She took him through each minute of the afternoon: where he was, what he saw, what he was doing, who was around, which orders he filled. She was amazed at how detailed he was with his descriptions. He could remember everything, every little specific thing that happened. He was able to recreate the position of each person in the store.

"OK now," she soothed him, prompting him to continue the remembrance. "You are helping the customer."

"Uh huh. Number five. Extra ketchup and pickles. No lettuce. Large fries. Coke, no ice."

"Very good. What else?"

"There's Elvis."

"Tell me about Elvis." Love said neutrally. Had there been another Elvis sighting? At this point, nothing would surprise her. She tried not to lose her composure, as things had been going well thus far.

"Not really Elvis. Looks like Elvis. Black hair. Slicked back. Sideburns. Tight blue jeans. Marvin is helping him, since I had to heat some more buns."

"Who's Marvin?" Love asked. "Does he work with you?"

"Yeah, just one of the guys on the shift. He was helping Elvis. I remember we joked about it afterwards."

They proceeded step by step through the afternoon, and he continued to walk through the shift remembering every customer, every order he filled. And all throughout the narrative, the two women sat mutely, nodding their heads as if they were right there with him.

"Let's go back to Elvis for a moment," Love suggested, since that had been an incident that seemed especially rich in detail. Tell me again what is happening."

"Taking out the trash."

"Who is taking out the trash?"

"I'm taking out the trash."

"Tell me exactly what is happening."

Carl continued, "I'm going outside with three, no four bags . . . pretty heavy. One is leaking, and a drink, Coke—no, Dr. Pepper—is leaking out and . . ." He squinted his eyes as if to see better.

"OK, that's fine. Just fine. Take it slowly. You are going outside with four bags, and Dr. Pepper is leaking out. Describe what you are doing outside."

"I'm putting the bags in the dumpster. The Dr. Pepper made a big mess. I have to clean it up . . ."

"That's great. You're doing a great job. Now, from the dumpster, I want you to look back in the restaurant and tell me what you see."

"Suzette is working the drive-through window. She's having problems with her headphones."

"OK. What else do you see?"

"Just Marvin."

"OK. What's Marvin doing?"

"He's standing by the register. Just standing there."

Suddenly, Carl's demeanor changed. He began to look frightened.

"What's happening now?" Love asked him. She was surprised that he was not more excited by the revelation of solving the mystery. Apparently, Marvin had been the culprit, the only one who had access to the register while Carl had been gone. But instead of looking relieved, he looked really scared.

"I'm drifting away," he said in soft voice that indeed sounded if it were fading. "I am leaving this earth. Now I am in space. I am one with the universe."

Love's anxiety started to rise for a moment until she remembered that he had warned her this would happen. That's why he had brought along the guides, specifically for this purpose.

"Is now a good time for your guides to come?" she asked him, and herself. He nodded with a relaxed smile. She responded by saying, "Just relax, feel safe and comfortable knowing your guides are close by."

Then she addressed the two women. "I'll ask each of you as Carl's interstellar guides to reach out and place a hand on his shoulder . . . gently but firmly. Very good. . . . Now I want you to guide him back to Earth. Just nod your head when you are all three back on earth and back in the room with Dr. Love."

About forty-five seconds passed and then one by one Carl and the two women nodded their heads, as if they had practiced this before.

"I'd like you to indicate," Love addressed Carl, "by nodding your head, when you feel yourself firmly back on Earth."

Ten seconds. Fifteen. Twenty. Then a slight nod.

Love took a deep breath. This space travel was exhausting.

All three of them were brought out of the trance. A posthypnotic suggestion was included that the client would remember everything they talked about, especially the identification of Marvin as the probable thief. They all left extremely happy about the outcome, and Love later heard through the grapevine that the management at the restaurant had indeed identified the offender through Carl's help. She never heard, however, whether the young man from outer space ever returned to his job.

Love learned a lot from this case, not the least of which was how important it was for her to trust the inner wisdom of her clients. That has always been one of her cardinal rules as a therapist—once she thinks she knows what's best for people, that's when she gets in trouble, or at least does not do her best work.

"What I love about doing therapy," Love says, "is that I become the student as much as the teacher. I know some might make the case that this guy was delusional, but he came to me with a simple task that I could do. When someone comes to me for help, I pay very close attention to what they ask for in their opening line.

"When this guy came in, I didn't make any more or less of what he asked for. I honored his reality. I respected that he knew what he wanted and needed, and I paid close attention to how he wanted me to work."

CHAPTER NINETEEN

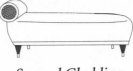

Samuel Gladding

Beauty and the Beast

Sam Gladding is one of the premier textbook authors in the counseling profession. He has written books for many of the courses required for graduate training, including Community and Agency Counseling; Becoming a Counselor: The Light, the Bright, and the Serious; Counseling: A Comprehensive Profession; Family Therapy: History, Theory, and Practice; Group Work: A Counseling Specialty; *and* Ethical, Legal, Professional Issues in the Practice of Marriage and Family Therapy. *Sam also specializes in using creative strategies in counseling, as described in his book for practitioners,* Counseling as an Art.

Gladding is Professor of Counselor Education at Wake Forest University.

—⁓—

They were an extremely good-looking couple in their early thirties, so Gladding's premonition was that they were most likely having minor marital problems, such as arguments about who might be entitled to use the aerobics machines or styling gel more. Never would he have picked them at first blush to be one of his most memorable clinical cases. Yet they have dwelled in his thoughts many years now, somewhat the way that a fictional couple out of a novel lives in your mind long after you've finished the book.

After greeting the couple at the door of his office, Sam observed that they sat together but with enough distance between them to drive a small pickup through. He had seen this seating pattern before but did not expect it with a couple who might be experiencing small adjustment difficulties. It dawned on him that behind the beauty of the bodies and faces before him might lie hidden in the shadows a beast of a problem. To test his new hypothesis, Gladding threw out a benign open-ended question that he knew would attract a response that would inform him of the severity of the situation.

"So what brings you here?" he queried.

Almost instantly, Joe, the husband, who was both a golf pro and a sports nut, answered in a loud voice that caught Sam's attention and must have startled anyone within a hundred yards of his office.

"She's just not behaving," he bellowed.

"Behaving?" Gladding replied softly and calmly. "Tell me more."

Joe, a brawny, crew-cut, blond-haired former drill sergeant in the Army, looked at Sam as if he must have been mentally impaired. Joe was used to telling people what to do and having them obey like the new recruits he once instructed or the golfers he now taught as a pro at one of the neighboring country clubs.

"Behaving," he repeated with a deep scowl on his forehead and a touch of sarcasm in his voice. "Like doing what she is told. Now do you understand?"

Before answering, Gladding glanced over at Mona, Joe's wife. She appeared to be frightened, and diverted her eyes away from his. Yet even at such an anxious moment, it was plain to see that Mona was truly beautiful. She was also a blonde with shoulder-length hair that fell down gracefully to her shoulders as if each strand had been individually trained. Her blue eyes and slender figure were absolutely stunning. But far more than her physical gifts, she presented the image of perfection. Her makeup was perfect, and her outfit looked as though it had been selected by an expert from an exclusive New York boutique who was totally devoted to making Mona into a fashion statement.

"So Mona," Gladding said, "Do you think that misbehaving is the reason why you have come to therapy?"

However, before she could speak, Joe interrupted and, moving threateningly toward Sam, barked with displeasure.

"What are you doing? I'm the one who called you. I am the source of information here. I can't get through to her anymore. She's not holding up her end. She won't listen. She just doesn't seem to care anymore. Just look at her. You don't need to question her. The evidence is as plain as the nose on my face."

Gladding tried not to stare at Joe's nose, but was tempted to do so. He knew his invitation was to scrutinize this porcelain doll of a person named Mona instead and to come back to Joe with the revelation that he understood what Joe was trying to tell him. However, as Sam briefly examined Mona, who looked like a favorite toy that was kept in a closet and brought out only on special occasions, he was puzzled as to what Joe saw the problem to be and where Mona might be in this relationship.

"I'm not sure what you mean," Gladding said cautiously to Joe.

"Do I have to spell it out for you?" Joe answered in an even louder, more commanding voice than before. It reminded Gladding of his days of basic training in the Army at Fort Bragg, North Carolina, a time of intimidation and tension.

"Look, when I found her, she was poor, backward, and bony. She had no class or sophistication. She was Eliza Dolittle but without the British accent. I made her what she is today. I pulled her out of that trash she called a family and taught her how to be a woman of means and style."

As Joe spoke, Mona crossed her arms and stuck out her tongue at her husband, a behavior that Gladding thought might be symbolic of the maturity of the couple and the respect Mona had for Joe. However, he noted that as soon as Joe gave Mona a certain look, she straightened up like a soldier coming to attention and resumed her doll-like posture.

"I wonder if you, Mona, if you—" However, before Gladding could finish his invitation for Mona to speak, Joe cut him off again.

"I'm not done," Joe said. "I want to tell you more. Here are my main complaints. Listen!! We don't have sex anymore! She doesn't like to go out or do anything! She doesn't even take much effort with her appearance anymore! I like my wife to look good when I take her out, and she should want that for me and for her! I entertain a lot of important people in this city, and my wife has to reflect well on me."

Joe reached over to put his arm around his wife, as if to show that he cared about her, but she pulled away.

"Well thank you, Joe," Gladding tried again. "I appreciate that you called for help in your marriage and that you explained your side of what is going on. But I really need to hear from your wife now. Mona, could you tell me what's going on from your point of view?"

In the silence of the moment, Mona spoke slowly but forcefully.

"He just wants everything and is willing to give nothing. I'm home alone all the time. He doesn't even let me keep a dog or cat for company. I'm a person, not an object!"

"Honey," Joe pleaded, apparently missing the significance of Mona's last sentence, "you know that animals shed. There would be hair everywhere if we had a cat or dog in the house, especially if—"

"Excuse me, Joe," Gladding redirected, "but I think Mona was saying something important, and it wasn't about furry creatures."

"You see," Mona lashed out, seeing an opening and speaking to Sam as if she hoped to win an ally. "You see the way he treats me?"

"Go on," Gladding prompted, not siding with her but making sure she was heard. "You were saying that you feel alone and only valued for how you look and act on certain occasions."

"Yes!" she almost screamed, adding a new intensity to the conversation. "You heard how he wants me to keep myself. Well, let me tell you it is not just me he wants to keep bright and shiny like a new penny, it is the house as well. If you can believe it, Joe does inspections every day. He uses white gloves like they do in the Army and checks for dust on the shelves and other places. He makes sure the beds are made properly. He wants to bounce quarters off of them. He thinks I'm some recruit that he can whip into shape because he outranks me and because he gives himself credit for turning me into what he calls one of the 'beautiful people.'"

"Honey, honey," Joe said, "You know I only care about you. I want you to look your best. I want our home to be—"

"You see the way he is?" Mona turned to Gladding with fire in her eyes. "You see what I have to live with?"

"I see that it is difficult for you to . . ." Gladding began.

"Wait. That's not all. In addition to everything else, I'm supposed to cook his meals according to this schedule he prints up each week— a meat, two vegetables (not just one), bread, dessert—and it's got to be on the table at 6:35 each night. Not 6:30. Not 6:40. But exactly 6:35. And it has to be hot and tasty. Do you know how many meals I've had to throw out to please this sergeant?"

Once started, Mona went on at some length about the list of standing orders she was under. And with every complaint she named, Joe became more and more edgy sitting in his chair. His already ruddy face turned ever redder. At one point, Gladding wondered if he was going to explode. But somehow he managed to keep himself under reasonable control, except for the occasional grunts of disagreement that shot out like bullets meant to silence the disruptive force facing him.

"Are you through yet?" he said to Mona forcefully, leaving it clear that her turn was now over.

Mona just crossed her arms, stared straight ahead, and this time in clear sight of Joe stuck out her tongue again.

"I have nothing more to say," she replied in an almost pouty voice.

"It's just not right," Joe said reasserting himself and shaking his head in apparent disgust, "that a woman acts this way. She's my wife. I married her. I own her. She's mine. Every part of her being belongs to me, and she needs to understand that and obey. I took her away from the most awful place you can imagine, and I made her a thing of beauty. I taught her skills like how to keep a house clean and how to perfect her cooking. The woman should be grateful for all I have done. But does she thank me? No! She just . . ."

"I should be grateful? I should be grateful for how you've kept me like a thing not a person? I should be grateful for how you pick out my clothes and check my makeup every day, how you hover over me and watch me every single minute? How you regulate my life from sleep to exercise? I don't think so, soldier!" Mona shot back.

Joe just shook his head, then looked at Gladding with an almost desperate expression on his face. "Now do you see what I'm talking about?"

A GROWING RESTLESSNESS

After that first session and the next several that followed, Gladding had plenty of time to learn more and reflect on matters. He learned that Joe and Mona had been married six years and that the conflicts between them had steadily grown worse. Mona was no longer willing to be obedient as she had in the beginning. She was standing up to her husband now. She felt she deserved more freedom and respect, and her attitude and assertiveness were driving him crazy. He saw her as becoming undisciplined and failing to recognize his superior rank.

However, the problem went deeper than that. Joe's life had revolved around winning. He had won honors while on active duty, including several citations as the best drill sergeant in his battalion. Now as a golf pro he was not content to merely teach golf to others; he played in tournaments on the weekend. He was driven to accumulate victories. Trophies sat on the fireplace mantle, a testimony to his prowess. He defined masculinity as being the best in everything he did, which included marrying the prettiest woman around.

Mona was his most valued trophy. He showed her off every chance he got. Her good looks and charm made him feel important, and because of his lack of self-esteem that sprang initially from his own background of poverty, Joe needed her in a way that a person who is alcohol dependent needs a drink. She was not just his possession but also his obsession. After the initial first few years of making sure Mona reached what he saw as perfection, Joe began spending hours making sure her appearance was as perfect as the house she kept or the meals she prepared. He agonized over what she should wear. He did inspections before she left the house. He even weighed her once per week to make certain that she maintained her perfect figure.

Mona now reminded Gladding of an erupting volcano. She just wasn't going to take it any longer, and a secret part of him admired her for standing up to this controlling, unreasonable guy. Yet another part of him realized that Mona and Joe might actually have a life together worth saving if Joe could admit he was as insecure as Mona had been when he first met her. The problem now was Mona's anger and whether she could direct it constructively or whether it would simply erupt and bring about an explosive end to the marriage.

THE AMBUSH

The answer as to which way Mona would go came suddenly and unexpectedly in between the sixth and seventh sessions. Mona called Gladding on a Saturday morning. Immediately he thought it was some sort of emergency, as he had instructed the couple only to call him in such cases. Had Joe finally lost his temper and physically assaulted his disobedient wife? Had Mona bought rat poisoning to put in Joe's food? Yet as he listened to Mona, Gladding noted that she didn't really have anything much to say. She was just chatting about things almost aimlessly.

"And the reason you called me at home?" Gladding finally said to her after about ten minutes of listening. "I'm asking because you are telling me everything under the sun but not why you called."

"Oh, I'm sorry about that. I guess I just felt like I was in the mood to talk, and I was pretty sure you would listen. I'll see you later in the week." Then Mona abruptly hung up.

What the heck was that about? Gladding wondered. He noted that it was unusual and nonproductive behavior. Did it have a purpose? Was there a reason for the call that went beyond the obvious? Gladding was mystified as he went back to his weekend chores. However, he would soon find out that this had been a "call to arms."

That revelation came as soon as Joe and Mona sat down in Gladding's office for the next session. Instead of waiting for Gladding to ask a question or make a comment to set the tone for the session, Mona uncharacteristically started speaking.

"First of all," she began, "I want to thank you, Dr. Gladding, for talking to me about Joe over the weekend."

"Talking about Joe? What was she referring to?" Gladding thought. All he could remember was that she went on a long rant about how much work she had to do to get the house ready for the next inspection.

"You called him without my permission?" Joe challenged her.

"That's right, I did!" she countered. "And he agreed with me that you are overcontrolling, insecure, and a pitiful person. He can see right through you, just like I can. It's got something to do with your feelings of inferiority . . ."

"What are you talking about?" Joe roared. Then he turned toward Gladding accusingly. "Did you put her up to this? Did you betray me like this? What an unethical, unlawful, disgraceful, disrespectful, and downright disgusting thing to do!"

"No, no," Sam tried to explain to head things off. "I did talk to Mona." Then to Mona he said, "We did talk last Saturday, but all I did was listen. You really didn't say anything. Rather, I got the impression that you just really wanted to read me a laundry list of complaints that you had voiced in previous sessions, and I finally ended the conversation with you because it was not of an emergency nature."

"Oh, Doctor," she said in a saccharine sweet way, "you are being too modest. Truly, you really helped me like nobody ever did before." With that, she looked meaningfully toward her husband.

"And besides," Mona continued, now talking directly to Joe, "he agrees with me that you are the one with the problem. If you didn't feel so inadequate as a man, if you . . ."

"What? Joe bellowed. "That's ridiculous! Mona, have you gone mad?"

Well, the fact was that Mona was mad, and now her madness had turned into meanness as she ambushed both her husband and the therapist. It was a painful thing to experience, especially because it came so fast and so furious. Gladding seriously wondered whether Joe was going to turn on him in a physical way, the way Mona had turned on him verbally. He didn't think so, because Joe had been clueless about the attack and was more stunned than anything else. Yet Gladding quickly surveyed the best escape route to the door and the phone.

"And you know what else?" Mona screamed at Joe. "I ate a whole box of chocolate yesterday and gained two pounds! When I get home today, I'm going to eat another box of chocolate. And there isn't a thing you can do about it!"

"How dare you!" Joe sputtered, feeling as if he had lost control of Mona and was losing control of himself. He looked stunned and scared, like one who is retreating from the midst of a battle he was not prepared for. Mona's ambush had worked. Joe's authority had been challenged and essentially defeated.

Mona sensed the sweet victory her surprise attack had won, and with just a little fanfare signaled her farewell to both Joe and therapy by standing up, pressing the wrinkles out of her skirt, and walking quietly but confidently out the door. Both Joe and Sam sat there dumbfounded.

"How could you do this to me?" Joe accused Sam. "How could you turn her against me like this?"

Before he responded, Sam realized that Mona had set him up. She had declared her independence by taking an innocent phone conversation and converting it into an event. Before a counterattack could occur she had seized the day and declared victory by leaving the scene of the encounter. The beauty had become the beast and exposed the marriage for what it was: a trap with outer boundaries but no inner core.

Hardly sheltered from such verbal abuse, Gladding listened more as Joe reeled forth an impressive variety of swearing words and terms that came from his experience as a drill sergeant. As he swore, the cords in Joe's neck stood out and the vein that ran just below his forehead pulsed rapidly. But the words were in vain, and all of a sudden, with his mouth still open, all the energy seemed to drain out of Joe. He turned and walked out the same door his wife had left a few minutes earlier. But with one last mustering of energy, Joe slammed the door so hard that two of the side walls vibrated.

AFTER THE FIGHT

Gladding never saw the couple again, at least in his office. But he did hear later that Mona had cleared out her clothes from the couple's house before the therapy session. Upon hearing this news, he realized even more what a skillful strategist Mona had been. She had made much of the "nothing" telephone call and had used the structure of seeking help to begin a new lifestyle by walking out on Joe and later divorcing him.

In time, Mona remarried. Gladding even ran into her in a department store several years later. She was with her preschool-age son picking out a GI Joe toy. Gladding was struck by how her appearance had changed. She was certainly still an attractive woman, but she no longer wore makeup or an elaborate outfit. She had gained considerable weight, but she looked happy. Although they did not speak, when Mona saw Gladding she smiled.

As for Joe, he kept collecting wives along with his golf trophies. At last count, Gladding figured Joe had been married and divorced another three times. Each new recruit to a Joe marriage arrangement was a pretty but initially unsophisticated young woman from a rural area and with little education. Joe's divorce record indicated that it was hard for him to keep good recruits once they gained a certain level of sophistication. In fact, it might be said that as in the case of Mona, Joe brought the beast out in each of his beauties.

Gladding found out that Joe never entered marriage counseling again, nor did another of his wives gain her freedom through a therapeutic ambush. The old soldier that was Joe never really learned new ways of controlling either his brides or himself. He apparently became more accepting or resigned to his patterns of interaction as time went on, and it was said that golf became as important as women to him. Although he continued to take pride in his achievements, he never explored the roots of his patterns of interaction.

As for Gladding, one ambush was enough. He reinforced the emergency rules for calls that came to his house. He also gave his couples in therapy several hotline numbers they could dial if needed. He also became an avid reader of Civil War history. The latter interest helped him understand more fully the strategies that are involved when one is waging a fight against a real or perceived oppressor. It also informed his therapeutic perceptions and strategies in unforgettable ways.

CHAPTER TWENTY

Gay Hendricks

The Lie That Hid
in His Back

Gay Hendricks's career has included work as a faculty member at the University of Colorado, a corporate consultant, a relationship skills trainer, and a best-selling author of books about love and relationships. He combines a spiritual focus with communication skills and the use of body awareness, breath, and movement in his therapeutic work. What this means is that he helps people connect their somatic experience to personal growth and connections to others. He also employs an unusual structure for therapy in which he prefers to see people for intensive two- to three-day periods rather than the usual weekly sessions.

In his books Conscious Loving *and* The Conscious Heart, *he helps couples deepen the intimacy in their relationships by asking them to consider a series of questions: What do I admire and appreciate most about my partner? How can I better appreciate those qualities? What can I do to make myself more available for appreciation? What commitments can I make that will allow the relationship to flourish?*

Working with his wife, Kathlyn, Hendricks travels extensively doing workshops on more conscious living. In fact, Gay is so much on the move that he conducted this interview on his mobile phone while cruising over the mountains into Santa Barbara.

—*vv*—

There were two cases that Hendricks wished to speak about, both of which centered around the themes of fidelity and trust in marriage. Gay and his wife often work together with couples who fly in for a few days at a time to experience their intensive therapy. They developed this approach partly because they are both rarely in town for prolonged periods, but also because they have found that these concentrated sessions work well with executive teams that come in for coaching sessions. He finds that he can accomplish more with a couple or a team in a few days than most others could do in a year. Sometimes, if time is limited or a crisis is looming, they might even work together for twelve-hour stretches, well into the night.

WHAT IS THE LIE YOU'VE BEEN HOLDING IN YOUR BODY?

The first case occurred when a man arrived as part of a business group to work with Hendricks for several days on team building. Tommy had been married twenty years to his second wife, and she had come along on the trip as well. Tommy was a very successful entrepreneur and also quite wealthy, so they were on solid financial footing; in fact, they were in the process of building their dream house. "On the surface," Hendricks said, "they had it made."

During the course of the interview with the fellow, however, it quickly came out that he was both unhappy in his job and experiencing some health problems. He had chronic back pain that had become so severe that he was being evaluated for spinal fusion surgery.

Gay and Kathlyn have a fairly standard way that they like to work with couples. After bringing Tommy and his wife, Caitlan, in for a lengthy session, they began by asking him their usual commitment question: "Would you be willing to solve the back pain problem?"

"Well," Tommy answered slowly, "I didn't exactly come here for that, but, heck yeah, I'd do anything to take away this damn pain. I can barely function."

This was a man who was used to being in total control of his business and his life, and it bothered him to no end that his body was betraying him in this way. He was in terrible agony, both physically and emotionally.

Convinced that psychological problems are strongly connected to physical symptoms, Hendricks believed that one important question could be useful in unlocking the origins of Tommy's back pain. The challenge, however, was that this inquiry could easily be taken as intrusive and threatening.

"I was wondering," Hendricks said carefully, "what lie you have been holding in your body the last few years since you first began feeling the back pain?"

"Excuse me?" Tommy said, taken aback. He began turning a bit red in the face. "Are you saying I'm a liar?"

"Not at all," Hendricks said, and then explained his premise that Tommy might be holding something back that was quite literally lodged in his back. Hendricks believes that just as cats and dogs raise the hackles in their back when they are aroused, so too can humans hold their psychic pain there.

Still, Hendricks didn't really expect Tommy to answer. "When you ask a powerful question like that, ninety-nine times out of a hundred the person doesn't open up and answer the question. But how the person responds is quite revealing; it says a lot about his personality. In other words, people will respond to that question with the same mechanism that they have used throughout their lives to get their needs met and to defend themselves against pain."

In this particular case, Tommy became incensed that Hendricks would dare challenge him like that. "This let me know right away that I was on the right track," he says. "If we can get *that* big a reaction from that kind of a question, we know we are on the trail to something useful. I always tell my students that that is the moment therapists are getting paid for. It's kind of like the moment a salesman is getting paid for is when the client says, 'No, I don't want to buy that.' Well, in therapy terms, that moment we are getting paid for is when the client digs in his heels and says, 'No, you are on the wrong track here.' That is a moment that I savor because I know that I am on the verge of a breakthrough."

CONFESSION

Hendricks stuck with that same issue and kept pressing Tommy for the next hour. He pointed out to him that whatever he was already doing was not only failing to work but also actually seeming to make matters worse. Eventually, the man's resistance began to wear down, and he confessed—reluctantly, haltingly—that the lie he was carrying around was that he was having an affair with another woman. Interestingly, his back pain began about the time that this relationship first started.

"Once he was willing to acknowledge his lie and speak the truth to his wife," Hendricks explained, "problems like that can be solved in ten seconds. But it has to be a ten seconds where you are really communicating the essential thing. So he was able to say that he was having this affair, but he was afraid to say anything about it because he knew his wife would get angry. And of course she did. There were a sweaty couple of hours while we helped them work through all of that."

The couple left the session resolved to continue working on their relationship. Tommy agreed to be more honest, and Caitlan would try to forgive him. Sure enough, his back pain began to diminish almost immediately. Tommy did not need surgery, and he felt better than he had in years.

As if this aspect of the story were not a compelling enough example of the ways the body can "hold" psychic pain, Caitlan began to notice some dramatic changes of her own once the couple returned home. One of the problems in their relationship all along was that she had been overweight; she had been trying to lose the same stubborn thirty pounds over the same years that her husband was having the affair.

"Caitlan wrote me a letter a few months later," Hendricks told us. "She said that the weight basically fell off of her body. She hadn't even needed to go on a diet—the weight just came off by itself. Things just shifted in her, and as a result of this moment of truth, she was able to get back into a more healthy relationship with her body."

It was the quickness of these responses that most surprised Hendricks. He has seen other cases before in which people have made these sorts of connections, but never another instance where the responses were so dramatic and instantaneous. It wasn't until Tommy decided that he was willing to surrender his back pain that he was prepared to face his wife's anger and disapproval. And it was not until Caitlan was able to confirm her suspicions and forgive her husband that she was able to shed her excess pounds.

EXPRESSING ANGER

Hendricks told us of another case similar to this one in that it also dealt with issues of trust in a marriage. In addition, it brings up a rather unusual example of reoccurring patterns in family legacies, a situation in which family history is passed on from one generation to the next, often without the participants' even knowing about the repetitious and inherited scripts they are playing out.

This was a case, Hendricks told us, of a couple who also arrived for a three-day intensive series of sessions to deal with problems in their marriage. They had been married for fifteen years. About a year earlier, an issue came up between them that they could not get past. They were now at the point where they were seriously contemplating divorce.

"Trent was a big guy," Hendricks described the husband. "Six feet two, over two hundred pounds. He had been an athlete, a football player, when he was in college, so he was a very sturdy fellow with a big, booming voice. His wife, Jane, was quite slender by comparison. She was very down-to-earth, very plain spoken, and plain looking in the sense that you could easily picture her on a farm or something like that. You would picture Trent down at the Kiwanis Club as the guy making the speech at the Tuesday luncheon. They were both in their forties and did not have children, so that gave them a sense that their professions were the main focus of their lives. And they were both very accomplished people in their respective fields."

After describing their appearance, Hendricks mentioned that it took little prodding to find out the central issue that brought them to such a precarious stage in their relationship: Jane had developed a sexual interest in another man.

"This had been a very short-term sexual liaison, and she had ended it soon after it began. Yet it had been a really powerful and quick infatuation that was over and out very quickly. Although the relationship had long been ended, Trent had become obsessed with it. He couldn't forgive and forget and move on from it. In fact, the more she apologized for it and the more she said she was sorry and would never do anything like that again, the more angry and abusive he became. This brought out an emotionally abusive element to him that she had never seen before and that really scared her."

Because Trent couldn't manage to forgive his wife, and his anger blossomed, Jane had decided that she had had enough. They had tried therapy before. They had prayed in church. But nothing could help them get past the point of being stuck.

"In Jane's family, if you did something bad, you apologized and people moved on from it. Yet the more she tried this with Trent, the less it worked; if anything, her contriteness seemed to enrage him more. This is the point where they showed up in the office."

Gay and Kathlyn tried just about everything they could think of with the couple to break through the impasse. They tried teaching them active listening in which each partner is forced to listen carefully to the other and respond at a level that proves that the person was heard and understood.

"OK," Gay tried coaching them, "Trent, I want you to tell your wife how you are feeling right now. Wait. Wait. Before you begin. Jane, while Trent is telling you how he is feeling, I want you to listen as non-judgmentally as you can."

Both of them nodded, as if they understood the directions but still found it hard to do what was asked.

"Are we clear this time?" Gay asked again, making sure that they would not end up in the same mess as previously, when things spun out of control.

"I'm really angry," Trent began in a level voice.

"Look at Jane as you speak to her," Gay directed him.

"I said I'm really, *really* angry." This time his voice rose in pitch.

"Good, Trent. Now it's your turn, Jane."

"OK. I hear that. I hear that you are angry."

Before Gay could intervene again, Trent jumped in. "You're damn right I'm angry! And you know damn well I have a good right to be!"

Hendricks explained to us that in his experience people usually melt a little after a few rounds of this, becoming less brittle and more understanding. He fully expected that Trent would reach a point where he might admit his fear of losing his wife, or his deep feelings of hurt, something other than pure anger. In this case, though, they just kept doing the same thing and nothing happened. There was no magic. No catharsis. No turnaround. If anything, Trent just got angrier and angrier as time went on. Then he turned his rage on the therapists.

I'M AFRAID OF YOU

"You mean to tell me," Trent said to Hendricks in a menacing voice, "that we flew all the way out here, and spent all this fucking money, and this is all you can do for us?"

"Calm down now," Hendricks tried to soothe him.

"Don't you tell me to calm down! I'm not the one who was screwing around behind someone's back. And why the hell do you keep taking her side?" As he said this, he pointed his finger in the way that witnesses do when they identify perpetrators for a jury.

"We are not taking anyone's side. We are just helping each of you to speak your point of view. We're helping you hear one another."

Trent just crossed his arms and scowled. Hendricks realized that his client was close to bolting out of the room.

Gay and Kathlyn were now certain that this listening exercise was a total flop. They kept hitting a stone wall each time they tried a slightly different way to get things on a deeper level.

"In our philosophy," Hendricks told us, "one of the things that we are known for is to invite people to take 100 percent responsibility for whatever is occurring in their lives. Even if it looks like it is somebody else's fault, we still ask people to assume total responsibility for the problems."

Gay and Kathlyn looked at one another, giving the kind of subtle signal that can only take place between cotherapists who not only have worked together for so long but also live together. Kathlyn set up the next intervention by calming Trent down and reassuring Jane to keep trying. She then signaled Gay to begin.

"I was just wondering something," Hendricks directed toward Trent.

"What's that?" he said suspiciously. His arms were still folded, and he refused to make eye contact.

"I was just wondering: Why do you think it was absolutely required for you to create this event in your life?"

Trent's cheeks and forehead started to turn pinkish and blotchy. The knuckles of his right hand, the one that was crossed over his chest and holding his other arm, turned white. He looked as though he was about to explode. "How dare you speak to me in that way. Are you saying that I made her have this affair? Are you saying that I made her go out and pick up some guy—"

"That's not what happened," Jane protested. "And you know it. I didn't—"

"Tell somebody who cares," Trent mumbled and looked away from his wife. He was pouting again.

"Do you see?" Jane said, glad she could score a few points. "This is exactly what he does at home. He scares me."

Hendricks had to admit that Trent *was* frightening in these circumstances. But he refused to back off.

"Look," Hendricks addressed him in a hurt voice. "When you act like this, when you raise your voice and act so threateningly, I feel scared. I can feel my throat tighten and my belly tighten, and my heart starts beating quickly. I really feel afraid of you right now."

As soon as he said this, Trent started to back off. He started to melt.

"I don't think anybody had ever talked to him like this before," Hendricks says. Jane had been responding to him by either running away or trying to shout back at him; neither one of those strategies had worked very well. I just think that my being able to calmly look him in the eye and tell him I was afraid gave him a model of how another strong man could say a vulnerable feeling. I think that was good modeling for him because of what happened next."

Trent just sat quietly, taking this in. His breathing slowed down. His knuckles and cheeks gradually regained their natural colors. There was total silence for a minute. Then Jane chirped in.

"You know, didn't this happen with your first wife too?"

HIS WIVES HAD AFFAIRS

Gay and Kathlyn were both stunned by this new information. It is one thing for something to occur once, but when something repeats itself, there may be a meaningful pattern.

"What do you mean?" Trent said, knowing exactly what his wife meant.

"Just what I said. This same kind of thing happened with Michelle, your first wife. Now that I think of it, I didn't even put that connection together until just now."

After that moment, everything in the session shifted.

"Yeah," Trent admitted. "I guess so. But what does that have to do with anything?"

"Well, you tell us," Kathlyn invited Trent.

"I . . . I don't know. I really don't know."

Whether that was true or not, Hendricks decided to help him along. Trent looked like he had been body-punched.

"What Jane is saying, Trent, is that when two similar things happen in two different marriages, it is best to pay attention to what that might mean. Where would such a pattern come from?"

"How should I know?" Trent said, angry again, but too tired to put on the usual display.

Everyone else just waited.

"Wait a minute. Are you trying to say that this is *my* fault? I'm not the one who had an affair. I'm not the one who betrayed this marriage. I'm not the one who . . ."

"We hear you Trent. We really do," Hendricks said. "But back to Jane's point. Did your wife, Michelle, also have an affair? Unless I'm mistaken, we have two relationships, fourteen years apart, and yet the same thing happened in both of them. That's kind of interesting, isn't it?"

Trent just shrugged. But they could tell he was thinking about this.

"So," Hendricks continued, "let me ask you something else. Have you ever known anybody in your life who had anything like that happen to them?"

As it turned out, Trent was part of a large family of eight children. When he was just a child, his mother ran off with another man. He had been the baby of the family, so he had grown up living with his embittered, lonely father complaining constantly about how untrustworthy women were, how they would always let you down, how when you least expect it, they will dump you and leave you holding the bag.

"There was never a successful female role model in the house again," Hendricks explained. He was stunned by the clarity of how this multigenerational theme had played itself out when even the participants had not realized it. They were living a script that had been written for them by others.

"This was absolutely stunning," Hendricks said. "This is the kind of thing I had suspected had a deep grip on us, but I had never seen it in real life until this moment. I saw how the context of our early programming can be so compelling. It is like a fish swimming in water. Later on, you ask a fish to tell you a little bit about this water stuff, and the fish says, 'What do you mean, water?' That was exactly the kind of response that he had to it."

Although insight and understanding don't always make a difference, in this case as soon as Trent realized the pattern he was living, everything seemed to change. He no longer felt as though he were being blamed. It was as if he had no choice.

"No wonder I couldn't forgive you," Trent said in anguish to his wife. For the first time in the two days they had spent together, he expressed a feeling other than anger.

This story, like the other one that Hendricks shared, had a happy ending. This breakthrough allowed the couple to examine more closely their patterns and do something about changing them to be more in line with the lives they preferred to live. When he checked in with them years later, Hendricks learned that they had been able to maintain their relationship on a more equal footing. Trent was no longer watching his wife for betrayal, and Jane was no longer terrified of his anger.

CHAPTER TWENTY-ONE

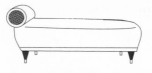

Howard Kirschenbaum

The Client Who Wanted His Therapist to Be Someone Else

Howard Kirschenbaum has achieved eminence through two distinctly different but equally important missions. Earlier in his career, Kirschenbaum was known primarily as the biographer of Carl Rogers, the preeminent founder of humanist psychology. In his book On Becoming Carl Rogers, *Kirschenbaum told the twin stories of Rogers's life and work and how one influenced the other. Subsequently, he coedited* The Carl Rogers Reader *and* Carl Rogers: Dialogues.

In his own right, Kirschenbaum is a leader of the values clarification movement in counseling and education. Simon, Howe, and Kirschenbaum's best-selling book Values Clarification: A Handbook of Practical Strategies for Teachers and Students *has been used as the primary resource on values realization by generations of educators. This book was accompanied by many others, such as* Advanced Value Clarification, One Hundred Ways to Enhance Values and Morality in Schools and Youth Settings, *and* Wad-Ja Get? The Grading Game in American Education.

Kirschenbaum is Chair of the counseling and human development department at the Warner Graduate School of Education, University of Rochester.

—∿—

It was Howard Kirschenbaum's work as the biographer of Carl Rogers that brought Billy to seek him out for therapy. The man had been a devotee of client-centered therapy for many years and had managed to enter therapy with many of the major practitioners of the humanistic approach, which makes use of empathic listening and an authentic relationship in order to promote deeper-level self-understanding. He had read Kirschenbaum's book *On Becoming Carl Rogers* and decided that he would try out this supposed expert on client-centered therapy.

THE CLIENT PRESCRIBES HIS TREATMENT

"So, you're an expert on Rogers, I understand," Billy began the conversation, in Kirschenbaum's university office.

"Well, I was fortunate enough to have worked with him for some years," Howie replied modestly. In truth, there is probably nobody who is more recognized as an authority on Rogers's work.

"I read your biography," Billy continued, "and I must say you did a decent job."

"Well, thank you," Kirschenbaum answered cautiously. This was a peculiar way to discuss a possible counseling relationship. "So, then," Howie said, "how can I help you?"

"I regard this as a good opportunity to work on some issues in my life. I feel stuck and not living up to my potential. I'd like to be in a position like you are. I think if I could get over some problems from my past, I could be free to move forward. And as I mentioned, I do have a long-standing interest in Rogers's work. Over the years, I've worked with some very famous client-centered therapists whose names I know you'd recognize." As he said this, Billy seemed proud of himself, which Kirschenbaum noted with some misgiving.

"It sounds like this has been a long-term interest of yours."

"It has. So will you work with me?"

In truth, Howie was not seeing any clients at the time, as he was fully immersed in the academic arena. In fact, he didn't even have an office for private practice. Yet Kirschenbaum was excited about renewing his clinical work, so he decided to accommodate this new client as best he could. However, he felt the need to explain to his prospective client that he was not completely a "Rogerian."

"Well, yes, I'd be open to working with you, but before we commit to anything, you should know that I don't actually practice client-centered therapy exclusively. I use an assortment of approaches depending on what is needed."

"Hmmm," Billy said, indicating that this was not an answer he approved of.

Maybe it was because Kirschenbaum didn't want to lose his only client, or perhaps because he also relished the challenge, but even with his misgivings, he agreed to work with Billy in a client-centered framework. After all, even though he had moved beyond this approach as his sole form of counseling, Kirschenbaum still maintained an immense respect for the power of empathic listening as a tool to help people deal with their unresolved problems. Still, he wondered if he really should let the patient prescribe the treatment, particularly when it meant restricting his interventions to reflective listening and deep-level empathy. Certainly these were powerful methods, but would they be enough?

SESSION ONE

Kirschenbaum arranged to use the offices of a therapist friend who had some extra space. The setting was spectacular, located in a spacious Victorian home with its own professional suite. The client filled out an informed consent and release form, and they began.

After talking about background information and launching into a discussion of his goals, it became apparent that Billy was certainly a well-trained, responsive Rogerian client. In no time at all, he was describing his presenting problem and responding readily to Kirschenbaum's prompts and reflections.

"I just feel like I'm in a box," Billy said with sadness. "I can't seem to move forward or back."

"It's like a prison for you, a place where you feel stuck."

"That's it! My parents never gave me much support. It feels like they assaulted me my whole life. They were sadists."

"You've felt alone for a long time, as if you have to carry these burdens all on your own."

Billy began to cry silently for a moment, then wiped away the tears and looked to his therapist. "You really seem to understand me even though we've only just met. You support me in a way that my parents never did."

Billy smiled as he said this last thing, and Kirschenbaum couldn't help but feel good about how well things were proceeding. As he had observed so many times before, he was impressed again with the power of acceptance and empathy in helping people express their feelings and inner struggles.

"You look relieved just now," Howie continued to reflect, "as if you feel lighter, freer."

"I do feel a sense of freedom. But it's scary."

"You're frightened of the responsibility that comes with this freedom."

"I feel like I'm dissolving in a way. But it's good. It's the defensiveness that's dissolving."

"It's your *defenses* that are dissolving," Kirschenbaum clarified.

"Yes! When I'm free like this, I can say anything I want. I could say, 'I hate you, Howie.'" He laughed nervously. Kirschenbaum smiled with understanding and acceptance. He went on. "I feel like I'm real. Thank you. Thank you for supporting me like this."

They'd spent less than an hour together but had already covered so much ground. Howie was really enjoying the kind of deep-level connection that resulted from practicing client-centered counseling in a way that he had not done in years.

SESSIONS TWO AND THREE

"With my parents I was smashed to oblivion. I feel like I have been smashed in my head and shoulders and stomach. I am scared that I will always feel imprisoned in this cage and go through life unable to be myself. I feel like an enormous stake has been driven into me holding me down and keeping me powerless. I also feel rage for having been treated this way, but I feel distant from my rage. It doesn't come out."

Never had Kirschenbaum encountered a client so fluent in the language of feelings. Never had he felt himself so fully able to enter into his client's world with compassion and understanding. Billy went on at length about the depth of his hurt and resentment toward his parents. And then he turned his anger toward his therapist.

"I hate all you fucking authorities. If I could just have one decent conversation with people like you who think you're important, then maybe I could be someone. I could emerge and feel things."

Not taking the bait, Kirschenbaum remained in his assigned role of being ultimately accepting and supportive. "You feel such anger toward people who seem to have it together when you feel so controlled, so unworthy."

"My parents kept me that way," Billy said, raising his voice. "And all you fucking authorities are trying to do the same thing. You're keeping me immobilized."

Kirschenbaum just nodded, encouraging him to continue.

"But when I say 'Fuck you' to an authority figure, I feel like the person who has power over me vanishes."

"You feel that way toward me right now. My power over you is lessening."

"Yes, and that gives me hope."

"Hope that some day, as you've said, you'll be able to get out of your box, your prison, and make something more of yourself."

Kirschenbaum had learned that although Billy was quite bright, he worked in menial jobs because he claimed he didn't have the confidence to move higher. He was filled with envy toward professionals, people like his therapists, who had become what he wanted to be.

Toward the end of this second meeting, Howie realized he liked Billy. He felt connected to him. He appreciated how sincerely he was trying to work on himself. And he also felt satisfied with the way things were proceeding so far. He recognized that he was playing a role, of course, by confining himself to only client-centered responses, but it was a role that he could play quite sincerely, and, as it seemed to be working, there seemed no sense in changing the plan.

In the third session, as Billy continued to talk about his resentment toward experts and authority figures, Kirschenbaum continued to reflect back the deeper, underlying feelings. He did everything he could to communicate that he was tracking and understanding what Billy was saying.

"This feels so good," Billy said gratefully. "I feel more substantial. You validate my experiences and feelings. I feel like the real me is strengthened. It isn't just that you understand but that you care about me. I think I see you clearly, and you do care. I feel stronger because of this."

"You're feeling stronger, more real. You believe that I really care about you and that makes you feel stronger."

"Yet it also makes me feel dependent. So I hate you for again dominating me and making me feel like I have to do the right thing here, do what I'm supposed to do."

As the session ended, Kirschenbaum thought they were really getting to some deep issues. He also noted that there were some strong transference issues at work. Billy said quite clearly how close he was feeling to his therapist and yet how frightening this was for him and how much he resented it. This was all reflected back to Billy, letting him know that he was fully heard and understood. Kirschenbaum was delighted with how well the sessions were going. He even wondered if Rogers himself could have been any more empathic and accepting than he, amused at his own hubris.

SESSION FOUR

"It would be best if you didn't use so many words when you reflect my feelings."

"I'm not sure I understand," Howie said. They had been in the middle of exploring his feelings of being oppressed by his parents, when Billy abruptly began critiquing his therapist's technique.

"It would just work better if you were more direct and concise. I want a simpler relationship with you. I want to feel you understand me. But sometimes I get lost in your words."

So now Billy was directing Kirschenbaum's behavior even more. He was telling him exactly how he wanted him to be. He had some perfect image of what he wanted his therapist to be, and he was trying to mold Kirschenbaum to fit that role. Kirschenbaum felt like pointing this out to his client, gently confronting him with what he was doing. Yet that would not be strictly "client-centered." He felt it was now too late to change the tacit agreement.

"That is my goal as well," Kirschenbaum said, "to understand you and to help you understand yourself."

"This is good," Billy answered.

"Good?"

"Yes, it's good that you didn't attack me. I was always attacked for criticizing or questioning authority."

So this was a test? Kirschenbaum thought. But then he started to feel a little less confident in his reflections. Perhaps he should learn from his client's feedback and abbreviate his responses if that was what was most helpful to him. So he continued to stay with Billy as best he could.

"I feel like the wall that has kept me frozen out is thawing a little," Billy admitted. He moved around in his chair a lot as he said this, uncomfortable with what he was feeling. Then tears began to fall.

Kirschenbaum leaned forward in sympathy. He wanted to reach out and touch Billy in his pain but sensed this would not be well received. In fact, even his simple movement triggered a strong reaction.

"Could you please move back?" Billy directed. "Move back!"

Kirschenbaum was startled by this sudden response. All of a sudden Billy was breathing hard and his face was flushed.

"I don't feel safe with you now."

"You don't feel safe?" Kirschenbaum repeated, puzzled by the abrupt switch. One minute they were in the midst of an apparent breakthrough, and now Billy looked as though he had been attacked. All because Kirschenbaum had leaned forward a few inches. But he remained empathic, keeping his reflections shorter, and that seemed to help Billy relax and explore his feelings again.

The session ended with Billy saying, "I feel the wall thawing again."

SESSION FIVE

Kirschenbaum now realized all too well how much he had boxed himself in by agreeing to be a Carl Rogers clone instead of himself in the therapy. He was now stuck trying to live up to an image, an icon, that he could not possibly reach. If he were working more naturally, he would confront his client or invite him to engage in a wider variety of methods, but according to the contract he had agreed to, he was only allowed to operate as a "Rogerian." In fact, Billy had already made it clear that he'd seen the best client-centered therapists he could find, so Kirschenbaum had damn well better be at least as client-centered as they, if he were to measure up. He didn't feel that he had much choice but to follow through on their agreed-on plan. When Billy returned, he continued to be critical of his therapist's interventions throughout the session. At times, it almost reminded Kirschenbaum of counseling supervision, but of course no competent supervisor would be as harsh as this client.

"You are reflecting my feelings," Billy scolded him, "but I don't get the sense that you really care enough about me. I am worried that you are not understanding me as much as I need to be understood."

Again, Howie was taken aback by the turn things had taken. In the previous sessions, they seemed to have done a lot of rich work. Their relationship had been solid. A lot of good issues had come up. Repeatedly, Billy had talked about how much he had been helped and felt cared for. And now he was doing his best to take apart the connections they had created between them.

Kirschenbaum again regretted the bargain he had made that restricted his therapeutic choices. "This is just not me," he thought to himself. "I feel like I am in a box just like him, but I am being forced to play a role. I'm not being congruent. He wants a client-centered therapist, yet above all else, such a person has to be real and genuine in the relationship. I need to do something that feels right to me now."

Kirschenbaum looked at his client. "I appreciate what you are saying, but I don't think it gets more empathic than this. I think you are placing unrealistic expectations that I—or anyone—could not possibly meet."

If he thought that his attempt at authenticity, this confrontation, would somehow turn the tables again, Kirschenbaum was disappointed. It just made Billy feel defensive, as though he were being attacked for having unrealistic expectations and a bottomless need that no one could ever fulfill.

"Now I really don't feel safe with you anymore," Billy said, physically moving his chair back. "You should have accepted what I said. Instead you got defensive. I can't trust you any more."

Kirschenbaum had the presence of mind (and heart) to realize what was going on, so he did not feel particularly defensive. But he also realized that no matter what he did or said next, it would probably escalate things further. If he continued to be authentic and direct, Billy would view this as defensive, not being client-centered, and a violation of trust. Yet if he returned to empathic responses, he would continue to be criticized as not empathic or caring enough. He thought about saying this to Billy, but instead stuck to the script and reflected back what he understood. It did not suffice.

"I'm sorry," Billy said, shaking his head, "but this is not going to work. I feel really, really uncomfortable with you. I don't feel safe, as I told you. I need to stop now."

"So you're saying that you don't want to go further with our counseling? You want to call it quits?"

"Yes, that's what I said. I really need to stop now. I'm feeling claustrophobic and I have to leave!"

"I'm genuinely sorry, then, that this isn't working out for you. I certainly respect your need to take care of yourself."

With that, Billy stood up to go. Kirschenbaum invited Billy to call him if he'd like to schedule another session. Billy acknowledged this, and they left the office together.

BACK IN PRISON

The office was located in the upstairs part of the suite, which was otherwise empty, as Kirschenbaum's therapist friend was out of town. As they walked down the stairs and toward the exit, Billy remained stiff and uncommunicative. He refused to look Howie in the eyes or even speak to him.

They got to the front door, in a small vestibule, and Kirschenbaum punched in the alarm code to turn off the security system that unlocked the door. For some reason, each time he punched the keypad, the signal indicated that the alarm was still armed.

"What's wrong?" Billy asked in a panic. "Is there something wrong? I told you I have to leave. I have to leave right now!"

Kirschenbaum was trying to concentrate on remembering the right code. Had he reversed the numbers? Maybe he didn't push the keys hard enough. He tried again. Same result. The solid red light indicated that the alarm system was still activated. If they tried to open the door, the siren would rouse the whole neighborhood. Besides, what would he tell the police? That he was a friend borrowing the house? (Just what Billy needs—a trip to a *real* prison.) And why wasn't the damn code working?

"I told you already," Kirschenbaum heard vaguely as he tried to concentrate on his task, "I *told* you I have to get the hell out of here. And I mean right now!"

He realized with a sickening feeling that they really were trapped in the house together.

"Look," he tried in a soothing voice, "I hope you have your sense of humor, because you won't believe this, but we're locked in."

"I don't find that funny one bit," Billy said coldly.

"I didn't really think you would," Kirschenbaum said with his best attempt at a reassuring smile. "But the fact remains that we're going to have to call for help because I can't get us out of here until someone comes to release the alarm."

It was more as a distraction than as any serious attempt at escape that Kirschenbaum next led his client through the house to explore other exits. But he knew that they couldn't leave until his friend's daughter came to rescue them. So they were trapped together for the better part of an hour, Billy mumbling the whole time about how this was the worst experience of his life.

After they were released from the house, and after it became clear that Billy was not going to call again, Kirschenbaum sent a letter to Billy letting him know that he was sorry things had not worked out the way they both had hoped. He summarized the main themes they had explored together and wished him the best in his future plans. He also returned Billy's last check. A week later he received the following response:

Dear Howie,

Thank you for your thoughtful and supportive letter and for re-turning my check. I believe that you are empathic but I didn't feel this in your reflections (and as guiding *what* you reflected). Am I seeking more than anyone can give? I don't think so because two others once provided that. Please believe that I am not saying this to make a point or score over you somehow. You are a good guy. It was good of you to wonder if I was seeing you as just another untrustworthy professional given my past. I don't see you that way. It just occurs to me that I see you as Rogers was before he went through the crisis you describe in your book. You seem emotionally blocked, and as Rogers found, I be-lieve that the therapy you do would also deepen without that block. It means a lot to me that you contacted me and wrote what you wrote.
Sincerely yours,
Shalom, Billy

LOOKING BACK

"I should have seen it coming," Kirschenbaum reflects, "For me, this case was just a wonderful example of why a therapist has to be him-self or herself rather than to play the role called for by a particular model. It just doesn't work to try to be someone you are not or to be only a part of who you are. The irony is that one of the main tenets of Carl Rogers's thinking was that the therapist must be congruent. I had clearly trapped myself in a situation where, by definition, I wasn't going to be congruent with my own feelings in the moment or with my own integrated approach to therapy. Even though I played that role very well, it wasn't enough. I didn't trust myself enough to make a contract with the client that worked for me, as well as for him."

Certainly Billy had considerable ambivalence about making major changes in his life. He had been hoping for a breakthrough, yet on some level, he *wanted* therapy to fail so he would not have to undertake all the hard work involved in learning something new. Like many people, he had been accustomed to his misery and had adapted to his situation. He wanted to be different, yet he feared the consequences of what would happen afterwards. So he structured things as best he could such that his various therapists could never meet his expectations, never be a perfect Carl Rogers.

"In retrospect," Kirschenbuam admitted, "I should have known better instead of walking into this trap. It's a shame because this was some of the best work I've ever done."

CHAPTER TWENTY-TWO

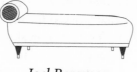

Joel Bergman

The Bride Wore a Tuxedo, the Groom Wore a Gown

As one of the significant figures in developing brief approaches to family therapy, Joel Bergman has been instrumental in training therapists for the past thirty years. He is provocative, playful, and, characteristic of his New York City roots, quite challenging when inviting his clients to consider the question, "Why are you here?" After people then proceed to tell the story of what they see their problems are, Bergman will persist in asking that question over and over again until they get the point that there are multiple ways of looking at their situations and many different ways of framing what is wrong.

In Bergman's classic book, Fishing for Barracuda, *he plots the systematic, strategic ways that therapists can produce lasting changes in relatively short periods. For the last decade he has concentrated on producing training videos for therapists that demonstrate creative, evocative ways to help people.*

Bergman is a psychologist in private practice in Manhattan.

This interview went a little differently than the others. Because one of the qualities that made this case so memorable to Bergman was the repartee and dialogue that took place with his client, he took the time to recreate the conversations as they occurred. The first part of this chapter is thus written in the first person as Bergman described what happened.

Bergman began the description of his most memorable case by saying that his client, James, was initially pretty skeptical that therapy could help. Nevertheless, he was so panic-stricken that he called for an appointment. Bergman began by asking his favorite question: "Why are you here, and how do think I can help you?"

"Well," James replied, "I'm here for a couple of reasons. What really scares me most is the possibility of my girlfriend leaving me. I'm afraid that one day she'll come home when I'm not expecting her. She will be so repulsed by what she sees that she'll leave me."

"What will she see?" I asked, wondering myself what he had in mind.

"I'm ashamed to tell you," James mumbled as he lowered his head. "I'm afraid you'll laugh."

"I only laugh when something is *very* funny."

"Well it's not funny at all. In fact, it's rather sick, and I don't understand it," James trailed off. With genuine anguish he looked up at me and added, "But I can't help myself."

"Try me."

James nodded, knowing that this was inevitable. "I keep a box of women's clothes hidden on the top shelf of my bedroom closet. Every once in a while, when my girlfriend Jennie leaves the apartment, I dress up as a woman. I put on women's panties, a bra, a blouse, makeup, a skirt, high heels, earrings, perfume—the whole bit."

"And then what?"

"I make believe I'm this gorgeous babe and prance around my bedroom admiring myself in the mirror."

I nodded casually and urged him to continue.

"You see, the problem is that to arouse myself even more, I take it a step further and tie myself tightly into a chair."

I tried hard not to smile. I hear wonderful stories each day in my practice, but I had never heard anything like this before. Naturally I was curious. I was also trying to picture how technically James was able to tie himself tightly into his chair.

"So," I prompted him with a straight face. "So what's the problem?"

James looked at me indignantly, shaking his head. He was wondering if I was a notch crazier than he was. In a slightly shrill voice, he said, "What do you mean what's the problem? If Jennie walks in and finds me in a dress, tied up in a chair, she'll think I'm some kind of pervert. She'll leave me for sure," he added in a pitiful voice.

"So," I suggested innocently, "why don't you lock the bedroom door when you're doing your thing?"

Again James gave me a puzzled look. When he could see that I was serious, he pleaded the obvious. "Then she'll ask why the bedroom door was locked."

"Well then," I quipped, "why don't you tell her you're tied up for the moment, and you'll be with her shortly."

MOTHER'S PHONE CALLS

James expected me to react the same way he feared Jennie would—with revulsion and rejection. But I was more curious than put off by his behavior. I wondered what this compulsion was really about.

As I learned more about James's childhood, his behavior began to make a lot more sense. He was a very gifted violinist, a prodigy in fact, whose natural talent, hard work, and an ambitious mother led him to enjoy a distinguished musical career.

"From as far back as I can remember," James explained, "I've been the sole focus of my mother's life. She wanted me to become a great violinist. As an only child, I was doted upon and sent to the best conservatories. My mother bought me the finest violins, hired the most gifted teachers, and made all the right moves to further my career. She attends all my concerts—even the world tours—and remains my biggest fan.

"She's been there for me whenever I've needed her. She's always showering me with expensive clothing, birthday and Christmas presents, as well as those little gifts she thinks will touch me."

"Sounds like a pretty terrific mother to me," I agreed.

"Well," James quickly interjects, "it wasn't all that terrific. Throughout my childhood, she'd confide in me about her own problems, and I listened for hours because no one else did. She divorced my father when I was five, and she never stopped complaining about how miserable he made her. I believed pretty much whatever she told me about him until my father and I began seeing each other again when I was around twenty-five."

Talking about his mother in this way reminded James of some of the intrusive things she would do to control every facet of his life.

"My mother would constantly burst into my bedroom without knocking. When I was ten, I put a lock on my door. She was insulted by that, so she removed it claiming that she wouldn't be able to get into my room in case of an emergency. Come on! What kind of emergencies do ten-year-olds have? Every night she'd lay out my clothes for the next day because she wanted me to have a certain look.

"She was critical of my friends to the point where I became isolated and lonely. For years we were the only people in each other's lives."

James hesitates for a moment, then adds with embarrassment, "It felt like we were more like husband and wife than mother and son."

"When did things change?" I asked him, trying to get him to elaborate more on this enmeshed relationship with his mother.

"Things changed after I moved to New York to play with the orchestra. Mother became morose and even more needy. For the past six months now, she's become impossible. Ever since Jennie moved in with me three months ago, my mother has turned into an absolute terror. I get frightened when she tells me she has nothing more to live for. She calls me two or three times a week, sometimes in the middle of the night, complaining that she's scared or can't sleep. When Jennie picks up the phone, my mother hangs up. Jennie now thinks I'm having an affair."

Again stating the obvious, I asked him, "Why don't you ask her to stop calling in the middle of the night? Maybe you could gently suggest that she see a psychotherapist."

"She's already in therapy and on *Prozac*."

"Well then," I tried again, "what about saying that these phone calls are frightening you?"

"I can't do that. That's too cruel and selfish. I'm the only one who cares about her. If I turned my back on her now, there would be no one. I'm afraid if I'm not there for her when she needs me, she'll do herself in, and then I'll feel guilty about that the rest of my life."

"What about asking your relatives for help?" I suggested as another option. In my style of therapy, it was not so much giving advice as looking for some kind of leverage to change this unhappy pattern. It is always interesting to me why people don't take the most obvious, direct path to solving their problems.

AN UNUSUAL PRESCRIPTION

James admitted that his mother did have four sisters who even lived in the same city, but—no surprise—she was always fighting with them. At any given time, his mom may be speaking to one of her sisters, but that would not last long.

I decided to try one more time. "Well, James," I said, "the next time your mother calls in the middle of the night, the best thing for you to do would be to call your father, or her sisters, and tell them that you're frightened, worried, and don't know what to do."

"I can't do that! It would kill her if I did that."

Yeah, I thought to myself, but if you don't do that, she'll kill you.

When I next met with James, things were even worse, and he was feeling more desperate. Not surprisingly, he had refused to follow my directive to call his aunts or father. His mother, sensing some resolve on the part of her son to put distance between them, was escalating things even more, threatening suicide. I knew I had to do something fairly dramatic to break this escalating cycle, which was not good for either one of them.

"James," I said to him in a soft voice, "I know that if you called your father or aunts after each of your mom's midnight calls, she'd eventually stop frightening you. On the other hand, I understand how your loyalty and love keep you from doing that. So at this point, it looks like you've got one of two choices. You can either call your father or aunts after each midnight call, or go see her and do what you've been thinking about doing for years."

"You mean sleep with my mother?"

Well, this wasn't actually what I had in mind, but I kept my expression neutral. "Well, you've told me how close the two of you are. Ever since your mother divorced your father, you describe your relationship as 'unnaturally intimate.' You've mentioned how beautiful she is and how attractive you think she is, so maybe it's time to get all this fantasy stuff out of the way, fly out there to see her, *and do it!*"

I expected James to jump out of his chair the way I would if a therapist recommended the same to me, but I was surprised when he turned pensive as he considered this possibility. He reminded me of Jack Benny when a robber shoved a gun into his back and said, "Your money or your life!" Long seconds later, Benny replied, "I'm thinking . . . I'm thinking."

Two days after I proposed this Hobson's choice to James, he finally called his father *and* his aunts after one of his mother's midnight calls. Sure enough, her terrorizing calls suddenly stopped. Ever since then, she calls mostly on Sunday afternoons, always with a miraculously calm air about her.

FROM MOTHER TO LOVER

James began therapy because he feared losing his girlfriend (through revulsion and abandonment) and his mother (through suicide), and ending up totally alone. Part of his problem was that he tried to separate from his mother by means of his compulsion. The cross-dressing and, more important, the secret about this behavior, was James's little island of self, marked out as a child to protect himself from being totally absorbed by an overly possessive mother. He never developed an identity of his own, a sense of me-ness, of James-ness, which was uniquely his and different from his mother.

When James was little, he didn't select his own toys, clothes, friends, or even his favorite snacks. His mother did everything for him in the name of love. James placed his mother's need to be needed above his own needs for autonomy, choice, space, and privacy. He seldom spoke up for himself, which is why his voice didn't develop. He had no father or siblings to complain to, or collude with, against his mother's intrusive ways. James was too dependent on his mother to speak up, risk quarreling, and be thrown out like his father had been.

It was too dangerous for James to experience normal adolescent rebelliousness by saying no or doing the opposite of what his mother wanted. Instead he rebelled through his secret. As a child, James dutifully wore the clothing his mother laid out for him each night. But secretly, he rebelled by wearing women's clothes without his mother's knowledge. The cross-dressing also protected him from his own incestuous fears, since his mother would never be sexually interested in someone who wore women's clothes.

Without a clear voice or identity of his own, James predictably got into trouble after his girlfriend moved in. His passivity, dependency, fear of abandonment, unclear emotional boundaries, and fear of intrusiveness and possessiveness that terrorized him growing up in his family reappeared with Jennie. He began losing himself to Jennie in the exact same ways he did with his mother. If you are wondering if this is mere speculation on my part, I should also mention some rather compelling evidence for this hypothesis: the cross-dressing stopped when he moved out of his mother's home but resurfaced a month after Jennie moved in.

Once we were able to stop his mother from calling, the next step was to work on his relationship with Jennie. I asked him one day what it was about her that he found so difficult.

"Her anger scares me," James confessed, looking sheepish. "Jennie gets angry when I don't do what she wants. If I want tuna fish on white toast and she thinks whole wheat is healthier, I'll eat the whole wheat even though it makes me gag."

"What would happen if you insisted on the white bread?"

"She'll get pissed."

"So what's so terrible about that?"

"Lots of things. First of all, I don't like confrontations. Second, when Jennie gets mad she stays mad and makes me suffer so much that I end up doing what she wants. Besides, I'm afraid that if she stays unhappy too long she'll leave me."

"If you can't have your way with white bread," I pointed out to James, "then how are you going to deal with important differences like career, money, sex, and children?"

"Well, that's why I'm here. You see, I'm a very easygoing guy, so I don't mind Jennie feeling stronger about things than I do. Most of the time I give in without being resentful. But she does scare me when she doesn't get her way." He looked thoughtful for a moment, then added, "In many ways, she's like my mother."

Whereas a psychoanalyst may have applauded at this point, as a strategic therapist I was far more interested in helping him change the pattern rather than merely generate this insight. I confronted James with the idea that he was not really afraid of her anger as much as her dramatic tantrums. As long as he gave in to her, he was continuing to "reward" her for behavior that proved to be a highly effective way of getting her way.

James insisted that he was not so much giving in to her as respecting her feelings. The truth of the matter was that he feared if he did not give in to her, she would leave him. We went around and around about this until he admitted that he would like to get his way on occasion, and he'd also like to feel less resentful about always doing things Jennie's way.

"Then you have to speak up for yourself," I told him like a coach cheering on an athlete. "You have to stick to your guns and negotiate. You know, like binding arbitration where both sides are forced to negotiate until they both come up with something you can both live with."

As expected, their quarreling increased the next few weeks. James was now taking a more assertive position, which Jennie did not greatly appreciate. This frightened James terribly, always fearful that Jennie would leave if she didn't get her way.

BRIDE AND GROOM

James asked if it might be appropriate to bring Jennie in for one session, because the quarreling was getting worse, and James was afraid Jennie would soon leave him. I readily agreed, excited at the prospect of being able to work with both of them together, even if for a single session.

When Jennie arrived, I wasn't surprised to find her warmer and more amiable than the way James described her. I invited her to share her version of the story, asking her what she thought their biggest problem was.

"He's too passive," Jennie said. "He defers too much and doesn't tell me what he wants. Sometimes I deliberately wait for him to initiate plans. And then I wait and wait until I can't wait anymore, and then I finally suggest something out of desperation."

"That's kind of surprising to hear that," I said, deciding to be blunt because of our limited time together. "James tells me you can be bossy and need to have your way all the time. He says that when you don't get what you want, you have terrible tantrums."

"I know," she said with a smile. "He tells me that too. But I'm really not that bossy. Usually, I wait until James decides to come up with an idea. When he doesn't, I get frustrated. When I can't wait any longer, I come up with something because I'm afraid if I wait for him, we'll wind up doing nothing. I react more out of exasperation than anything else. You have no idea how much money we waste on airplane fares because when he finally decides what he wants to do, the fares are twice as much as they would have been if we bought them two to three months earlier."

"What about your anger?" James challenged Jennie. I felt proud watching James speak up for himself.

Jennie turned to face James. "When I feel angry it is because of what you do when you're mad at me. Instead of telling me you're hurt or angry, you withdraw and stop talking to me. Sometimes you ignore me for days. Then I'm feeling so rejected and alone that I explode. My explosions are what you call tantrums."

We ended our meeting by negotiating an arrangement whereby James agreed to speak up for himself more, and Jennie would tell him more explicitly what she was feeling. The plan was for them to stop withdrawing from one another when they felt hurt.

Sure enough, there was an immediate shift in their relationship as James began speaking up more and Jennie began to listen. James called me a few months after the therapy ended to let me know how things were going. He was excited and wanted me to know that he and Jennie had just gotten married. James's mother predictably refused to attend the wedding. And there were two ceremonies: the public one with Jennie wearing the gown and James the tuxedo, and a private ceremony held in their apartment, where the bride wore the tux and the groom the gown.

REFLECTING ON THE CASE

After Bergman told us this story, we were curious what it was about this patient that was so memorable to him. After all, cross-dressing is not all that unusual in New York City, even the variation that included tying oneself tightly to a chair.

"I think the fact that we were musicians," Bergman says. "He was, of course, a very accomplished symphony musician, and I am a jazz pianist who never made it past weddings and bar mitzvahs. But I felt a musical connection with this guy in some way."

Bergman also points out that he loved the New York one-liners and the back-and-forth nature of their conversations. He likens the feeling to two jazz players who are trading riffs back and forth, reading where each one is going next.

"Plus," Bergman mentions, "I empathized with this guy's passivity. I too was a very passive guy who had a very controlling, aggressive mom, and for many years I didn't speak up for myself. So there was a piece of me I saw in this guy that made it fun being able to coach him to speak up more for himself. I was convinced that the lack of his voice was the main issue more than anything else."

Bergman also felt challenged by this patient because he had not, to this point, ever worked with cross-dressing in any way. "I preferred to look at his behavior in a systemic way and not to see it as an identity disorder, which I think would be very resistant to change."

What Bergman means is that rather than looking at his patient as a sexual pervert, as someone with a sexual identity disorder, he instead conceived of the problem as a function of relationships in his life with his girlfriend and his mother. A big clue that this approach might be helpful occurred when Bergman realized that the cross-dressing had begun again only after the girlfriend moved in.

The other thing that sticks with him about the case is that he can't believe that he actually prescribed incest to his patient, even though it was the most effective strategy he could conceive at the time. Bergman could not get the guy to follow his therapeutic advice, which was to call his father or aunts for help. He had to find some way to provoke the man into taking action.

"I take pride in being a responsible, thoughtful therapist," Bergman said, "but somehow the case drove me to come up with these interventions." Drawing from his book *Fishing for Barracuda,* Bergman explained that because the patient was unwilling to do what would have calmed his family system down, what needed to happen was an intervention at the same level of drama as what he presented. Given the rather unusual set of symptoms, it took an equally powerful prescription to get through to him. Luckily it worked, and the patient was able to make the appropriate choice of behavioral change.

Because James moved away from New York City, Bergman hasn't seen him for many years, but they talk to each other from time to time, and James and Jennie are still married and have a family.

CHAPTER TWENTY-THREE

David Scharff

Recovering from Recovered Memories

David Scharff, psychiatrist and psychoanalyst, is one of the leading theorists in Object Relations Therapy. This contemporary revision of psychoanalysis emphasizes the attachments and emotional bonds developed between oneself and others, especially those from one's family of origin. By making use of transference and countertransference dynamics—that is, the authentic and projected aspects of the therapeutic relationship—Scharff focuses on helping people let go of entrenched dysfunctional ways of relating to others.

David is the author, coauthor, and editor of fifteen books. Among those coauthored with his wife, Jill Savege Scharff, are Object Relations Individual Therapy; Object Relations Couples Therapy; Object Relations Family Therapy; The Primer of Object Relations Therapy; *and, most recently,* Tuning the Therapeutic Instrument: Affective Learning of Psychotherapy.

Scharff is Director of the International Institute of Object Relations Therapy, Clinical Professor of Psychiatry at Georgetown University and at the Uniformed Services University of the Health Sciences, and a teaching analyst at the Washington, D.C., Psychoanalytic Institute.

—*⁓*—

This is a case that gave Scharff the feeling that it taught him almost everything he knows; it involved the kind of family that could teach *any* therapist just about everything he or she needs to know. As is typical for someone who does mainly long-term, psychoanalytic therapy that looks at underlying issues as well as presenting symptoms, Scharff saw this family for two and a half years. As one would expect from such lengthy treatment and from an approach that prides itself on how deep it goes, there was complexity and shaded nuance in the various issues and themes that emerged.

There are several reasons why this particular case stands out to Scharff among all those he has seen in a long career. Certainly the family was disturbed, but that in itself isn't the main reason. What struck him as so memorable was how articulate they were and how totally committed they were to their therapy over a period of almost three years. The parents were highly communicative, most certainly, but so were the children wonderfully expressive—both verbally and in their play. (The use of children's play is one of the hallmarks of his use of object relations family therapy.) This was a family that had so many problems, individually and collectively, that one couldn't begin to catalogue them, yet the family was also incredibly dedicated to improving their functioning.

Scharff could never really decide if this was a difficult case or not, because although the family members' symptoms appeared intractable and their behavior challenging, they tried so hard to be cooperative. Of one thing he was certain: there were no clients who ever taught him more about how to do therapy—and about what actually makes therapy work.

FOUR MINUTES TOO LONG

Scharff was working in a teaching hospital, doing demonstration sessions for psychiatric residents and other staff. One of the couples who volunteered to be interviewed was a husband and wife, Lars and Velia.

At first impression, they appeared to be polar opposites. Velia was emotional, expressive, given to dramatic embellishments in her gestures and speech; Lars was rather quiet and withdrawn.

"So," Scharff began the interview, "why did you come today?"

"I'm not sure," Velia said, then giggled. "I guess it's because I just hate sex."

"You hate sex?" Scharff prompted.

"Yes," she answered, then looked toward her husband and said to him, "That's all there is to it, right?"

Lars nodded.

"That's your view of things as well, that the trouble is that Velia hates sex?" Scharff clarified. He wanted not only to elicit the husband's own view of the situation but also to show the physicians and medical students present how important it was to draw out both partners.

"Yeah," Lars agreed, grinning sheepishly. "That's pretty much it." Pause. "Except that I also have premature ejaculation."

"How long do you last?" Scharff asked.

"Two or three minutes," he said.

"So then," Scharff said, "Is that why Velia hates sex? After all, how good can it be if you ejaculate before she experiences any pleasure?"

"No, no," Lars insisted. "I may only last three minutes, but that's four minutes too long for her."

All three of them laughed about that, quickly establishing rapport that made an easy transition into the part of the interview in which Scharff gathered some background from each of them.

FAMILY BACKGROUND

Velia had come from a dysfunctional family where there had been a lot of verbal abuse from the parents and some unspecified sex play among the children. She was quite forthcoming about the traumatic atmosphere in which she had suffered and the difficulties she had faced growing up in a place with such inconsistent, negligent, and abusive parenting.

When it was Lars's turn, he said he couldn't remember anything from his childhood. "It all happened a long time ago," he shrugged, as if to say that it didn't matter much to him. No matter how much Scharff pressed, Lars insisted it was all a blur; he left no doubt that this was something he either could not or would not talk about.

"Tell me about your parents?" Scharff asked him, deciding to stay with something reasonably safe.

"They got on fairly well, I guess."

"No problems, then?"

"Well," Lars hesitated, deciding whether to go on or not. Then, in the most casual way, he said, "My dad once got arrested."

"How old were you when that happened?"

"In high school. I was seventeen. I remember that part because I was starting my senior year."

"And what was your father arrested for?"

"Soliciting."

Soliciting? Wait a minute. Scharff thought they were talking about his father, not his mother. Unless he was talking about some kind of fraud.

"I'm not sure what you mean," Scharff said.

"He was arrested for homosexual seduction. You know, picking up a guy in a men's room. He went to jail for a while. He was gone for a few months."

"So your father went to jail then?"

"Yeah, but that was the only thing. Other than that, my parents got along fine. We had a good happy family . . . well, they split up after he came out of jail."

Scharff asked, "And did he come out as a homosexual then?"

"Oh, yeah," Lars said in his matter-of-fact way. "He's homosexual since then. He lives with a man now."

Deciding it was time to move on—he would come back to their families later—Scharff continued the initial assessment. "Besides the sexual problem you both mentioned, is there anything else you would like help with?"

"Maybe the kids," Lars said simply.

"Tell me about your children then."

Lars and Velia had three kids, ages seven, five, and three. The middle child, Sven, was very disruptive in his kindergarten classroom. From the sound of things, it seemed to Scharff that the boy was probably hyperactive with some sort of attention deficit.

Seeing time was running short, Scharff asked them if they wanted to bring their children with them next time for a family assessment. They agreed and set up a time for their next session that would reconvene in Scharff's office rather than this public forum.

PLAY TIME

The family settled themselves into the room, with Velia and Lars sitting on the couch and the kids playing on the floor. The two oldest children were boys—Sven, the five-year-old who was the so-called problem child, and Eric, an outspoken but well-behaved seven-year-old who came equipped with all sorts of combat action figures that he played with. The youngest one, Tiffany, was an absolutely adorable three-year-old girl, dressed in a little pink party dress.

It did not take long for Scharff to confirm his initial impression that Sven probably had attention deficit hyperactivity disorder (ADHD). The boy could barely sit still for more than a few moments at a time. He would constantly interrupt his two other siblings—Tiffany, who was quietly building a structure with Legos, and Eric, who was conducting elaborate war scenarios with his action figures, hurling them at one another, pitting good against evil, the outcome by no means assured.

Scharff also learned from the parents that in addition to his attention problems, Sven also had problems controlling both his bladder and bowels: he would wet his bed and sometimes need to change his pants during the day.

While the children continued to occupy themselves with their favorite toys, the parents talked about their own troubles. "It's really our conjugal relations that are our biggest concern," Velia summarized, wording things carefully with the kids present. "Sometimes I get so mad when Lars is interested that I just come out swinging."

"What would the children see?" Scharff asked. "How would they view things?"

"They'd just see us go in the bedroom, maybe, and then they'd see us storm out fighting mad."

Tiffany and Sven were playing together in the middle of the floor. Just as Velia spoke about the anger resulting from their sexual relationship, Tiffany took a toy fire engine and started driving it in and out of the long, low building she had assembled. Scharff was stunned how much this looked just like intercourse. He glanced up at the video cameraman who was taping the session, and prayed fervently that the camera had captured this striking image. He had never seen a more dramatic symbolic representation of how the child's play mirrored the parents' narrative. And this little girl was only three and a half!

Scharff pointed to the engine that Tiffany was moving recklessly through the tunnel-like building, now knocking it down, and asked Velia, "Is that what it's like for you? Does it feel like it tears you apart?"

"Exactly!" she laughed. Lars laughed, too. The children stopped their play for a moment and then resumed with new themes. Sven began building block structures and knocking them down, scattering blocks and cars across the floor. Eric was now sitting at a table drawing a picture of an intergalactic war. He told Scharff that the bad fighters were attacking the mother ship.

"Will they destroy it?" Scharff asked.

"I don't know yet," Eric answered, still drawing.

But it was little Tiffany who reacted the most strongly. As soon as her mother had laughed at Scharff's observation, Tiffany grabbed the largest baby doll from the assortment of toys Scharff had provided, and placed it over one of the smallest ones that happened to be a father doll. It looked like the huge girl was smothering the father by lying on top of him.

Scharff glanced over at Lars to see him holding his head in his hands, as if this were happening to him, as if he were the one being smothered. So Velia and Lars could readily see the obvious connection and could talk humorously about how their children's play acted out their own issues.

It was later in that same session that Velia and Lars were talking about their most frequent fights. They were interrupted by Sven, who started making "pooping" sounds and loud noises and then ran from one side of the room to the other, beating on the chairs. There was little doubt that he was extremely agitated even though the parents were quite calm—they had been talking about their fights only in the most civil way imaginable. Again, Scharff was shocked at how clearly the kids seemed tuned into their parents' problems and began symbolically to act them out as if they had been cued to do so.

BACK FOR MORE

Scharff prescribed a trial of Ritalin, which initially appeared to help Sven, the hyperactive five-year-old, control his impulsive behavior quite a bit, but even after Sven had been referred to a child therapist colleague, the boy did not respond well to individual psychotherapy. This seemed to parallel the experience of his father, who also couldn't seem to use therapy well either. Most of the time Lars would remain passive and speechless in sessions, allowing his wife to do the talking for both of them. It didn't seem that he was trying to be difficult in any way—quite the contrary, he was trying just as hard as he could—but he just didn't seem to be able to give words to what he was thinking and feeling. He seemed to have a defect in his capacity for insight.

Velia, in contrast, the one who was most disturbed in the family, seemed to respond the best. She had a history of mental health problems that seemed to add up to having a borderline personality disorder, a way of swinging between a cooperative attitude of concern for her family and a manipulative, self-destructive way of relating to them and to others. Although she often presented herself as giggly and smiling, inside there was a lot of rage and vulnerability. Velia began treatment with another psychiatrist, who worked with her individually in intensive psychotherapy. During the course of therapy, she had to be hospitalized briefly on two occasions and stabilized on medication because of depression and severe dissociative episodes—times when she would lose touch with reality and retreat inside herself as a protective defense.

About a year later, the whole family returned again for a consultation, and at that time Scharff offered them twice-weekly sessions, one for therapy for the whole family and one with the couple for sex therapy. The couple's sexual interaction had not improved, although Velia's individual therapy had awakened a longing for sex in her. Tiffany was now almost five, still adorable, but wearing a dress that seemed way too short. There had always been something about her behavior and appearance that struck Scharff as sexualized in some way. At times she seemed almost seductive in the way she responded to her brothers, to her father, and to Scharff.

Sven looked worse than ever. Although he had responded fairly well to the medication, his rambunctious behavior was more disruptive than before, and he was still soiling and wetting. Eric, the older boy who had so much boyish energy the last time Scharff had seen him, now seemed depressed. Whereas before when Eric would enact wars or draw them on pictures, good would triumph over evil. Now Scharff noticed a darker side to the scenarios: the bad guys always won. And this was the healthiest person in the family!

Scharff thought he could understand how this situation had come to pass when he witnessed the following episode in a family session a few weeks later. Sven was calmed down for a change and playing quietly when his brother, Eric, grabbed the toy he had been playing with and put it out of reach. This enraged the boy, who started screaming and hitting the wall in frustration, chasing after his brother to get the toy back.

"Now stop that right this minute!" Velia screamed at the boys, enraged and out of control. "Now you've ruined everything," she screamed at the boys. "Can't you two behave yourselves for a minute? Why do you have to act this way? We're trying to do something good here, and you are just ruining everything! Eric, you're going to be just like your grandfather!"

Sven went back to his game, but Eric looked absolutely devastated by the verbal lashing. The outburst had been sudden and vicious, and it looked like the sort of thing that had happened many times before. All throughout the explosion, Lars sat with his head in his hands just as he had a year earlier when he felt smothered during Tiffany's play with the large baby doll that covered the father doll. In her vulnerability, Velia had seen her "good son" Eric turn into the inner image of her abusive father, and her fright had turned into a rageful scolding that subjected Eric to the same behavior from her that she had hated so much from her own father. Lars acted helpless to protect Eric (and himself), just as he must have felt helpless with his own father.

Scharff knew he was witnessing a small episode in the intergenerational transmission of abuse. He was able to point out to the family that an ordinary sibling fight had been misunderstood in the light of previous trauma, and thus he offered a measure of protection to Eric while offering understanding to Velia and a new model of fathering for Lars.

RECOVERED MEMORIES

Progress with the couple went very, very slowly. They began serious work on their sexual issues; eventually Lars learned to hold back his orgasms, and Velia learned to enjoy sex a bit more. They also continued to explore their family histories in greater detail, looking for clues to explain some of their current problems.

"I was talking to my sister this week," Velia reported during a session, "and she told me that our father used to beat us up all the time. It's funny, though: I had no memory of that whatsoever, but I feel sure it's true, and I'm beginning to remember things about it."

"That's a pretty significant recovery," Scharff observed. "Had you talked about that to Lars during the week?" As he asked this, he looked directly at Lars.

"Yes, as a matter of fact she did," Lars admitted. "And when she told me about this, I suddenly remembered something too."

"What's that?" Scharff asked gently. He didn't want to scare him away, because Lars had always found it so difficult to talk about this past.

Lars started to raise his hands to his face, about to take on that tortured, smothered look again. "I remember once I asked my dad about sex, how it worked and all."

Scharff waited, hoping Lars would continue without having to be pushed further.

"Then my dad said to me, 'Here, I'll show you.' Then he put his penis in my anus." Lars looked down, unwilling to meet either his wife's or therapist's eyes. He added, "I think it happened twice." Then he was silent.

"It looks like there's something more you want to say about that," Scharff said hopefully. Lars's answer was even more surprising.

"I think then I did it to my brother." He stopped for a moment, then said, "I *know* I did it to my brother."

That was all Lars could remember, or at least all that he would say about the matter. He realized later that his parents had not been very happy with one another after all and that his father had probably been gay his whole life. He could accept that about his father, even accept the sexual abuse, but he still wanted to have some sort of relationship with him. His father had virtually cut off contact with him and his family, however, and this was the part that seemed to hurt more than anything nowadays.

INSIGHT AND OUTSIGHT

These disclosures became a breakthrough in the work they all did together. Velia and Lars were able to address some of their long-standing issues, both personally and interpersonally. Because both of them had been abused as children, it became important to deal with what was going on with their own children—not only Sven's problems (which had been gradually improving) but also Tiffany's sexualized behavior. This was actually their worst nightmare coming true, because the last thing they wanted was for their own children to experience anything like what they had survived.

Lars seemed to see very clearly what was happening with others in his family, but could not manage to develop any insight whatsoever into his own issues. Scharff calls this having a capacity for "outsight" rather than insight—when people can't see things in themselves but can understand the same issues when they see them in other family members. It is one of the great advantages of family therapy for people like Lars and Sven.

Even with his limitations, Lars tried hard to help pull his family together and help them come to terms with their own pasts, often recognizing his children's misinterpretation of events and helping them get things right. This was part of the process that let the whole family make major gains together, so that Lars felt better as a husband and father. He and his wife managed to have satisfactory sex. Eric grew sturdier (and the good guys generally won again); Sven stopped soiling and wetting, and was more organized in play and at school; and Tiffany no longer seemed to lead with sexuality. It was only Velia who still had not been able to complete all the work she needed to do, but she would continue that with an individual therapist.

After two and a half years, the time came for the therapy to end. It was Eric, the eldest boy, who seemed to express most clearly what they were all feeling. He had drawn a picture of a fierce but funny monster. He showed it to Scharff, who asked what it was.

"It's called therapy torture," Eric said grinning. "But there's another picture of him on the other side." He turned over the paper, where he had drawn the same monster with huge eyes, and tears running down his cheeks.

"What is he feeling so sad about?" Scharff asked.

"He's sad because he can't come here anymore."

Again Scharff was struck by how wise children can be, expressing through their play what their parents had been unable to talk about. Taking Eric's lead, the whole family was then able to share their sadness at parting from an experience that had helped them all.

FOLLOW-UP

Eight years later, Velia called Scharff. She asked if they might all come in one more time just to catch up on their lives.

When they walked in, Scharff saw a family transformed. He had trouble holding back his own tears because they looked so different, not only in the ways they had grown up but also in the ways they had matured. Eric had just been accepted to his first-choice college on a scholarship. Sven was not doing great academically in high school, but he was reasonably well adjusted and seemed to be enjoying life. Tiffany was now fourteen and still adorable. She was excited that she had gotten almost all A's and disappointed about her one B in school. Most of all, Scharff was relieved that she had appeared to turn out just fine.

Scharff continued to keep in touch with the family over the years. As of now, Eric is happily married, and Tiffany is engaged. They had both done well in college and were starting careers. Sven, the middle son, was in the military and doing well with the structure that helped organize his life. Lars had done something that had been missing from his life for years, resuming his strong interest in playing music. Velia was still having some ups and downs, but she had stayed in therapy to help with her vulnerability to dissociation under stress, was enjoying her job, and was enormously proud of her family.

"This family taught me so much about how people recover from ravaged development," Scharff recalled to us. "The case shows so clearly how parents, in spite of their own histories and limitations, can work together to help their children. This is a family that, eighteen years later, still believes that one of the most important things they had ever done was to share the connected times they felt first in therapy, and learned to keep the momentum going in the years since then."

CHAPTER TWENTY FOUR

Howard Rosenthal

Panic Disorder from Sewer Grates, Amusement Parks, and Sex with Ministers

Howard Rosenthal is the author of several practical books for therapists, including Before You See Your First Client; Favorite Counseling and Therapy Techniques; 51 Therapists Share Their Most Creative Strategies; Favorite Counseling and Therapy Homework Assignments; *and* The Encyclopedia of Counseling. *Although known primarily for his handbooks that supply exercises and techniques for practitioners, Rosenthal also works integratively with stress-related disorders.*

In addition to his books for professionals, he has written such popular books as Not with My Life I Don't: Preventing Your Suicide and That of Others *and* Help Yourself to Positive Mental Health.

He currently serves as the Coordinator of the Human Services Program at St. Louis Community College and teaches graduate courses for Webster University. On the lighter side, Rosenthal serves as a mental health hair expert on a website for professional hair stylists.

—*w*—

Before talking about his most unusual patient, Rosenthal remarked that perhaps his most bizarre case of all was with himself. He thought of a time in which the same kind of phenomenon that emerged with the person he was helping was something that he had also experienced personally.

TWO WEIRD SYMPTOMS

When he was in graduate school, Rosenthal decided to venture outside the theoretical domain that was being introduced at the time and pursue a course of study in psychoanalysis. To his surprise, he loved the training that emphasized making sense of the past and uncovering unconscious desires. This approach was distinctly at odds with the more action-oriented, present-focused therapy that he had been learning to that point.

A few of Rosenthal's classmates at his home institution would occasionally ask him about the psychoanalytic training he was undergoing.

"So," one of them asked, "who's your instructor in the course? Some guy with a beard?"

"Nah," Rosenthal answered with a laugh. "No beard like Freud. Not even a cigar."

"OK, so what's your instructor's name?"

"I'm thinking," Rosenthal pleaded. "I'm thinking. Give me a minute."

"You've been going to this class for how many weeks, and you don't even know the guy's name who is teaching you?"

Rosenthal stood there frozen. Most peculiar. He liked the class very much and greatly admired his teacher. But for the life of him, he couldn't recall the name of his instructor. And furthermore, this wasn't the first time this had happened; just a few days earlier he had tried and failed to remember the training analyst's name.

Rosenthal found this particularly disturbing because ordinarily he had a very good memory for names. To this day, he can even recall the maiden name of his kindergarten teacher.

As if this were not perplexing enough, he developed another symptom that was even more bizarre. Growing up as a kid in St. Louis, the bowling capital of the United States, he aspired some day to be a professional like some of his boyhood heroes. Although his fantasy had not materialized and he had ended up a therapist instead, he had continued to bowl recreationally. Even with his school commitments and extra psychoanalytic studies, he was unwilling to sacrifice his weekly bowling nights.

THE DOOR TO THE BOWLING ALLEY

The new problem he was experiencing was that each evening that he would approach the bowling alley, he would find himself becoming increasingly agitated as he came closer the door. It was an ordinary door, just the sort one would expect to see at the entrance of such an establishment—a glass door with a single metal bar across that serves as a handle. On the bottom was a steel mesh that was designed to protect the glass against the kicks of irate bowlers.

"Every time I'd see that door," Rosenthal said, "I'd focus on that steel mesh and it would make me crazy. I'd start cussing to myself and felt uncontrollable anger toward the door, especially that part at the bottom. I hated that damn door with a passion!"

Rosenthal felt especially embarrassed by his irrational behavior because he aspired to be the sort of therapist who had it all together. Instead he felt as though he were losing his mind—forgetting his instructor's name when he prided himself on having such a perfect memory, and now this crazy rage toward a silly door.

He tried everything that he knew to address these irritating symptoms. He tried talking to himself, applying what he'd do with his clients. He analyzed himself. He did self-hypnosis. He used imagery, desensitization, thought-stopping—anything and everything he could think of, and all to no avail. On top of everything else, he felt like a miserable failure in being his own therapist. About the only idea he could come up with was that maybe he was mad at the fence on the glass door because it reminded him of crime in some way. It was a stretch of a theory but all he could come up with.

EUREKA!

The cure to his problem occurred quite by accident, although certainly his immersion in psychoanalytic training had primed him for this insight.

One day, after Rosenthal had finished bowling and was taking off his bowling shoes, his teammate came over and slapped him on the shoulder.

"Hey, Howard," the friend said, "how about let's go get a pizza."

Rosenthal froze. All of a sudden he had a flashback from his childhood, a memory long forgotten. He recalled a time when he was about ten years old, bowling in this very same alley, on another Wednesday night league. It had been his custom after finishing his games to occupy his time playing chess while he waited for others to finish. He was thus involved in a game with one of his friends when a younger kid, known as a pest, came over to bother them.

"Get outta here, kid," the friend threatened him, "or I'll kick your butt."

Instead of noticing how annoyed Rosenthal's friend was, especially considering that he was losing the game, the kid knocked over a few of the pieces and then started to run away. The friend started chasing the boy through the alley until Rosenthal heard a loud crash, an ear-splitting noise that sounded like a bomb exploding.

In an effort to escape his pursuer, the boy had run right toward the glass door, which in those days didn't yet have wire mesh along the bottom. Because he was so small, he had managed to avoid the bar handle across the middle and run right into, and then through, the plate glass. He was covered in shattered glass and blood, surely dead from the impact.

"My God," Rosenthal thought, "he killed that poor kid. And I could have done something to stop it." It was just at that moment that his friend returned, put his arm on his shoulder (exactly like his teammate had done now) and said the same thing: "The hell with him. You want to go and get a pizza?"

So it seemed that this long-forgotten repressed memory had been reawakened by these cues that so resembled the original incident. Now Rosenthal knew why he hated that door so much. But what about the connection to his psychoanalytic instructor and why he kept forgetting his name?

Coincidence of coincidences, it turned out that the poor kid had the exact same name as the teacher!

Once he realized the origins of his symptoms, sure enough Rosenthal could remember his instructor's name and stopped hating the sight of the door. He also learned that day how powerfully the past can affect present behavior. This is a lesson that every therapist is taught in school, of course, but it is one thing to experience its power so vividly when a mystery is solved.

One more thing: it turned out that the kid recovered after all, although he had more than a few bruises, cuts, and scrapes to show for his attempted escape.

PANIC ATTACKS

In a case that paralleled that of his own strange recovered memories, Rosenthal was working with a graphic artist who had debilitating anxiety that interfered with her work and even the daily functioning of her life. This was first brought to the woman's attention when she found herself breathless and dizzy any time she would inadvertently walk across a sewer grate embedded in the sidewalk. Even with her most vigilant efforts, there were times when she was daydreaming or otherwise occupied and would step onto the grates that were positioned at most street corners. On such occasions she would become virtually incapacitated. She would find it hard to catch her breath. Her heart would begin pounding in her chest, beating so hard she feared that it might explode. She could feel herself become instantly sweaty. Her hands would shake. If things got really bad, she might even collapse into a heap on the ground.

"Any other times that you experience something like this?" Rosenthal asked her. He was searching for some explanation to account for her extreme reaction. Why did sewer grates elicit this response?

It turned out that indeed she had had a similar experience not long before. She had been at a local amusement park, walking around enjoying the day, when out of the blue, she had her worst episode ever. She became paralyzed with anxiety, absolutely frozen to the point that she couldn't move, couldn't speak, and then couldn't even breathe. She thought she was dying. The park authorities had to call an ambulance to revive her.

After any possible physical causes had been ruled out, it turned out that she did indeed have some sort of panic disorder that was triggered by these two disparate stimuli. There was something about walking on grates and strolling in amusement parks that triggered the uncontrollable attacks.

It would be reasonable to assume, just as in Rosenthal's own case of self-analysis, that some past trauma was causing this severe anxiety. The hard part involved trying to figure out the pattern.

THE MISSING PIECE

Just as with his own problem, Rosenthal tried a variety of methods to help the woman deal with her symptoms. He tried hypnosis to provide skills for dealing with the stressful situations she feared most. He used biofeedback to help her gain greater control over her bodily sensations. He introduced systematic desensitization to accustom her gradually to the stimuli that were most likely to spark an attack. He put her in an assertiveness training group hoping to boost her self-confidence. Even medications specifically suited for anxiety and panic disorder proved useless.

In the course of these treatments, it came out that there was one other situation that also provoked a severe attack. She was involved in a relationship with a man, a minister, that had been going on for some time. Although they otherwise enjoyed a good relationship, it seemed that every time they attempted to have sex, she would become breathless and pass out. It was clear that this was not exactly an expression of passion but of terror. Further, Rosenthal learned that she had been involved in relationships with other ministers as well, some of them married and some not—but all of them with unconsummated sex because of her panic response to the prospect of penetration.

Slowly, gradually, incrementally, sensitively, Rosenthal encouraged the woman to talk about her childhood. Something was buried there; something traumatic had occurred when she was small. But no matter how much and how often he probed, she could recall nothing significant that could explain this phenomenon.

Soon after this, the woman attended a professional conference. During the course of one presentation, the speaker told an off-color joke. Although normally this would not have bothered her in the least, this time it sent her into a rage, not unlike Rosenthal's own response to the glass door. She censured the speaker publicly and then scolded anyone else who came to the person's defense. Her response was particularly surprising to her because she not only enjoyed hearing a good dirty joke but also liked telling a few herself.

Frustrated and angry, she finally stormed out and retreated to her room. It was while trying unsuccessfully to sleep that she was visited by long-forgotten memories of when she was five years old. Her father was a minister, a respected member of the community, and a teacher. He was also molesting her.

Other pieces of the puzzle now began to fall into place. Certainly her aversion to sex with ministers and her attraction to them as embodiments of her father made for an easy interpretation. But what about the rest?

During the time when her father first began to touch her sexually, there was a train that had been passing by. The clickety-clack of the distant train going over the tracks sounded to her exactly like the sound of her own footsteps as they passed over a sewer grate. Each time she heard that sound, she could feel the terror just as she had when she was being molested.

But Rosenthal still wondered how the heck amusement parks fitted into this story.

The sexual abuse had taken place many decades ago, during a time when horses and buggies were still in evidence. She had actually been molested in a buggy that looked exactly like the ones displayed at the amusement park. Terrified and tearful, yet wanting to please her father, she had endured his sexual abuse while listening to the train in the distance and the buggy squeaking on its rusty springs. Whenever she heard that familiar but long-forgotten noise or saw the kind of place where she had been abused, she felt herself dying again.

THE CONFRONTATION

Upon retrieving the repressed memories, the woman decided to confront her parents, who were still alive and in their nineties.

"Mom," she said over the phone one day, "you aren't going to believe this. I've been seeing this therapist, you know, about my symptoms. For years I haven't been able to figure out why I get so weird every time . . . well, you know."

Her mother was unnaturally quiet, so the woman continued.

"Well Ma, I think I figured out what was going on."

"It's your father, isn't it?"

"My what?"

"It's your father. That's what you wanted to talk about isn't it?"

The woman was stunned. Apparently, her mother had known all along about the molestation but had kept silent all these years. This is not altogether an unusual configuration in sex abuse—the nonabusing parent knowing about what is taking place but ignoring it.

The woman attempted to confront her father as well, but he denied everything. He made jokes about her accusation, and when that didn't work said she was making it all up. He never did admit to what he had done, and that was disappointing, but the woman was still proud of herself that she had done everything she could to address the situation.

Just as in Rosenthal's own case, insight proved the cure. This is not always the case in therapy, and some of the other theorists included in this book might very well take strong issue with the idea that insight is enough to produce lasting changes. But in both these cases, uncovering the source of unconscious and repressed memories allowed both the therapist and his client to put the past behind them.

CHAPTER TWENTY-FIVE

Jay Haley

The Eighty-Two-Year-Old Prostitute

Jay Haley is, quite simply, one of the most influential theorists of the past century. His early research on schizophrenia was groundbreaking in its focus on how dysfunctional communication patterns within families actually helped drive some people crazy. He later went on to establish a school of strategic therapy that was based on research he conducted as well as on consultations with some of the most innovative thinkers of his time.

Haley's brand of family therapy was based on the principle that people get stuck when they persist in doing things that are not working. His strategy was to (1) help clients identify the kinds of problems that could be more easily solved, (2) reframe those difficulties so that they were more amenable to change, (3) design interventions that would disrupt the dysfunctional communication patterns, and (4) make changes in the plan according to the responses generated. As a practitioner, Haley was provocative, powerful, and creative, beyond anything that had been seen previously.

Haley's many publications span four decades and cover a number of significant areas. As the intellectual biographer for his mentor, Milton Erickson, Haley introduced the world to his brief therapy methods in such books as Uncommon Therapy *and* Conversations with Milton Erick-son. *He then described his own unique brand of therapy in* Problem-Solving Therapy, Ordeal Therapy, *and* Techniques of Family Therapy. *Many of his former clients might very well say about Haley that his be-havior was occasionally more strange than their own presenting problems.*

At the time we spoke to Haley, he was seventy-eight years old, semi-retired, and concentrating his efforts on making training videos for ther-apists. This conversation proved to be far more than a discussion of one case but rather a retrospective on his professional life.

—w—

Haley remembers a time when he was supervising a student who was working with a couple. He was, in fact, one of the pioneers who de-veloped the method of watching therapy from behind a one-way mir-ror and then intervening as necessary to direct the course of the treatment.

This was a couple in which both partners seemed to be extremely unhappy.

"So, what's so unusual about that?" we asked Haley. After all, that's why people come to marital therapy in the first place.

"They were quarreling a lot, everywhere they went," he explained. "They quarreled at home. They quarreled when they were with me. But most of all, they quarreled in front of the wife's mother." Haley paused for a moment, then added, "So I had them bring their mother next time."

Haley is famous for these sorts of direct interventions in which he likes to work on communication in families, especially adjusting the way power is distributed. As we already mentioned, he is also well-known for creating "ordeals," therapeutic tasks that are so annoying to people that they cure themselves just to avoid having to come back for further instructions.

When Haley asked the couple to bring in the eighty-two-year-old mother for the next session, both seemed reluctant, and Haley won-dered why. It turned out that this eighty-two-year-old woman was a prostitute and still earned a living servicing older gentlemen, and also a few younger ones who got a special kick out of having sex with a sur-rogate grandmother.

"That does seems unusual," we admitted.

"She was very tearful about it," Haley recalled. "She didn't like being called a prostitute but rather wanted to be called a call girl, which she considered a more honorable name for her work. She'd developed quite a clientele over the years and was reluctant to let go of her referral base."

"So, what did you do with this family?" we asked him.

"Well, we saw them for just two sessions. We tried to integrate the mother into the family, to have her play a bigger role since they both seemed to respect her a lot. That seemed to work pretty well."

Haley had managed to help the couple realign themselves in such a way that fighting was no longer a profitable way for them to communicate with one another. The mother served the role as a kind of mediator for them, a bridge of sorts.

"The only problem," Haley continued, "is that the grandkids didn't like to visit her when she had a few men sitting in the living room, waiting for their turn. So apparently, business was pretty good for her."

Eventually, they did work out a time and place where they could present their problems to the mother for mediation, and they phoned to tell Haley that their fighting had gradually decreased. They had worked out an arrangement whereby the mother would not entertain her gentlemen visitors whenever the kids were around, and this made everyone happy.

EIGHTEEN YEARS OF ANALYSIS

We invited him to recall other unusual cases from his half-century as a therapist and supervisor.

"When I first went into practice," Haley told us, "one of the first cases I handled was a lady who had been in analysis for eighteen years. What had happened was that she had gotten upset with her husband and went into analysis, and she was still there eighteen years later."

"And she was also still with her husband?" we asked him.

"Yes, but when she came to see me she was ready to leave him."

"Which one, her analyst or her husband?"

"Both. It was a package deal. But ultimately she couldn't do anything about it."

What amazed Haley about this case was not only that eighteen years of analysis had not helped her much but also that it had not seemed to do much harm either.

"The two relationships were linked," Haley explained. "She couldn't deal with one without the other."

"So, what happened?"

"She wouldn't come back to see me."

"How come?"

"Because I told her to leave her analyst."

Haley just couldn't believe the kinds of things that are done under the guise of therapy. "It was like it was a three-person marriage. In fact, the husband wasn't nearly as important to her as her analyst."

THE COUPLE WHO LIKED TO YELL

The cases that stand out most to Haley were the ones he found most challenging or the most difficult or that at least tested him in new ways. He remembers one couple, in particular, who argued a lot with one another, and there was nothing that Haley could do to get them to stop. This says a lot considering that he was the fellow who developed paradoxical strategies in which clients were sometimes ordered to do what they were already doing anyway—for example, to wake up at three in the morning and argue for an hour before going back to bed.

"They'd come to see me," Haley said, "and then as soon as they sat down they started to yell at one another. Then I would spend the hour quieting them down until it was time for them to leave. The next week it would start all over again. I tried everything with them—prescribing their symptoms; asking them to yell louder, then softer; trying to separate them. I had them face away from one another. I tried yelling at them myself. I told them they were amateurs and that if they really wanted to be good yellers, they had to practice more. Nothing worked. They just liked to yell. I've never seen anything like it."

"With all your inventiveness, there was nothing you could do for them?"

"I tried stopping the session early one time, and this really made them angry. They felt cheated because they wanted more time to yell. My office was a place where they felt safe enough to scream at one another. My problem was I had to decide whether this was OK with me or not."

"What did you decide?"

"Nothing. I just ran out of other ideas. I was exasperated."

Haley remembers this unusual case precisely because he felt so defeated. With all his resources and experience, he still couldn't get them to stop doing what they were doing.

Such inconclusive results were rare in Haley's experience, because he never subscribed to the usual assumptions about what is normal and what is crazy; he was not inclined to look at people as being strange in any way, but rather what was functional about their behavior.

CRAZY OR UNEMPLOYED?

At the very beginning of his career, Haley was working with Gregory Bateson and others on the social basis of schizophrenia. They viewed this condition not as a biological disease but as a social phenomenon that was influenced most by family communication patterns.

"I remember when this psychiatrist approached me once," Haley told us. "He came up to me one day on the grounds of the Veterans Administration Hospital."

"I understand you are studying communication," the doctor said to him. "Well, I've got a patient who really communicates in a strange way."

Haley volunteered to see the man and said he was willing to see what could be done.

"We sat down to talk and I learned that he had a whole interesting and difficult history. Our therapy sessions together lasted about five years. This was not unusual in these days, especially with someone who had such intractable, chronic problems."

Haley again experimented with everything he knew how to do at the time, but with little lasting effect. The man insisted he was from Mars. He used a dozen different aliases, all in the Martian language. Haley felt the two of them were getting nowhere.

Then, one day, he was in the man's room talking to him, trying to make sense of what he was saying in response. Haley heard another therapist in the room next door interviewing that patient. So he knocked on the adjoining door and suggested that since neither one of them could make much sense of what their patients were saying, maybe they should let them do therapy with each other. They tried that, and it seemed to work just fine. Both of them jabbered away to one another, each in his own language, apparently understanding perfectly what the other was saying. To Haley and the other therapist, it sounded like a pretty bizarre conversation, but to the two patients it was as if they were long-lost friends catching up on their lives, which is exactly what they were. Both these apparently noncommunicative, intractable patients were quite able to have a conversation that was happy and meaningful to them both, which taught Haley something crucial about human behavior and alleged pathology.

"This man was a loner in the world. I had been doing whatever you do when you are interpreting to people this and that. I put this poor fellow through all of this, and he went along with it because he was bored to death sitting on the ward. When I started therapy with him we got interested in his family background and how he ended up in the hospital. What had happened was that he was found out in the valley as a young man and seemed to be drunk. They arrested him, and the next morning, he didn't sober up. He just talked in a strange language. When they asked him where he lived, he said he was from Mars."

This was the one case that taught Haley to be more pragmatic in his approach. It was after this that he abandoned conventional therapy as it was practiced at the time—interpreting dreams, analyzing the transference, and so on. Instead, Haley began looking at problems as metaphors.

"This guy would use metaphors in interesting ways," Haley remembered. "He didn't speak regularly, so I got experimental with him. I took him home for dinner. I took him out to the local stores. He had been locked up for so long in a state hospital that he had forgotten how to behave in the outside world, so I decided I would help teach him this. The poor guy was getting shock therapy every week, so he was disoriented.

"Even after all the time we spent together, we never got his real name or where he was from. Then finally I was able to track down that he was from somewhere in the Northwest. I eventually figured out the town he was from and contacted his parents. The man's father sent him a note, after which the guy took off for home. He got to the town where his father was, got in a car, and sat in the car for a while until he was arrested. His father came to get him out of jail and said that his mother had died that very morning. So the sad thing was that he didn't get to see his mother after all those years."

Haley continued to follow this man's case, especially when he landed back in the VA hospital. As much as he hated being institutionalized, he enjoyed spending time with his therapist, the one solid relationship in his life. Eventually, the man was able to hold a job on the outside, even though he was still diagnosed as a chronic schizophrenic. Haley believed he was cured, as maybe that is what a cure is, when someone can find meaningful work and live on his own. The mental health establishment saw this guy as crazy; Haley simply viewed him as unemployed.

All the cases that Jay Haley told us about—the eighty-two-year-old prostitute, the yelling couple, the man from Mars—taught him important lessons about the variety of human behavior and the accommodations necessary to make a difference in people's lives. From these experiences, he was able to develop strategic interventions such as reframing, in which he learned to redefine presenting problems such that they were more easily solved. After all, what can you do for someone who claims to be from Mars? In Haley's work, he stopped seeing people as crazy or disturbed or anything else other than trying to communicate metaphorically in unique ways. In a book about unusual cases, Haley is perhaps best known as one of the most unusual therapists.

CHAPTER TWENTY-SIX

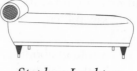

Stephen Lankton

Saved by a Ghost

Stephen Lankton is a social worker who has trained extensively in several broad areas. As an undergraduate, he studied engineering and chemistry but eventually settled in the social sciences, including psychology and linguistics. His training as a therapist was similarly varied—first in Gestalt therapy and psychodrama, later in transactional analysis, body therapies, neurolinguistic programming, and Ericksonian hypnosis. His writing in the field has reflected this eclectic background, combining features of several approaches into a deeper understanding of hypnosis and transformative change. Some of his best-known books include Practical Magic; The Answer Within; Enchantment and Intervention in Family Therapy; *and* Tales of Enchantment.

Steve lives in Phoenix, Arizona, where he works as an organizational consultant, trainer, and therapist.

"One case?" Lankton said to us as his opening remark. "I only get to pick one? There are so many interesting people I've seen. How am I going to choose just one?"

"Which ones are you considering?" we wondered.

The first one that came to mind was that of a woman who was referred by a physician because nobody else could do anything for her. Many of Lankton's referrals originated from physicians and other therapists who were stumped by the unusual features of a case and had all but given up. It was often Steve's job to try alternative, creative strategies that might not occur to more conventional practitioners.

THE WOMAN WITH A PAINFUL PULSE

"So, what's the problem?" Lankton asked the woman as soon as she settled herself.

"I've got this powerful pulsating pain in my wrist, in my left wrist, and I can hardly stand it. Nobody can fix it."

"You've consulted physicians about this problem?" Lankton wondered, trying to figure out why this woman had been referred to him in the first place.

"Yeah, sure, I've seen lots of doctors, but none of them can do a thing for me. But the pulsating hurts so bad I can hardly stand it."

"The pulsating?"

"Yes, it's like a pulsation of pain all on my left side."

"Well, it sounds dreadful, but I'm not sure I understand what you mean by pulsating."

"Let me tell you something," she said in a conspiratorial whisper, "that I haven't told any of the other doctors. I know you won't think I'm crazy because of the way you are acting toward me."

"What do you mean?" Lankton asked, now quite curious.

She hesitated for a moment. "You know, like hearing strange stories."

"And you've got one of those?"

She nodded her head gravely. "You see, I died in the operating room. I didn't tell the other pain doctors because I knew they would think I was loony."

"You died? Well, tell me all about it!"

"Uh huh. I was clinically dead. My heart stopped and everything. I was aware of the doctors around me trying to get a pulse because the machines were making that high sound that says that the person is not breathing and has no heartbeat. I could feel myself floating upwards, so I could look down at all the doctors in the operating room, and I could see them scrambling around trying to get a pulse."

"What were you feeling," Lankton asked her, "as you were looking down at yourself?"

"Kind of calm and serene. Peaceful."

"Makes sense. What else were you feeling?"

"Just that I sure hoped they could find a pulse."

"So then what happened?"

She shrugged. "Next thing I knew I woke up in the recovery room alive. But I've had this pain in my pulse ever since. Only on the left side."

Steve thought for a moment and announced to her that he thought he could fix the problem. After putting her in a trance state, he returned her to the operating room. Once she was floating out of her body above the doctors, wondering once again whether they would bring her back to life or not, Lankton told her to turn down the sensitivity of her pulse as it was turned back on. He figured that she had returned from the dead with an oversensitive physiology on one side, so he just asked her to adjust the volume control, so to speak.

"And that was the end of her pain," Lankton concluded simply. "So, should I talk about this case, or one of the others?"

"What else do you have?" we wondered.

SHE WANTED TO KEEP THE PHONE IN THE REFRIGERATOR

Lankton saw another woman who was extremely depressed and suicidal. She was a recluse as well, isolated from the rest of the world. When she first showed up, she was virtually mute. Her hair hung in front of her face as if she were hiding behind it. During those rare times when she would speak, her responses were all too brief. When she did respond verbally in some way, her remarks were sometimes puzzling and always spoken quietly. Several weeks of therapy ensued. Violet, the client, had made a number of notable changes in that time. Slowly and gradually, she and Lankton began to make some progress in the sessions. However, one day, while complaining about noisy telephone interruptions, Violet mumbled something about quieting them down by putting them in the refrigerator. Violet had been talking about how much she hated the telephone ringing; she wished everyone would just leave her alone.

"That's strange," Lankton said.

"What? Putting my phone in the refrigerator?"

"No," he answered. "I wasn't really thinking of that. I was just remembering that this is the second time you've said something uncommon about refrigerators in the last couple of weeks. What's with that?"

The woman shrugged, but something was triggered by the image of refrigerators. She couldn't quite get a hold of the memory that was just out of reach, so she decided to ask some members of her family about that. Maybe they knew what triggered the association.

When she asked her mother if there was anything in the past about refrigerators in the family that she should know, her mother just broke down in tears and walked out of the room. Now *that* was strange, she thought. Next she tried calling her sister.

"Don't you remember?" her sister said. "You almost died in a refrigerator when you were two years old. When we finally found you, you were practically frozen into a little ball. You didn't even talk after that for the longest time."

When the woman returned to session that evening, she related what she had learned about being trapped in a refrigerator. Lankton helped her go back in time to that day when she was two. It was her sister's birthday. She felt ignored and neglected, so she went to the neighbor's garage and played in the boxes. She climbed up into this smooth, cool box and played inside. The door snapped shut, and everything was dark inside. She spontaneously recreated the same position she had been in by positioning herself on the floor with her knees drawn up to her chest and her arms around her ankles. Just like that first day, her hair fell in front of her face. She became totally still and mute. This time, however, Lankton encouraged her to make noises and cry out instead of waiting helplessly for rescue.

Violet screamed and flew off the chair as though she were being ejected from a spring-loaded seat. She flopped around like a wet dishrag making strange sounds. But at least she was making noise instead of surrendering to her fate. She was now angry, and she was scared. And—she was speaking out! She was also transformed, never again so helpless, depressed, and mute.

"So, what about *that* one?" Lankton asked us. "Do you want more detail on this case?"

"Definitely intriguing," we admitted. "What else do you have?"

THE DRESSER

Lankton received regular referrals from local psychiatrists and physicians for pain control. He quite enjoyed his work with these clients because they were highly motivated and had been well prepared by their doctors for what to expect.

Peter was in his early thirties, casually and neatly dressed. He looked like someone employed in some sort of trade, perhaps a mechanic or plumber. He was a no-nonsense kind of guy who was a little skeptical about the value of hypnosis. Eleven years previously, he had been in a car accident and had been in unremitting pain ever since. Like so many people in this situation, he was desperate because nothing else had worked for him. Yet he was still uncomfortable with the idea that his chronic pain could really be controlled by his mind. This was a guy who was used to solving problems by replacing broken parts. Nevertheless, he agreed to give hypnosis a shot.

"Nothing to lose," he said, "right, Doc?"

Lankton prefers to use a form of self-hypnosis that makes it possible for the person to get back into trance later in order to practice pain control methods. When someone like Peter is not particularly educated about hypnosis, Steve's strategy is to help the person select some object or image from childhood that can act as a simple meditative device that he can return to later. Typically people come up with something like sitting in a rowboat during a fishing trip.

"Peter," Lankton began the trance, "I'd like you to close your eyes and think as carefully as possible about some time prior to this car accident, before you were in pain, where you were in a situation that was so intense in your mind that you can remember it vividly. This could be some sort of object that reminds you of feeling comfortable in that situation."

"Yeah," Peter said without a moment's hesitation. "Got one."

The instantaneous response surprised Lankton because usually it takes a minute or two to come up with an appropriate image.

"OK then," Lankton continued in a soothing voice. "I want you to concentrate on that object or image as a positive experience."

Peter said it was a positive object. The induction continued with Lankton's asking him to become more and more absorbed in the image. "Move your eyes around it," Lankton instructed him. "Follow the lines of that experience as you examine the object carefully. Look carefully at its height . . . and width . . . and depth . . . and the colors you see. Notice the feeling in your body that you had not realized at the time . . . the relaxation and the pleasure you feel. Let your mind recall the things that you were thinking at the time, and any of the sounds that you heard."

This beginning induction continued to become the pain control session and went on for about twenty minutes, with Lankton taking Peter through the process of enriching the memory so that later he could use it to bring back the trance state. Next, Lankton offered suggestions that would help Peter replace the pain sensitivity with the means to dissociate himself from those unpleasant feelings.

Upon Peter's awakening, Lankton assessed the impact of the procedure. It was important at this juncture to find out the extent to which the hypnosis had worked before proceeding further with deepening techniques.

Peter opened his eyes and looked around. "That's funny," he said, with a puzzled look on his face.

"What's that?"

"Weird. I don't have any pain anymore. It's totally gone! Wow, it worked. I'm kind of surprised."

"Me too," Lankton admitted. "Usually people don't respond so quickly. You must have had something that you were concentrating on that was extremely absorbing for you and pretty memorable."

"Yeah, I did."

Lankton was intrigued with what that might be, but because Peter didn't volunteer anything more, he wondered if he should let it go. Partly he wanted to find out if the image selected was appropriate for their purposes (although it was hard to argue with success), but he was also really curious about what had worked so well. "So Peter, can you tell me about what you thought about?"

"A dresser."

"A dresser? You mean like a clothing dresser for socks and sweaters?"

"Yeah. It was the one in my room when I was a kid."

Lankton had heard a lot of choices over the years, but this one was certainly the most unusual. He asked Peter about it. "Was there something really special about this dresser? It must have been very beautiful."

"No, it was pretty ordinary. Just wood. With drawers. That's it."

Deciding to be more direct with this man who was so concrete, Lankton pressed Peter about why he settled on this ordinary dresser for his comforting image.

"Well," he said hesitantly, clearly reluctant to talk about it. "It was part of something that happened when I was a kid. The whole thing was kind of odd."

THE INTRUDER

Steve couldn't help himself when he asked Peter for more detail.

"I was eight years old and in my bedroom. My father and mother slept across the hallway. We had this old house that was somewhat in disrepair."

"There were really thick—like five or six inches thick—plaster walls and ceilings. My room was sealed off from the hallway by a heavy door. I had closed the door, gotten into my pajamas, and crawled into bed." Peter stopped at this point, deciding whether or not to go on.

"Is that it?" Lankton asked, not wanting to intrude but still curious about what was going on.

Peter shook his head. "So I was in bed, and I had just closed my eyes, when I heard something."

"You heard something?"

"Yeah. I don't know if I had drifted off to sleep or not, but when I opened my eyes there was a guy standing at the end of my bed. I've never been more scared of anything in my life."

"That must have been terrifying."

"Believe me, it was."

"So then what happened?" It sure wasn't easy to get the story out.

"I screamed. I just let out a yell 'cause I was so surprised. The weird thing was that the guy was just standing there looking at me, not saying a thing. So I screamed louder and louder."

THE ENGINEER

Peter's father burst into the room wondering what the hell was going on.

"Dad, Dad," Peter sobbed. "There was a man in my room. Honest. He was standing right there." Peter pointed toward the end of the bed.

"What do you mean there was a guy in your room?" Peter's father started looking around trying to see if anyone might be there. He noticed that the window was closed tightly and the closet door was closed.

"Dad, honest, there was a man here. He was right there."

"What'd he look like?" he asked, not knowing what else to say.

"He was like a railroad man. He had overalls on like one of those guys who runs a train. He had a beard and a striped hat. And he had something—like grease or soot or something all over him."

"You mean like a railroad engineer?"

"Yeah, yeah," Peter said excitedly. "And he was carrying a lantern of some kind."

"Look honey," Peter's father soothed him, "it was probably just a bad dream. Just go back to bed—"

"No Dad, listen to me! I'm telling you there was guy really here." Peter became more agitated when he realized his father didn't believe him.

"OK, OK, Son. Let's look under the bed and the closet and then you can get back to sleep."

"Dad please!" Peter insisted. "You gotta believe me! I'm telling you that he was a railroad man with a beard and a hat and some old blue, greasy overalls. And he was wearing a funny shirt, like a plaid shirt, and . . ."

There was something about this description that froze Peter's father in his tracks as he had headed out of the room. There was something familiar about this mysterious man. But he shrugged and invited Peter to come and sleep in his parents' room.

So Peter crawled in bed between his two parents. Just as they got settled, they all heard a roaring crash like an explosion that rocked the whole house. They carefully went to investigate and discovered that Peter's room, where he had been just a minute earlier, had been totally destroyed by the old plaster ceiling that had caved in. All the heavy chunks of plaster, like huge boulders, had crushed everything in the room. The bed where Peter had been sleeping was totally destroyed. The aquarium was shattered into thousands of pieces, the fish flopping around on the floor. The chair, the nightstands, the toys—everything had been crushed. The only thing remaining in the room was the dresser. Somehow, miraculously, it not only had survived but also didn't have single scratch on it. The whole room was in ruins, yet there stood the dresser as if on a protected island.

FAMILY PHOTO

"Is there more to the story?" Lankton prompted Peter eagerly. He could certainly see how Peter could have become attached to the dresser as an object of safety. But again, Peter seemed reluctant to continue.

"Yeah," Peter admitted. "There's more."

"Would you like to go on?"

"Somehow we all went back to sleep," Peter continued. "The next morning when I woke up I could hear my dad rattling around upstairs in the attic. I figured he was inspecting the damage or something. But as soon as he heard me moving around, he called down to me."

"Peter," he called out, "come on up here, will ya?"

Peter climbed the attic stairs to find his father kneeling over an old trunk, rummaging inside it. He pulled out an old leather case of some sort that had pictures inside.

"Whatcha got there, Dad?"

"Come here, Son. I want to show you something."

Peter's father opened the leather case, which turned out to be a photo album. Among the old family photos, there was an eight-by-ten sepia-toned picture of a group of men. They were all railroad men, dressed in overalls and caps.

Peter's attention was instantly drawn to the man in the front row, third from the left. "That's him!" Peter cried out. "That's the guy who was in my room last night!"

Peter's father put his face in his hand to muffle a sob. Peter was frightened, almost as much as the night before, because he'd never seen his father crying before. Clearly something was terribly upsetting to him.

"Dad, what's wrong?" Peter asked, on the edge of panic.

"The man you pointed out," he said, wiping his wet cheeks with his arm. "This is my father. Your grandfather. He died when I was eight years old, exactly your age."

GHOST STORY

As he heard this part of the story, Lankton felt a creepy chill crawl up his spine. "Gee, Peter, this is like a ghost story. Your grandfather was separated from your father by an untimely death when your father had been your age. It's like his spirit won't rest unless he has somehow done his duty to set things right in the world. He returns to rescue you from certain death at the exact same age that your father was. This is spooky stuff, Peter."

Peter looked at Lankton for a second with a serious, deadpan expression and said, "I don't believe in ghost stories!"

"You don't believe in ghost stories?"

Peter shook his head.

"Well hell," Lankton agreed, "I don't believe in them either. But then I never lived through what you did."

Lankton didn't feel it was his role to talk Peter out of his beliefs, but he was still flabbergasted that he would say what he did. He *lived* a ghost story but said he didn't believe in such things! It was amazing that this experience had not shaken the whole foundation of his belief system. To this day, this story still gives Lankton the shivers.

Peter did leave the treatment a satisfied customer. He reported that all his pain was gone, and he never returned again. Lankton was never able to learn what happened to him.

SHRINKING VIOLET

Speaking of the end of the story, we wondered whatever happened to the woman trapped in the refrigerator.

This woman, Violet, had faced a lot of adversity in her life long after the early trauma. Always shy and timid, she had trouble remaining employed. She had a baby who had been born with deformities. Her husband abandoned them soon thereafter. And all throughout these difficult times, she remained silent, just as she had been when trapped inside the refrigerator.

After Violet's cathartic experience on the floor, reliving the refrigerator episode, she began dating again. She became much more verbal and assertive, even expressive of feelings she had been holding on to for her whole life. She made great strides in every aspect of her life, so much so that the time came to end the sessions.

Violet was extremely reluctant to end therapy; it felt like her lifeline. "How can I possibly survive without you?" she wondered.

"Oh, Violet, how could you possibly fail? In fact, next week, our last session together, I want you to come back prepared to talk about how you could fail to follow through on what you've begun."

When she returned for the final session, Lankton put her in a trance and asked her to imagine that it was now three years in the future. Once her eyes were closed and she was fully focused on this fantasy, Lankton changed out of the jacket and tie he was wearing and pulled on an extra sweater he kept in the office. Now when she was instructed to open her eyes, she saw her therapist dressed differently than before, just as one would expect after three years have passed by.

Violet recounted all the wonderful successes she had experienced in the preceding three years. She appeared happy, and her whole demeanor was completely different from when she had first showed up, and even significantly transformed from a few minutes earlier when she had been in the present. Her vision of the future contained nothing but hope.

"Now I want you to close your eyes again, Violet," Lankton told her, "and I want you to return to the present. Let me know when you are there again." While she was reorienting herself from her journey to the future, Lankton again changed outfits, putting his tie and jacket back on so that he would look the way he had appeared when she first walked in.

The one thing that Violet had not managed to work on to her satisfaction was her ability to find stable employment. While she was in the trance state, Lankton had told her that this too would happen "at the proper time."

A few years later, Steve made plans to leave his job at the social service agency. Before his last day, he received a call from Violet, who had heard that he would be moving on.

"Hi, this is Violet," she said on the phone.

"Hi there!" Lankton replied, recognizing her voice immediately. "What's going on? How are you doing?"

"I need to see you," she said. "I heard you were leaving."

"What's this about?" he asked her.

"It's the proper time," she said, "to see you."

What she wanted to tell him was that, indeed, the hypnotic suggestion that Lankton had planted so long ago—that she would find meaningful employment when she was ready to do so—finally came to pass as the last part of Violet's transformation. As was true for the woman with a painful pulse and the man who didn't believe in ghost stories, hypnotic trances allowed Violet to resolve long-standing difficulties that had previously been resistant to change.

CHAPTER TWENTY-SEVEN

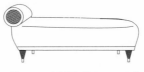

James F. T. Bugental

He'll Always Be Black

James Bugental is one of the most influential psychotherapy theorists. Passionate and articulate, Bugental continued the work of Carl Rogers, Rollo May, and Abraham Maslow, with whom he worked, advancing humanistic psychology beyond its roots to encompass a more global, flexible, culturally responsive approach. His book Challenges of Humanistic Psychology *has been the classic book in the field for over forty years.*

Recently, he has again collected the most important scholars and clinicians into a single volume, Handbook of Humanistic Psychology: Leading Edges in Theory, Research, and Practice. *Among his other important works are* Intimate Journeys: Stories of Life-Changing Psychotherapy; Psychotherapy and Process; The Search for Existential Identity; The Search for Authenticity; The Art of the Psychotherapist; *and, more recently,* Psychotherapy Isn't What You Think: Bringing the Psychotherapeutic Engagement into the Living Moment. *Bugental's trademark in all his books is his own authentic voice that invites clients, students, and readers alike to explore more deeply their innermost subjective experience.*

Bugental is Emeritus Professor at Saybrook Institute and Stanford Medical School.

—⁓—

This chapter is constructed differently from the rest. Jim Bugental, now eighty-seven, admits that he doesn't remember many of his cases. "Too many years have gone by since I last practiced," he told us. "It was a place where I once lived, and I really liked that place, but there is no possibility of going back to it now."

Jim was such a good sport, however, so willing to accommodate us as best he could, that he did agree to look back on his distinguished career. What we discovered, however, was that he had less to say about any individual client he saw, memorable or not, and wanted to speak instead about the meaning of his life's work.

Nevertheless, the case that Bugental does recall best was that of a woman in her late fifties. She was divorced, with no children, and worked as an administrative assistant for the dean of a college. She was despondent. She tended to alternate between flamboyant displays of her various complaints and genuine, incapacitating depression.

What struck Bugental most about the way the woman presented herself was that she was trying to get the most from therapy without becoming too involved. This is a familiar pattern, but nevertheless it was a challenge for him to engage her.

"My ex-husband came over last night with his new girlfriend," she said casually, "and then he expected me to be friendly to her. All I could think was that I wanted to blast him and blast her and get them out. But I felt like I had to pretend to be nice."

There was real underlying fury as she was telling this story, but the woman was so cut off from her feelings that she acted as if this whole visit didn't matter. Sure her ex-husband was an insensitive jerk, but it was no big deal.

The woman continued with one complaint after another, all similar illustrations of the same basic theme: she tried so hard, but people didn't understand or appreciate her. They took advantage of her. She found her ex-husband worst of all. They had been constantly having fights, breaking up, getting back together, and then splitting again.

This struck us as an utterly ordinary case of couples counseling, nothing whatsoever unusual about it, so we wondered why this one stood out among all the thousands of people that Bugental had seen in his life.

Timing was one factor for him. "This was fairly early in my career after I left teaching. I had just gone into full-time practice, and this was one of my first cases."

The second factor was the strong transference that the woman developed toward Bugental and also the strong feelings he developed toward her. These were by no means all positive reactions, as she was difficult for him to deal with at times. She was constantly complaining about her life and citing example after example of all the injustices that were done to her. Bugental observed that she reminded him a lot of his mother. "My mother wasn't quite as lacking in reality," he said, "but they shared certain things in common."

She was also memorable to him because he worked so hard to save her. Bugental badly wanted to fix things for her, as if this would somehow make things right with his own mother. Yet he was frequently frustrated in the relationship because he didn't feel he was doing her much good.

"Looking back on it now," Bugental admitted, "I see how much I learned from her. She taught me a great deal."

"What's that?" we wondered. "What did she teach you?"

Bugental's answer surprised us. We expected a list of three or seven things, all mapped out. After all, he has had a half century to reflect on this case, and he *is* one of the most articulate and poetic writers in the field.

"I just don't have a neat answer," he said.

"What about a messy one then?" we prompted.

"I think I learned to allow the patient to keep her misery. I learned to stop trying to rescue people, but to allow them to use the opportunity to work through their own suffering. I hadn't really thought about this beforehand, but now I realize that this was one of the milestone cases in my life. I learned to work through process, particularly in dealing with the transference and countertransference. Some place along in there I also began my own personal therapy, and that made a big difference."

Apart from this one case, we wondered who else stood out among all those Bugental had seen throughout the years. We remembered one of his cases, for example, in which he had been approached by a black man who wanted Bugental to make him white.

Bugental smiled fondly at the memory. "Yes, he was a very dear man. I grew very attached to him. I was so sorry that I was not able to help him more. That was . . . I feel a little choked up right now just remembering him. It was such a hard thing for him to finally accept himself that he was black and would always be black."

Moved ourselves by the passion and caring that he still felt for those he has known and helped, we mentioned what a legend he is.

"Yeah," he added, his humor intact, "with an emphasis on *end*."

CHAPTER TWENTY-EIGHT

Michael Mahoney

"I Wouldn't Mind Being That Guy in the Mirror"

There have been two significant contributions credited to Michael Mahoney. In the early years of his career, he was one of the leading researchers in cognitive therapy. His book Cognition and Behavior Modification *was instrumental in combining the work of cognitive theory and behavior therapy into an integrative model. His book* Human Change Processes *continued his efforts to synthesize ideas from a variety of sources into a coherent framework.*

More recently, Mahoney has turned his attention toward writing in the area of constructivist therapy, an effort culminating in several influential books, such as Cognitive and Constructive Psychotherapies *and* Constructivism in Psychotherapy. *In this approach, Mahoney and several colleagues have developed a theory that helps people create meaning from their experiences through the use of metaphors, cognitive reflection, and a collaborative relationship.*

Mahoney is Professor of Psychology at the University of North Texas in Denton and Distinguished Adjunct Professor at Saybrook Graduate School and Research Center in San Francisco.

Although Mahoney had been well trained in his internship and early years of supervision, he felt challenged by the complexity of some of the cases he was seeing. He was operating as a behavior therapist in those days, and some of his clients were just not behaving as they were supposed to according to the texts he had studied.

For example, when Adam first came to see Mahoney, he had by then completed twenty-two years in therapy with seven previous therapists. During Adam's last stint in an inpatient ward, the doctor there told him that probably his only hope was to see someone like Mahoney, who might approach things in a way that was different from his previous therapists. Even now, Mahoney isn't sure what the guy meant by that, but he understood that this was probably not the best thing to say to someone who already was quite frustrated with the profession.

THE PHONE CALL

"Where did you say you work again?" Adam asked Mahoney during their initial phone contact.

Mahoney explained that it was about a four-hour drive from Adam's location. He also learned that his new client suffered from a variety of problems, including chronic depression, debilitating anxiety, obsessive-compulsive disorder, and an eating disorder. Mahoney was intrigued by this last difficulty, because although anorexia and bulimia were not that unusual in young women, it was quite rare to find these disorders in men. In fact, it would be safe to say that this was unheard of at the time.

"Well," Mahoney responded to the new referral, "you have quite a lot to deal with. But it's also a long way for you to commute."

"That's OK," Adam said. "After everything I've been through, maybe the drive will do me some good. So, Doctor, will you take me on as a patient or not?"

"How about let's try this: Why don't you come for a consultation and then I'll see if I might refer you to someone closer to your area?"

As he hung up the phone, Mahoney was feeling pretty good about his charitable gesture. He'd see Adam for one session, do an assessment, and then based on what he discovered, he could make the best referral.

THE CRITIC

At the appointed time a week later, Adam showed up. He strode into the office, ignoring Mahoney standing at the door, tossed his keys onto the desk, and slumped into the nearest chair—which happened to be where Mahoney liked to sit.

"Well, Adam," Mahoney addressed him, "I would—"

"Do you know I got a speeding ticket on the way here?" Adam said as he looked at his new doctor with a scornful face.

Expecting to see someone who would be eternally grateful for his noble gesture to do this intake, Mahoney was shocked to find that the new client was so hostile.

"I can see that you are upset," Mahoney agreed. "So, what can I do for you?"

"What can you do for me? *What can you do for me!* What the fuck can you do for me that is any different than the other seven doctors I've seen?"

Still relatively young and easily intimidated, Mahoney could think of nothing to say, so he sat there dumbly.

"You're all a bunch of fucking frauds, if you ask me. How do you live with yourself taking money for the shit you do?"

Mahoney just sat there paralyzed. What the heck was he supposed to do or say now? He considered and rejected a number of options, everything he had ever learned, but somehow he'd never been taught what to do with a guy like this.

"Look *Doctor*"—Adam said this complete disdain—"I have been psychoanalyzed, Jungian analyzed, and a bunch of other things I can't even remember. It's all a bunch of bullshit. What are you going to say to me that those other clowns haven't said?"

Mahoney was wondering if the guy expected an answer or not. Finally, he mustered his courage and cleared his throat. "What are you ready to hear?"

"Oh, that's a good one!" Adam countered. "Where did you learn that cute technique? I like the way you ask that ambiguous, open-ended question, waiting for me to draw out enough rope to hang myself. Shit, I was in Gestalt therapy for *years;* I know all those tricks."

Mahoney had rearranged his schedule in order to help this ungrateful guy, and he was starting to feel angry by the unprovoked attacks. Realizing that he had lost his center, Mahoney began to calm himself with deep breathing. Once he had regained his composure he felt ready to proceed.

"I recall on the phone that you told me that you had been depressed for quite some time."

"Very good. So you remember that. So what of it?"

Mahoney looked at Adam thoughtfully, then said, "I was just wondering what it would take for you not to be depressed?"

For the first time, Adam declined to respond critically and admitted that it was an interesting question that he hadn't considered before. Immediately, Mahoney felt proud that he, a beginning therapist, had thought to ask something that none of the other therapists had investigated in the previous twenty-two years.

"Well," Adam said cautiously, "my first response is really crazy."

Mahoney leaned forward and asked, "Crazy or not, what is the first thing that comes to your mind?"

"For me not to be depressed," Adam said, "I think I would have to be a different person."

Mahoney finally let out a breath. It seemed that they had made contact after all. There was something in this response that struck him as totally authentic and real. For the first time in their conversation, Mahoney felt that they could work together after all.

THE EXPERIMENT

In considering how to approach the whole collection of symptoms that Adam presented, Mahoney realized that they would be working less on each individual symptom and much more on Adam's identity. This was going to be less about therapy for the compulsions, the eating disorder, the anxiety and depression, and more about who Adam was as a person and how he had ended up that way.

Adam responded well to this approach and became so committed to working on himself that he moved closer to the town in which Mahoney resided so he wouldn't have to commute eight hours round-trip. This became Mahoney's first real case of long-term, depth-oriented therapy in which they worked on their relationship with one another as much as anything else.

Each time Adam showed up for a session, Mahoney knew he had to be on his toes. Adam was always in crisis even though the content would change. During one session, the latest disaster seemed to resolve itself in just a few minutes. Adam was left with nothing else to talk about, as if his crises were what organized his thinking. Mahoney was struck by how, if he was without a major problem, Adam seemed to lack energy. He was a skinny guy, rail thin, with unkempt, wiry hair, and when he ran out of problems to talk about, he just seemed to fold in on himself. He was like a long balloon that had become deflated.

"When I started therapy with you," Adam said, "I was depressed. Now I feel even worse because I don't feel anything at all." As he said this, he remained hunched over in his chair, looking down.

"Not feeling anything?"

"Nothing."

What Mahoney so enjoyed about his work with this client was that Adam pushed him to invent and try things that he'd never used before. Many of these strategies that evolved, even when they didn't prove useful with Adam, worked stunningly well with others. Mahoney sometimes wasn't sure if he was helping Adam, but he knew that he was sure learning a lot as a result of their relationship.

"Well," Adam pressed, still bent over staring at the floor, "aren't you going to say anything?"

Mahoney remained quiet and still.

"You're just like my psychoanalyst!" Adam threw out, as if this were the worst insult he could imagine. Actually, Mahoney did take it that way and felt provoked to challenge his client.

"Adam, would you mind doing me a favor?" As he said this, Mahoney had no idea where he was going with it, or what he would do next.

Adam looked up at him. "What?" He tried to act perturbed but couldn't quite pull it off. His voice sounded drained.

"I'd like you to stand up. Would you mind standing up?"

Adam looked at him with an expression that said, Are you crazy? But at least he was doing something, trying something. After all, a psychoanalyst would never ask such a thing.

"You really want me to stand up?" Adam shook his head in disgust, as if to say, Is this the best you can do?

What the hell am I doing? Mahoney asked himself. He's either going to stand up or he isn't. But then what do I do next?

"You want me to stand up?" Adam asked again.

By now, Mahoney was committed to this action. "Yes," he said, with more authority than he felt.

Adam laboriously, painfully, pushed himself up out of the chair. He looked like an old man, bent over and arthritic. He put his hands in his pockets and stood there, slumped and swaying. "Now what?"

"I don't know," Mahoney said honestly.

"You don't know? You asked me to stand up, and you don't know why the hell you did it?"

Mahoney just smiled and looked at him with a sheepish grin. "Nope. No idea."

"Man, you are more nuts than I am. I can't believe that people pay you for the crap that you call therapy. You should be paying me!"

Mahoney found himself almost agreeing, but he let the rant continue. Adam's rage built into a full-fledged storm. In the middle of one of his ongoing insults, Mahoney interrupted with a soft question. "Adam, are you still feeling nothing?"

Stunned by the obvious, Adam muttered, "You sonofabitch!" and sat back down in the chair.

This exchange led to a fruitful discussion of taking the risk of doing something, even when you're not sure why or what might happen. Adam thought that it was a trick pulled out of some textbook, but Mahoney explained that he had never done it before. Sharing his own inner process, he told Adam that he had felt the need to ask him to do anything in order to move beyond that earlier moment of impasse. It was a safe risk, and their relationship survived it.

THE MIRROR

Soon after this session, Mahoney saw another client, an adolescent who had been referred by the court for possession of marijuana. The kid's mother had turned him in to the authorities when she discovered some pot in his underwear drawer. She figured it would be good to scare him by getting the police involved. Little did she realize what she had set in motion: the judge ordered the boy to undergo psychological evaluation and required four sessions before he would decide on sentencing. This was the third session Mahoney had had with the boy, and one of the main themes they were working on had to do with trust.

The boy wasn't talking much, even less than usual. Mahoney was frustrated, feeling that he wasn't making much progress; they only had this and one other session left, so there was a lot of pressure to produce quick results. They sat in silence for a while, but it was kind of a comfortable companionship. There was no way that Mahoney was going to pressure this boy to do anything that he didn't want to do.

Just as the time was running out, the boy reached into his pocket and pulled out a small hand mirror. He held it out shyly to Mahoney, who examined it. The words *Harley Davidson Motorcycles* were engraved on the top.

"You can have this if you want," the boy said, smiling shyly.

"For me?" Mahoney was really surprised and touched by this gesture of friendship. This meant that the boy did trust him; this was an offer of goodwill. He wondered if it would be OK to accept such a gift, but then decided that it would be worse to decline, especially considering this meant so much to the boy.

"Yeah, you can have it. If you want, I mean."

"Of course I do! Thanks a lot."

"I won it pitching softballs at a carnival. We went there this weekend." Then he stopped, as if that were all he was going to say about it.

Mahoney looked at the mirror again and then, knowing how important his next move was, he walked slowly over to his bookshelf and placed the mirror in an honored spot. When they parted, it had seemed as though this might be a breakthrough.

THE REFLECTION

Mahoney had an hour to prepare himself for his next client: Adam. He found that he needed time to get himself centered before he would encounter this man who could be so infuriating and yet so interesting.

Adam was in crisis as usual. About five minutes into the session, Mahoney noticed him darting his head from side to side, as if he had some sort of strange tic.

"What the hell is that?" Adam said, pointing at the mirror on the bookshelf. "That wasn't there before."

"No, it's new."

"Well, I don't like it. I keep catching a glimpse of myself in the mirror and then I lose my train of thought. Would you mind moving it?"

"Not at all," Mahoney replied, standing up to retrieve the mirror. As he walked back to his chair, something possessed him to hold the mirror up to Adam's face.

"What are you doing?" he screamed. "Take that thing away!"

"What's wrong?" Mahoney asked innocently.

"If looking in a mirror is a requirement for being in therapy with you, I am out of here."

"No, Adam, you don't have to look in the mirror. But could we talk about what is going on?"

Adam stood up and started pacing nervously around the room. Mahoney had placed the mirror face down on the table, but Adam kept staring at it as if it were some kind of snake that might strike out at him.

"I apologize, Adam. It is clear that I have done something that really upsets you, and I am sincerely sorry. Help me understand what I have done and what you are feeling."

Adam paused in the pacing. "It's just that I have spent so many hours of my life suffering in front of a mirror. Poking at pimples.

Looking at how ugly I am. I am not going to come in here and spend good money being miserable."

"As I said, I do apologize. I just hadn't realized the significance of the mirror to you."

THE BREAKTHROUGH

Later that day, Mahoney was talking to a colleague about what had happened in the session with Adam. He showed him the mirror, and they both started playing with it, holding it up to one another as he had done with his client. They were both intrigued by the kinds of thoughts and feelings that were elicited when you are forced to look at yourself in the mirror in a therapeutic context. This sparked an idea that has become a consistent part of Mahoney's therapy ever since: he installed a full-length mirror on the inside door of his office. He ended up using this "mirror time" with most of his clients, asking them to look in the mirror, then close their eyes and tune inward to describe what is happening in their bodies.

The next time Adam came in, it surprised Mahoney that Adam asked if he still had the mirror around.

"Yeah," Mahoney answered cautiously, not sure if this was a trick question. "In fact, I have a few more mirrors. Why?"

"I can't stop thinking about my reaction last time. I think I need to look in it again."

Looking in the mirror ended up being a major part of the work they did afterwards. As Adam gazed at himself, it reminded Mahoney of a little kid peering into a dark closet, expecting to confront a monster hiding within. Adam would actually approach the mirror from the side rather than head-on, as if to sneak up on it. Then he'd lean forward to see if it was safe, sneaking a quick peek, then a longer one.

"You know," Adam said, "the guy in the mirror doesn't look as fucked up as I feel."

"Can you say more about that?"

"I wouldn't mind being that guy in the mirror."

That was the beginning of the breakthrough in his therapy. As they worked together for the next two years, Mahoney came to respect and like this man like few others he had ever encountered. They came to appreciate one another in endless ways.

"He was so bright," Mahoney told us, "so very psychologically minded and very alive to his inner life. He really stretched me in so many ways. He clued me into styles of being therapeutic that I had never tried before."

THE FEAST

Adam's eating disorder had taken its toll on his body over the previous ten years. He had a very peculiar set of rituals and procedures associated with food. First he would go to his favorite market, where he would select the finest ingredients available—the freshest spices and herbs. Then he would spend several hours following elaborate recipes, many of which he had never tried before. He would make a five- or six-course meal, just for himself. Next he would set an elaborate table with his finest serving pieces, crystal, and silver. He would take an hour or more to luxuriate in the feast, tasting all the delicacies, savoring the rich flavors.

It would be nice if the rituals ended there, but unfortunately, this is where they really began. After he cleared the table, but before he washed the dishes, Adam would next head to the bathroom, where he would kneel on the tile floor and vomit up the whole elaborate meal into the toilet bowl. Then the coup de grace: he would give himself an enema and purge anything left in his lower intestine. Next, he would shower carefully and spend the better part of an hour sticking a finger up his anus to test for any residual fecal matter that might have been left inside. If there was even a tiny speck, he would then begin the cycle again, probing with his finger over and over.

After hearing about these compulsive bingeing and purging episodes in such detail, Mahoney despaired that they would ever address this last of his major problems.

THE PHONE CALL

It was 4 A.M. when the phone rang.

"Mike, are you awake?" the voice asked.

"Awake? Sure, I'm awake. Who is this?" Mahoney is the sort who denies that he was sleeping when awakened in the middle of the night or early in the morning.

"Mike, it's Adam. Can you talk?"

"Talk? Now?"

"Mike, you'll never believe this, but guess what?"

Silence.

"Mike, are you still there? Mike?"

"Yeah," Mahoney said, almost drifting back to sleep. "I'm awake. You said there's something I won't believe."

"Listen. For the first time in over ten years I didn't binge and purge last night."

"Wow. That is something."

"And guess what else? I am just getting home."

"You're just getting home. From where?"

"I was at a party, and I met a woman and I spent the night at her place and it was wonderful." The words just tumbled out and he'd never sounded more happy.

"Oh," was all Mahoney could think to say.

"Wait. There's more. She actually wants to see me again. Can you believe it?"

"That's just great, Adam," Mahoney said, now fully awake and almost as excited as his client was.

"Listen, Doc, I want you to surgically excise my bulimia because if this woman knows what I do in the bathroom she will never want a relationship with me."

"How about let's talk in the morning, after I wake up."

"That's fine, Doc. I just wanted to tell you the good news. I don't care if you hypnotize me or do whatever you need to do, but you have to get me over the bulimia. And I mean right now! This could by my first shot at a real relationship."

"Let me see if I understand this. It has been ten years, and every night you have binged and purged."

"Yeah. Yeah."

"You have been through behavior modification. You have been through psychoanalysis. You have been hospitalized. They tried shock treatment to get you to stop vomiting and sticking your finger up your butt."

"Yeah, you know that."

"And now, spontaneously, this behavior begins to change, and you want me to do something about it?"

"You aren't going to do anything, are you?"

"It seems to me," Mahoney said, "that it is beginning to change by itself."

"Damn," Adam said with a chuckle, "I knew you would say something like that."

Adam ended up telling the woman about the issues he had around food, and surprise, surprise: it turned out that she had an eating disorder as well! They actually had this in common, and it brought them even closer together.

"I may never be to the point where I won't binge and purge," Adam admitted later, "but it is so much less interesting than it used to be."

THE LESSONS LEARNED

Even twenty years after seeing Adam, Mahoney is still learning things from their work together. It wasn't just the interesting conversations they had but that this was the one case where Mahoney learned to trust his intuition. He remembers another example of this when Adam came in and announced, "You know, I don't feel so bad today. I wish you could just nail me here."

"Nail you here?" Mahoney responded with surprise.

"Yeah, I'm in a good place. If you could just nail me here, and keep me in a good mood, I would be OK."

For some reason that he couldn't explain, Mahoney decided to give Adam a homework assignment of spending some time hanging around a pendulum clock. Mahoney's intuition was that there might be a lesson to be learned by watching a natural cycle close up.

There happened to be a tall pendulum clock down the hall in the lobby of a law firm. Adam, of course, thought this assignment was ridiculous and became irate over the absurdity of the task. But he complied and began spending his lunch hours there, watching and listening to the clock.

Some time later, Mahoney heard the following message on his answering machine: "My dear little shrink. Today I was wasting another lunch hour looking at that fucking pendulum clock and trying to figure out if one side was good and the other side was bad. Or maybe I was counting the seconds I was alive, hoping the movement would keep going. As I stood up and was folding my lunch bag, I realized that there is only one place on the shaft where you can see both the good and the bad and that is at the top where it rotates. There is still a part of me that wants to be the mouse that runs down when it is a good day and runs up and hides when it is a lousy one. But I hadn't realized the importance of perspective before. I hadn't realized that was in the assignment."

Mahoney reflects again on what he learned from Adam at a time in his career when he was just beginning to find his stride and his confidence. Even with their battles together (or perhaps because of them), Adam is still the one client who he thinks about the most. After all, he was the person who helped Mahoney realize the limits of his narrow behavioral approach and expand his interests in the direction of helping people create meaning in their experiences.

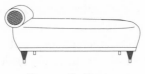

CHAPTER TWENTY-NINE

Laura S. Brown

The Three-Year-Old
Who Was an Alcoholic

A feminist theorist and an expert on sexual abuse, Laura Brown represents a cutting edge in therapeutic practice. Her approach deals more explicitly than traditional therapies with issues such as power, ethics, sexual harassment, gender roles, sexual orientation, and body image. Her work in recovered memories and tireless work on behalf of social justice issues related to gays and lesbians have been groundbreaking.

Among Brown's most significant works are the following books: Subversive Dialogues: Theory in Feminist Therapy; Recovered Memories of Abuse; Fat Oppression and Psychotherapy: A Feminist Perspective; Personality and Psychopathology; *and* Diversity and Complexity in Feminist Therapy.

Brown is based in Seattle, where she maintains an active therapy and consulting practice and is Professor of Psychology at Argosy University Seattle-School of Professional Psychology.

———

When Brown thinks about the extraordinary people she has known in her life, there is one person who stands out. This was a woman she has not seen in therapy for over six years but with whom she still keeps in touch on occasion. What makes her story so remarkable was not the unusual nature of her problems, or the adversity and obstacles she faced that would have killed a lesser soul, but rather her resilience in managing to recover from the trauma she faced.

CHILDHOOD FROM HELL

Gloria visited Brown to deal with issues related to her ongoing struggle with her size and her relationship with food. ("I would never use the word obesity!" Brown told us.) She reported to Brown that she recalled starting to use alcohol at the age of three, when her family was living in London, and this was corroborated later by other family members. It seems that one day both her parents had been passed out drunk. The toddler managed to crawl into the open liquor cabinet and began tasting from various bottles until she found something to her liking. What she liked was that the liquid in the bottles eased her terrible pain. From that day forward, she used alcohol and other drugs as she found them to numb herself against the almost daily abuse she suffered at the hands of her parents.

Gloria's father was the "good" parent, the one who was predictable, stable, caring, and loving. He was so "loving," in fact, that he introduced his daughter to sex from the time she was in elementary school. Heavy petting soon led to penetration and regular intercourse.

Mother was so unstable and unpredictable that she probably had a multiple personality disorder, that kind of dissociative condition in which she would literally present a half-dozen different people for the young child to cope with. One of these personalities was chronically angry at her daughter and took every opportunity to beat her with a broom handle. Sometimes Gloria would be awakened in the middle of a deep sleep to find her mother standing over her with some apparently benign object that would be used to "punish" her for some imagined transgression.

Gloria's earliest memory is of being in a crib with her mother leaning over to smother her with a pillow. To this day, Gloria has a strong posttraumatic reaction to a particular popular perfume because that was the scent favored by her mother when she would try to strangle her.

Although Brown would never recommend alcohol as a form of self-medication for childhood abuse, it did seem ironic that it was the drinking that probably saved Gloria from a severe dissociative disorder, if not outright psychosis. When the alcohol was not enough to numb the pain and block the memories of constant emotional, physical, and sexual abuse, she also turned to amphetamines and hallucinogens. Gloria believed that this is what got her through her childhood and adolescence, even with all the negative side effects. Gloria used drugs until she could find the thing she truly needed—a safe emotional haven among other people.

A CHOSEN FAMILY

Brown muses that Gloria had no reason whatsoever to turn out to be a decent human being. Because her father was in a job that required frequent moves, she rarely lived in one place for a long time. Not only was her home such a dangerous and disordered place, but because she was constantly on the move she had little opportunity to maintain stable relationships that might compensate for her bizarre family dysfunction.

Because her father was in a prominent position and demonstrated otherwise caring parental responsibilities, the abuse she suffered was invisible. White, upper-class families were not suspected of abusing their children in the 1950s, when she was growing up. So she managed. She learned to block out memories of being beaten, strangled, and molested. Of course, drugs and alcohol certainly helped her to substitute oblivion for the hellish reality she faced.

Both parents were active alcoholics. Although Gloria's father tried to protect her as best he could from the mother's violent rants, he was not particularly effective because of his own betrayal of her trust. There were other times when he left Gloria alone with her mother for days at a time while he was away on a work assignment. The best that could be expected was that maybe the mother's catatonic personality would emerge, the one that would remain frozen in place for the duration. At worst, his times away would be days of terror for Gloria, days when she stayed at school as long as she could, hung out in neighbors' yards, and in general did her best to stay alive.

Even with any deterioration that must have taken place as a result of chronic substance abuse, Gloria emerged as a remarkably bright, precocious young woman with superior intellectual and interpersonal skills. It is her resilience that Brown still finds one of the most amazing things she has ever seen.

One would reasonably predict, even expect, that someone subjected to this type of continuous, long-term abuse would have to suffer a major attachment disorder. Most of the research in this area indicates that such victims find it difficult to connect with others, to trust others; often they never recover from their early traumas. Frequently they develop severe personality disorders and multiple personality disorders, strategies that help them avoid being wounded in the future. Yet Gloria not only recovered from her traumas but flourished. She was a "mensch," a decent human being, against all odds.

As a participant in therapy, Gloria was a very responsible client who never pushed boundaries. She didn't go into crisis when Brown was on vacation. She didn't call her late at night during emergencies. She didn't test people as a way to avoid intimacy. She had every reason to be crazy but had somehow turned out to be a lovely human being. It was only the overeating that continued to plague her.

Gloria became active in Alcoholics Anonymous. She sponsored newcomers to the program. She remained in a long-term relationship with her partner that has now lasted almost twenty years. She was a pillar in the lesbian and gay community, active and giving. The way Laura speaks about her client, you would think she was talking about a trusted colleague—and that's exactly the way Brown thinks about her, and the way she would prefer to think about most of her clients—as colleagues and collaborators in change.

"Gloria has an innate capacity for connecting to people," Brown told us. "She appreciates people, values people, and finds healthy people with whom to affiliate. It is just amazing. For example, when she went to college she found a peer group in the English department where she basically fell into a group of gay men who took care of her. She didn't know yet that she was a lesbian. It took her a very long time to come out to herself, but she fell into this group of very protective men who wouldn't hurt her and were loving toward her. They gave her a chance to have emotionally intimate, safe relationships, and she ate it up. She still maintains those friendships today, thirty years later."

Gloria discovered that she could choose her own family, this time one in which she could feel safe and protected. And she has built a family that is a model of love, connection, and honesty.

A NEW MOTHER

Brown worked with Gloria, on and off, over a period of ten years. They continued to work on her body image and eating patterns, making slow but steady progress. In some ways, Brown functioned as a mentor, a healthy role model, and another source of support for remaining sober. She also helped Gloria come to terms with the abuse she suffered in the past, first accessing previously unavailable memories, then living with them in such a way that she could accept that which could not be changed.

Although Gloria had come to therapy already stabilized and mostly healthy, she was very overweight as a result of being a compulsive overeater. Food had become her addiction after she surrendered the use of drugs and alcohol as her main coping strategy. The therapy thus focused, in part, on attempts to rein in this external means of giving herself comfort.

For Gloria perhaps the most challenging part of therapy was to take the enormous risk of developing a deep, emotional relationship with a woman, even if she was a professional and the therapist. Although Gloria was a lesbian, women were quite dangerous to her on an emotional level. Having been sexually abused by her father was a terrible thing, certainly helping her to mistrust men, but she felt even more caution in her relationships with women. After all, her mother had tortured and almost killed her. She was counterphobic toward both genders, and with good reason; the task of developing a deep transference relationship with her female therapist was an enormous leap of faith.

Brown considers herself quite skilled at developing mother-child transference relationships. In part this is because she actively steers herself away from any awareness of sexualized transference. Another component is her huge reservoir of warmth and openness. Laura invites people to trust her because she demonstrates such complete respect and caring toward those she helps.

Once maternal transference was developed in their relationship, Gloria felt safe enough to remember some of the things that had happened in her life. Remarkably, she could do this without going back to alcohol and drugs. "She developed enormous compassion for herself as a child," Brown explained, "which was one of the pieces that was missing. She was compassionate to other people as well—loving and caring and kind."

Gloria worked as a supervisor in a local social services agency. She had one of the most challenging jobs imaginable—the office was understaffed and without resources—yet she was universally loved by her employees and adored by her supervisors. She would frequently bring her job evaluations in to show Brown, as if she couldn't believe that the person they described was really her; she was stunned by how much others appreciated her work.

FEEDING HERSELF WITH LOVE

As good as she could be toward other people, Gloria had not yet learned how to be good to herself. She was feeding herself with food instead of love.

"In order to feed yourself in a loving manner," Brown explained, "you have to be willing to act as though you love yourself."

"What do you mean?" Gloria wondered. "You're saying that because I don't love myself, that's why I'm too fat?"

"Well," Brown suggested, "let's look at this more. What is there not to love about you?"

Like a lot of abuse survivors, Gloria had no sense of herself as a child. "I think perpetrators see children as miniature adults," Brown explained. "Not only do they lack empathy for their victims, but they lack the capacity to appreciate that children are cognitively and emotionally different. I think that victims of severe childhood sexual, physical, and emotional abuse internalize that image of themselves as shrunken adults. Somehow, they believe that they could have, or should have, engaged in the behavior that an adult would if under attack."

Brown helped Gloria retrieve an image of herself as a child, without being terrified during this process. She helped her understand how little and vulnerable she had been, as well as to redirect the anger she felt toward herself. Brown introduced several strategies to assist Gloria with this. She asked Gloria to bring in photos of herself as a child, so that she could be confronted with the incontrovertible evidence of her having been little. She encouraged Gloria to do something she had always feared, which was to spend time around children, so as to get an experiential feel for what kids really can and can't do in the face of adults. Gloria had long feared that she might be dangerous to children. What she came to realize was that the only child at risk from her was the child inside herself. As Gloria used these and other strategies for knowing that she had once truly been small, she softened toward herself. Her constructions of her childhood coping behaviors became more compassionate and appreciative. She came to internalize Brown's view of her as a child who survived against the odds, rather than as a weak wimp.

Slowly and gradually Gloria was able to change her eating habits, although her body size did not significantly change. She began an exercise program, which was particularly frightening for her. For a four-hundred-pound woman, it is a scary thing to appear in public in a bathing suit or workout clothes. She became more aware of her body's needs for care, and began to learn how to meet those needs, rather than avoid or numb them.

As Gloria continued dealing with her early trauma, her resolve to remain sober was tested as well. This was the first time that she was able to deal with what happened in such a way that she did not emotionally distance herself. She was able to develop compassion and love for herself, realizing the kind of strength it must have taken her to hold all these feelings inside as a child without totally destroying herself in the process.

MORE THAN JUST SAY NO

Kids see advertisements to prevent drug and alcohol abuse. They are told it is a simple matter of "Just Say No to Drugs." Yet in Gloria's case, it was actually the drinking that helped save her. It numbed her. It allowed her to dissociate from the craziness that was happening around her, the abuse that was directed toward her, without having to completely and permanently separate from reality. She was able to survive by medicating herself until she could protect herself, or at least until her mother died. What needed to be addressed in Gloria's family, was the abuse inflicted by her parents. Without that abuse, she might have had to make the choice between substance abuse and inner disintegration.

Gloria taught her therapist a lot about the capacity people have to turn horror into something transcendent. "This taught me a lot," Brown said, "about trusting my clients and where they were going in the work even when it was sometimes temporarily destabilizing. This taught me to pay attention when someone says, 'This is where I need to go next.' I learned to follow them."

In addition, Laura got a much deeper appreciation for the restorative powers of coming to terms with the past, not in a Freudian sense but in a way that leads to forgiveness. Eventually Gloria was able to confront her father and ask him about what happened. He confessed to his role in the abuse and confirmed the kinds of abuse that she had suffered. In the years that he had left, he was willing to work with his daughter, corroborating events and helping her remember what took place. Gloria was able to claim the good in the relationship without having to deny the harm, which allowed a greater degree of connection.

Once Gloria understood where she came from and what she had lived through, she could make better sense of her characteristic patterns.

She began to see the world differently. This was not because Brown pushed her to confront the past, but because Brown gently supported and encouraged Gloria to go as far as she wanted.

"I truly believe," Brown explained, "that people know what they need to know in order to function at any moment. Their knowledge of their own biography helps them to have a more complete story. It helps them give meaning to their pain."

Gloria has built a life that is full of meaning. She and her partner have created a family of choice. They have become foster parents, caring for children who remind Gloria of herself as a child. "Gloria is committed to giving back," said Brown. "She is trying to create a world that is safe for children, and taking an active part in that endeavor." By knowing and owning her past, she has been able to live in peace with herself. Brown encounters Gloria from time to time at events in the lesbian and gay community. Every time, Gloria seems more alive, more energized, more open.

CHAPTER THIRTY

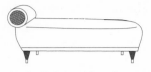

Donald Meichenbaum

Every Parent's Worst Nightmare

Donald Meichenbaum is one of the originators of cognitive behavior therapy, and his contributions have been recognized by his colleagues, who have voted him to be one of the ten most influential psychotherapists of the century. He has emphasized the interdependence among the patient's thoughts, feelings, and behavior and their resultant consequences. Born and raised in New York City, where, he noted, many people "talk to themselves," he has highlighted that one goal of therapy is to help people learn to talk to themselves differently and to tell themselves and others more constructive adaptive "stories." But such stories must be based on behavioral change. His books include several classics, including Cognitive-Behavioral Modification: An Integrative Approach; Stress Inoculation Training; Pain and Behavior Medicine; Facilitating Treatment Adherence; Treatment of Individuals with Anger-Control Problems and Aggressive Behaviors; *and, most related to the case discussed in this story,* A Clinical Handbook for Assessing and Treating Adults with Post-Traumatic Stress Disorder.

Meichenbaum is presently Distinguished Professor Emeritus at the University of Waterloo, in Ontario, Canada, and Research Director of the Melissa Institute for Violence Prevention and Treatment of Victims of Violence, in Miami, Florida.

—⁓—

Monica had all of the characteristics that predict a favorable prognosis. She was a prototypical "YAVIS"—Young, Attractive, Verbal, Intelligent, and Successful. Monica was a thirty-six-year-old mother and teacher, married to a successful businessman. Although her husband, Bruce, traveled frequently as part of his work, they had a solid marriage and an excellent relationship with their eleven-year-old daughter, Vickie. They lived in a comfortable suburban area where they felt insulated from the dangers of urban living.

Although Monica was fortunate to live a "privileged life," as she described it, she entered the therapy office depressed to the point of contemplating suicide. Distraught, listless, and fearful, her life had turned around on a dime. Meichenbaum wondered to himself what events could have so affected an individual that her life had changed so quickly and profoundly. He invited Monica to tell her story.

THE HOME INVASION

Monica spent a great deal of time at home with her daughter. With her husband traveling so much, Monica and Vickie enjoyed an even closer than usual mother-daughter relationship. Vickie was a bright and precocious girl, "wise beyond her years," as her mother described her, which allowed them to relate to one another on many different levels. It had been their custom to talk about their lives and share intimacies, catching one another up on their respective days before they would prepare themselves for bed.

It was late one evening while her husband was out of town when Monica was suddenly awakened in the middle of a very deep sleep. She listened carefully for a minute or two, drifting back to sleep, when the noise repeated itself again. She bolted upright in bed, now convinced that there was somebody else in the house. Their home had been invaded by burglars.

Monica could distinctly hear the footsteps of people rummaging downstairs. They didn't even seem to be trying to cover the sounds of their work downstairs. Utterly terrified, Monica's first thought was for

Vickie. Somehow she had to protect her. After dialing 911 to call for help, she carefully crept into her daughter's room to wake her. They hid in the closet until the burglars left.

PROTECTIVE ACTION

Fortunately, the burglars never did come upstairs. They took the stuff they wanted and left before the police arrived. Both Vickie and Monica were severely shaken by the experience, but came away relatively unscathed.

As one would suspect after such as event, the family engaged in a number of protective acts, including changing the locks and having an alarm system installed. As a last resort, Bruce convinced Monica to purchase a handgun.

Although these protective measures made Bruce feel more secure, Monica continued to live in fear that her house could be attacked again. She was also afraid of the ugly-looking handgun in her nightstand, reluctant even to look at it, much less touch it. When her neighbors reassured her that they too kept firearms in case of robbery, she felt a little better about the situation but still apprehensive.

Several months went by and routines in the house had returned to normal. Bruce was again on the road, leaving his daughter and wife alone. It was a stormy night. The wind was howling, and the rain was beating heavily against the roof and windows. The trees were making whistling sounds. The shutters were pounding against the side of the house.

A strange noise awakened Monica, different from those of the storm. Where was the sound coming from? Could it be that the burglars were back? Was it the harsh rain, the whistling trees, the clamoring shutters? Monica concentrated more and more; it was obvious that someone was in the house once again. Yet that couldn't possibly be so! How could they get past the new locks and the alarm system? She tried to remember if she had indeed set the alarm.

Monica sat up in bed, terrified, straining to discern the sounds from below. She thought she heard footsteps. Could she be dreaming? No, it was someone. Thank God, Monica thought, I have the gun.

She bolted for the nightstand, ripped open the drawer, lifted out the handgun. It was heavier than she remembered, not at all easy to hold in her trembling hand.

With her heart pounding and fear overwhelming her, she took the gun in hand and headed for Vickie's room, where they could hide once again. Now she felt protected by the gun.

The next part happened very quickly. The next thing Monica knew was that her bedroom door was suddenly thrown open and she heard the sound of a deafening boom. It was her gun. The gun had gone off when the bedroom door hit her hand.

There was a body lying on the floor, wedged in the doorway. A spreading pool of blood flowed from underneath the head. Monica, stunned and disoriented, looked down to see her daughter Vickie lying crumpled on the floor. Her brain matter, bits of bone, and blood were splattered across the opposite wall.

Monica was found twenty-four hours later by her husband, upon his return from his business trip. Monica was sitting on the floor in a catatonic state, with Vickie's body in her lap.

HEALING THE TRAUMA

When Meichenbaum heard Monica's story, he found that he could barely listen without being moved to tears. With four children of his own, he could not imagine what Monica went through in losing her daughter in such a tragic manner. No wonder she was depressed and suicidal.

The challenges were immense. How could he help Monica stay alive and continue functioning? Her daughter was gone. Her husband, who felt responsible for the tragedy, had left. Her life was in ruins. She could no longer work. She was totally without hope.

Friends and family had tried to console Monica. She was reassured repeatedly that what happened was not her fault. Doctors had pre-scribed antidepressants, but her sense of loss and feelings of guilt and hopelessness were unremitting.

"As every day passed," Monica observed, "I realized more fully that I had not only lost my daughter and my husband, I had lost the very purpose and shape of my life. Depression is winning and I am losing." On that tragic night, Monica lost not only her family but also her basic assumptions about the world, herself, and the future. Prior to the tragedy, Monica had a sense of a "story-book life," as she described it. The present, the past, and the future were bright.

In a situation like this, there are no words that can heal the pain or cure the aftermath of trauma, so the first task of Monica's therapy was to establish a therapeutic relationship in which she could tell her story, at her own pace, in as much detail as she wished. Meichenbaum noted that the goals of treatment were not only to help Monica with the bereavement process and to help her address her feelings of responsibility and guilt but also to help her find meaning in the experience of loss, allowing her, one would hope, to come to see herself as a survivor and not merely as a victim.

In order to avoid becoming overwhelmingly dispirited, Meichenbaum reminded himself that the stories of those who had been exposed to traumatic events and loss, whether the Holocaust or the ravages of war and terrorist attacks, are tales of resilience and courage. Where and how do they find the courage, the will to go on, to create a new way of making a life for themselves?

Meichenbaum's strategy was to encourage Monica to talk more fully about her pain and loss, but to do so in a way that would permit and encourage her to get "unstuck" from the moment that the gun went off and the immediate next twenty-four hours of despair. He asked Monica to do something that would be very difficult—and she should feel free to say no: Would she consider bringing into the next session a picture album of Vickie? Meichenbaum has found that reviewing such photo albums is a useful way to help those who grieve to broaden their memories from the moment of a tragedy, to that of a consideration of a full life.

Although it was very painful for Monica to review the lifetime of family pictures involving Vickie, the reflective process also provided her with the occasion to observe that one of the things that impressed her most was that Vickie was "wise beyond her years."

"If Vickie was here right now," Meichenbaum said to Monica, "if she could curl up into those loving arms and look into your caring eyes, what advice, if any, would Vickie, who was 'wise beyond her years,' as you describe her, have to offer? Moreover, Monica, if you kill yourself as you are considering, what will happen to the memory of Vickie? Those memories will die with you. Is that what Vickie would want?"

Meichenbaum was trying to accomplish two things simultaneously. First, he was honoring Vickie's memory, holding a sacred ceremony of reviewing their lives together. Second, he was helping Monica find reason to go on. He used the "absent other" of Vickie as a way to help Monica collaborate in generating coping efforts.

"Before this," Meichenbaum observed, "Monica had tried to suppress thinking about Vickie. The more she would suppress, the more she would have intrusive disturbing thoughts and feelings." So rather than hiding from the painful memories, Monica needed to transform her memories. The absent Vickie was transformed into a "consultant," a co-therapist in the healing process.

Under the guise of soliciting what advice Vickie might offer, Meichenbaum guided and supported Monica in collaboratively developing a variety of coping efforts. These included ways Monica could address her overwhelming feelings of guilt and her penchant to continually engage in "what if" forms of contrafactual thinking; her tendency to avoid social contacts and ways to reenter life; and ways she could find meaning and develop a purpose in life. As Monica observed, "There are only so many if-onlies left. The only thing I can change is what I do now."

Meichenbaum helped Monica transform her pain and find meaning in her suffering. Monica concluded that if she could help prevent one more innocent child from dying from guns, then perhaps Vickie would not have died in vain. Monica decided to share her tragic story with anyone who would listen, including parent-teacher associations and church groups. She found meaning by highlighting the dangers of keeping guns in the house and the value of using gun safety locks.

SO THE STORY CONTINUES

Monica continues to struggle with grief and depression, especially on the anniversary of her daughter's death. But her work on behalf of parent education groups in her effort to prevent similar tragedies in other households gives purpose to her life. She and her husband remain friends, but they decided to divorce. She went back to teaching in order to give to others.

One loose end that you might be wondering about: Were there really burglars in the house that fateful night that Vickie died?

Indeed there were. Somehow they managed to break into the house even with the new safety system in place. They had been downstairs when they heard the gun go off and had taken off right afterwards. Monica found some consolation in that, knowing that the sounds she had heard that night were not all in her head. She had enough to live with already.

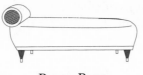

CHAPTER THIRTY ONE

Peggy Papp

The Third Sexual Identity

Peggy Papp is known primarily for her work examining how gender roles, beliefs, and expectations influence relationships and families. Her books, such as The Process of Change, The Invisible Web, *and* Couples on the Fault Line, *look at family therapy from the perspective of people's underlying belief systems. Throughout her career, she has been a strong and consistent advocate for examining problems within a context of how men's and women's experiences are both similar and different.*

Papp is Senior Training Supervisor and Director of the Depression Project at the Ackerman Institute for Family Therapy in New York.

The case that most challenged Papp's assumptions about romantic love, gender, and sexual identity forced her to reevaluate her understanding of male-female relationships. This was a case with so many nuances, and so much complexity in its issues, that Papp needed more than a decade to integrate what she learned. Part of the problem in even talking about the case has been the political atmosphere in the field of gender research, which makes a frank discussion difficult. Nevertheless, the implications of what took place with this couple cannot help but challenge anyone to consider that love is indeed a many-splendored thing.

ALL THE USUAL PROBLEMS

Wayne and Holly had a traditional relationship in many ways, presenting the usual complaints one would expect from a couple that had been together for two years—disputes about quality time, minor jealousies over friendship, negotiations over the frequency of sex, money issues, and the like. They had both been married before, so they wanted to make sure that they didn't repeat the same mistakes. They approached Papp because they wanted to do some preventive work.

They were a most attractive couple. Wayne was distinguished looking, slim, in his early forties, with a carefully trimmed beard. Holly was absolutely stunning, thirtyish, long blonde hair, casually but colorfully dressed. They were quite striking to look at and obviously taken with one another.

Holly had recently rented an apartment in Wayne's building so that they could be close to one another yet still retain their own space, literally and metaphorically. They had recently decided to take the next step and move in together, a big step toward their commitment as life partners.

As excited as they were about this new arrangement, both of them were a bit apprehensive about how they would organize their space so that they could be together yet still maintain some degree of privacy. They also spoke about some frustrations related to sex: Wayne wanted to make love more often, whereas Holly felt reluctant until they grew closer emotionally. It was all very familiar to Papp and to any therapist who has done couples work: the two of them were aligned along typical gender roles, the man wanting more physical contact and the woman wanting closer emotional ties. Holly also complained that Wayne had an overpowering personality, whereas she was very shy.

"He makes all the decisions," Holly complained, "about where we go out to dinner, or even what we watch on TV."

"That's not really true," Wayne said with a laugh. "Holly doesn't let me know what she wants. I can't read her mind."

"But I do try to tell him what I want," Holly insisted, "but I can't hold my own with him. He out-talks me and I end up going along with him."

"Well, you can speak up," he told her. "You just don't assert yourself. You leave everything to me, so I end up making the decisions. I don't like this arrangement, but I thought this is what you wanted."

"How does this affect your decisions around moving in together?" Papp wondered. "Are you allowing Wayne to make all the decisions about your living arrangements?"

Holly cast a meaningful glance at Wayne and nodded in agreement. Wayne looked surprised. "I didn't know you felt that way," he said. "What decisions am I making that you don't approve of?"

"Well, for one thing you made the decision about the extra room, and you also decided where most of the furniture will go in the living room." It was clear Holly was feeling left out of their decision-making process, and that became the focus of the discussion for the remainder of their time in this first meeting. At the end of the session they had reached some mutual decisions and agreed to try and follow through on them during the coming week.

A CHOREOGRAPHY

When they returned the next week, Holly reported she had been able to express some of her needs more directly. Likewise, Wayne expressed relief about knowing what was on her mind. Then there were long, awkward pauses, followed by superficial chatter and sidelong glances at one another. Papp had the feeling they were hiding something that was difficult for them to talk about.

After a period of rather aimless talk, Peggy suggested they do a communication exercise she has developed over the years that she refers to as couple's choreography. The exercise involves an enactment designed to help couples communicate on a nonverbal level by using metaphors, symbols, imagery, and physical positioning. They are asked to have a fantasy about their relationship and then to enact the fantasy together. Because the fantasies bypass the logic of language, they reveal in a more primal way the different aspects of the couple's relationship. Peggy suggested the exercise to Wayne and Holly as a way of helping them express through images what they seemed to be having difficulty putting into words.

"What I'd like you to do is close your eyes," Papp began the exercise. "Just relax comfortably and let your eyes close."

They both complied and settled into the couch they were sharing.

"Now, let yourself have a fantasy about the problem you are having together and imagine what symbolic forms each of you would take in the fantasy."

"I'm not sure I know what you mean," Wayne said, opening his eyes for a second.

Papp elaborated further. "You know how in dreams and fantasies people often don't appear as they do in real life but take on metaphorical shapes and images like characters in a storybook or fairy tale? It doesn't have to make sense. Just let your imagination run free. Then imagine how these two symbolic forms would interact with one another when they are trying to solve some of the problems in their relationship. When you have finished imagining this I would like you to just open your eyes without speaking."

Both Wayne and Holly sat silently, lost in their fantasies for a minute or two, and then Wayne opened his eyes, followed shortly by Holly.

"Good," Papp said. "Now, I'm going to ask you to do something that may seem ridiculous. I'd like you to act out your fantasies together. Wayne you opened your eyes first, so why don't you begin."

Wayne appeared a little reluctant.

"Come on," Holly encouraged him, "let's try it. It'll be fun!"

Papp liked to see Holly taking the lead, breaking the mold she reported was standard in their relationship. Wayne arose and said, "Well, I couldn't come up with any symbolic forms—the image is just very emotional—and very powerful—it's something that comes from here." He pointed to his solar plexus.

Peggy said, "OK, that's fine. Show us that."

"Well," Wayne continued, "I was a scared little boy, and I was running away from the relationship."

"Show that to us. Act it out. Where was Holly in all this?"

"She was just standing there looking—this may sound strange but sort of looking like an angel—a kind of self-righteous angel—and she was pointing a finger at me." Holly followed Wayne's directions and pretended to be the self-righteous angel.

"And how did the scared little boy react to the self-righteous angel?" Papp prompted.

"I kept running away from her," Wayne said enacting the scene, "but I couldn't go very far. I kept turning around to attack but then I noticed how scared and sad the angel looked. So I couldn't attack. I turned to run again, but I couldn't because I couldn't leave the sad angel."

Papp asked them to keep repeating the movements so that they experienced the situation physically. When Wayne turned away from Holly, Papp asked what the scared little boy was afraid of.

"Getting too close to her, I guess. I'm afraid of her disapproval. I'm probably afraid of committing myself; I'd be too vulnerable."

Papp then asked him to show what his ideal fantasy would be like, and he moved toward Holly and hugged her. As he held her, Wayne began to cry.

"What's making you cry?" Papp asked.

"It feels good," Wayne sobbed, and they both laughed at the contradiction. "I've turned and run too many times in my life. I don't want to do that anymore. I want to face the issues now."

Holly caressed Wayne and said through her own tears, "I'll try and help you not be so afraid."

One of the most powerful things about this method is that it allows people not only to see but also to *experience* the essence of their perceived interactions; further, they can do it in such a way that they don't feel so threatened that they shut down.

SURPRISE

Holly next presented her fantasy. "I pictured being in bed with Wayne, but he was a little girl. I was hugging her because she was hurt and angry and it was my fault. The little girl didn't hug back. I can't stand it when the little girl doesn't hug back. I try everything to get her affection. If the little girl stays hurt and angry, I think I will die."

Wayne, lying on the floor in Holly's fantasy bed, looked puzzled and said, "So you think of me as a little girl, huh?"

Holly seemed embarrassed, and they both looked at Papp sheepishly. Then Wayne went on, "I guess we'd better tell her, huh?"

Holly nodded.

"What's going on?" Papp asked them, puzzled by this interaction.

"We're both gay," Wayne blurted out.

"You're both gay? I'm not sure what you mean." Papp was both stunned and confused. How could they both be gay? It didn't make any sense.

"We're both homosexual," Wayne repeated with a smile of amusement. "Holly is a lesbian, and I am gay."

How could this be? Papp wondered. How could she possibly have missed this? They had struck her as the most ordinary of couples with conventional marital problems—all the usual issues. She was trying to get her mind around this: How could a gay man and lesbian woman be involved romantically and sexually?

This was during a time a number of years ago when it was the consensus in the field that once you were gay, you were always gay and only gay, and you never had a heterosexual relationship. It was all or nothing: you were or you weren't. If two people were in a marriage like this, or as Holly and Wayne had been for some time, they were covering up their gayness out of shame and fear of coming out of the closet. But these two had reversed that. And it took Papp's breath away.

"Maybe we'd better back up a bit," Papp suggested, trying to regain her composure. "How did the two of you meet and fall in love?"

"We met at a gay party," Holly began the story. "At the time, we were both involved in a relationship that had recently ended."

"A relationship?"

"Yeah," Holly laughed. "A gay relationship. I was involved with a woman, and Wayne had a boyfriend. They were pretty long-term relationships too."

"And so you were at this party, trying to stabilize yourself, when . . ."

"That's right," Wayne continued the narrative. "We were both in pretty bad shape. We were both grieving, so we cried on one another's shoulders."

"So you were friends at first," Papp clarified.

"Exactly," Holly agreed, and then looked at Wayne, who nodded his head for her to continue their story. "We became best friends. We have so much in common. We would go to museums. We'd go for bike rides. And picnics. We became real bosom buddies." They both laughed.

"So then what happened?"

"I'm not sure what happened," Wayne tried to explain, "but all I know is that every time I left her I felt more and more restless and lonely. Whenever I wasn't with Holly, I just missed her so. I've never longed for anyone as much as I did her."

"How did you explain it to yourself?" Papp wondered.

"I didn't for a long time. I wasn't sure what I was feeling. Then I denied all my feelings. How could this happen? What would my friends think? What would happen to my lifestyle? I mean I fought so long and so hard to come out, to embrace my gay identity. You can't imagine the pain I went through with my family and friends. I was very politically active in the gay community—I still am!"

"So here you are, a gay man, in love with a gay woman."

"Exactly. It's like I was a breeder."

"A breeder?"

Holly and Wayne both laughed again.

"A breeder is what gays call straight people," Holly explained. "It's not exactly a term of endearment."

"I see," Papp said. It's amazing what she was learning, turning her whole concept of sexual identity upside down.

"So anyway," Wayne continued, "I was walking back to my apartment after we'd been riding our bikes together all day, and I said to myself, 'Oh my god! I'm in love!' I couldn't understand this. At all. I'm not attracted to women, except as friends. To tell you the truth, I've never been sexually turned on by women, always by men. But here I was—completely, totally, passionately in love with a woman."

"So what was the experience like for you?" Papp asked of Holly.

"I knew before he did that we were both falling in love. But I just didn't think Wayne could handle this. He didn't even have a single straight friend. His whole life had been the gay world. I think it was easier for me to switch even though all my sexual experiences had been with women."

"What was the most difficult part of it for you?" Papp asked Holly.

"It was the reaction of the gay community. A lot of my friends turned against me, and some even blamed me for converting Wayne. I think they felt betrayed and threatened."

"How have you managed to deal with that?" asked Papp.

"Well, we still haven't come out as a heterosexual couple to most of the gay community," Holly continued. "It drives me crazy that Wayne and I are still telling people we're gay. How can we be gay if we're practically married to one another? We're madly in love with another, for Christ's sake!"

"This does seem a bit confusing," Papp observed mildly.

"We have been in denial about being in a heterosexual relationship," Holly said to Wayne, "and that stops us from getting closer because we are not admitting who we are. It just gets me very angry when you camp with all your gay friends. At gay parties you leave me all alone—as though you don't even know me. I feel excluded."

Wayne looked uncomfortable, and Papp asked him where he stood on this issue.

"Look," he said to her, and then looked at Papp too. "I believe that being gay is a state of mind, and I am still a gay man even if my lover is a woman. I have always been gay. I will always be gay."

"How can you say that?" Holly challenged him. "You can say it is a state of mind, but if you accept the definition of gay as same-sex attraction, then there's a bit of a contradiction here."

Holly talked further about feeling frustrated with Wayne, who was not willing to make friends with other heterosexual couples or even attend straight gatherings once in a while. "It's like you're ashamed of who we are."

Wayne described to Papp how his gay identity had been such a battle after decades of self-hate, denial, and even harassment by the police. He remembered how horrible his first marriage had been because he had denied the truth about himself. He was adamant that he would never do that again.

Papp was curious why neither one of them felt comfortable with labeling themselves as bisexual. This was before the word *gender-blender* came into being. "I just don't like that word," Wayne said, with anguish in his voice. "That's not who I am! I am a gay man, and I've always been that way." That's about as clear as he could be on the matter.

"It sounds like when you talk about losing your identity," Papp ventured carefully, seeing his discomfort, "it becomes a political issue for you. Because you struggled so long to come out, and it took so much courage, and you had to confront so many things to do it."

"Exactly!" he said with relief. "I am so glad that you understand this because Holly doesn't."

"I do understand, darling," Holly reassured her partner. "I know what you've been through. I know what I've been through with my own struggles to come out. But I also know that I need to fit in somewhere. We don't fit in the gay community anymore, but that's where all our friends are. And we don't fit in the straight community because we're gay."

For Holly, it was increasingly difficult for her to hang out with gay and lesbian friends because of how critical they were of her relationship with Wayne.

Papp thought for a minute as they sat in silence. "Maybe the two of you just need to be pioneers."

"What do you mean?" Holly asked. Wayne looked up with interest.

"Maybe it's time for you to create a third culture, a third sexual identity."

"A third culture?" Wayne repeated.

"Yes. You don't fit in the culture of the gay community. And you say that you'll never be—what did you say—a breeder."

They all laughed at that.

"But your relationship doesn't fit into any of these boxes. Why let yourselves be caught up in language and defined by conventional categories? You are both gay, but you are living in a straight relationship. So maybe it's time for you to take what you want from both worlds and create your own culture, a third sexual identity. That way neither of you has to give up your own identity, or your integrity."

They thought for moment about this, then nodded their heads—not that they agreed with the premise but that they would give it some thought.

A NEW SPACE

Over the next several sessions, they continued to talk about the uniqueness of their relationship. The idea of having the best of both worlds appealed to them, and they talked about how they could be enriched by each without having to forfeit their integrity or identity but rather expand it to include both. Eventually they did declare their love publicly and present themselves as a couple.

Just as expected, a few of their friends rejected them. But many were accepting of their situation. Not surprisingly, as soon as Wayne stopped denying that they were a straight couple, Holly's sexual desire came back, and their sex life was reinvigorated. She felt she wasn't being wiped out anymore. Over time, Wayne agreed to socialize with some straight couples and found, to his surprise, that straight men could be artistic and sensitive too. These were characteristics that he had associated only with gay men.

"I think I have finally created a space," Wayne said in one of their last sessions together, "where I can be both a gay man and a man in love with a woman. I can be a man who hasn't lost all of the qualities that I am most proud of being gay and still love Holly."

They made progress on the other issues between them as well. Wayne learned not to run away from Holly when he felt scared of their intimacy. And Holly learned to express her own needs without feeling guilty or responsible for Wayne's reactions afterwards.

BOUNDARIES ARE FLEXIBLE

This case, perhaps more than any other that Papp has seen, aroused her curiosity about the very nature and possibilities of love and sexual identity. The case had taken place during the 1980s when all the confusing and contradictory ideas of the culture were floating around in her head, but until this point, she had never been called on to sort them out for herself.

"I began to think about all the things I had heard or read about homosexuality," Papp said. "Years ago a prevalent psychodynamic concept of homosexuality was that it was caused by an intrusive mother and a distant father. I don't know where that idea came from, but since they were blaming mothers for everything I guess it was convenient to blame them for that. And the thing is, you don't have to challenge what you believe until you are confronted with a situation that demands it."

Papp abandoned that popular theory after reviewing the research that emerged in which it had been found that there was no correlation between the kinds of families that people came from and their sexual orientation. It was not a simple matter of family dynamics after all.

"After I saw this couple," Papp said, "I did a great deal of reading and research and I found that there were many conflicting ideas in the field about homosexuality. One of the ideas that was promoted by gay parents was that it was biologically determined. You were born that way, and there was nothing you could do about it. If you had been involved in any kind of relationship other than a homosexual one, then you were only covering up. I think that is still a prevalent thought in the gay community today. Then there is the other side that believes that it is a choice people make. The conclusion that I finally came to is that nobody really knows why people fall in love with the same or different genders and it's different for every person. It is probably a very complex combination of many different factors, including biological, psychological, historical, interpersonal, cultural, and genetic.

"Friends of mine who have switched say you can love different people at different times in your life, and it's the person you love regardless of the gender. They describe love as being on a continuum with flexible boundaries. I think that there is so much prejudice around homosexuality, and so much stigma and fear and so many political issues, that it is extremely difficult to do good empirical research on the subject. At this point in our history, the most important thing is to keep an open mind and not worry so much about putting relationships into categories. There are so many different kinds of love and so many different ways that it is expressed and experienced."

When last she had heard from Wayne and Holly, they had still been doing well and were talking about having children.

CHAPTER THIRTY TWO

Len Sperry

The Bird Colonel Who Turned into an Elephant

Len Sperry's education as a therapist has followed a circuitous route. Originally he studied counseling and organizational psychology at Northwestern University, where he received his doctorate. Wanting more specialized training, he completed analytically oriented psychotherapy training at the Alfred Adler Institute, after which he headed to the West Coast for a postdoctoral internship in marital and family therapy. Sperry then practiced both psychotherapy and organizational consultation for several years before returning to complete medical school and residencies in psychiatry and preventive medicine (partially as a result of the case described in this chapter). As you would expect from someone prepared in so many disciplines, Len is Clinical Professor of Psychiatry and Preventive Medicine at the Medical College of Wisconsin, as well as Professor and Director of the doctoral program in counseling at Barry University in Miami, Florida. He is board certified in clinical psychology as well as in psychiatry and preventive medicine.

Sperry is the author of more than forty books that reflect his interdisciplinary training and diverse interests in consultation, diagnosis, family therapy, brief therapy, leadership, spirituality, psychopharmacology, and health. Some of his best-known works include The Handbook of

Diagnosis and Treatment for DSM-IV Personality Disorders; The Intimate Couple; The Disordered Couple; Psychopathology and Psychotherapy: From Diagnosis to Treatment; Brief Therapy with Individuals and Couples; *and, more recently, books such as* Effective Leadership *and* Spirituality in Clinical Practice.

—*www*—

Len Sperry's story begins during the three-year period that he practiced in Southern California after having spent much of his earlier life in the Midwest. Although hardly having led a sheltered life, he found the California scene to be a bit bewildering and incredibly stimulating. He also encountered the kinds of cases about which he had never dreamed, much less ever encountered before. This included people involved in Satanic cults and others who believed rather strongly in the existence of UFOs. It is not that such groups were unique to the West Coast; it is just that Sperry had not had the opportunity to work with this population before.

Sperry was also amazed by the prevalence of certain diagnostic entities that would be considered rare anywhere else. He encountered quite a number of patients with multiple personality disorder and even more with borderline personality disorder, both forms of psychopathology that present consistently unusual, unpredictable patterns. We mention this for contextual purposes so that you can understand that Sperry is not easily surprised by much.

"In walked a smallish, sort of effeminate-looking man," Sperry began. "He was very boyish looking with a wispy little mustache and the air of someone who swaggers around. He had the stiff posture and the kind of immobile expression that you associate with military and police personnel. But if he had not been wearing a uniform, you would have guessed he was a stock boy or clerk. He reminded me of a tiny kiwi bird strutting around on the beach with its puffy chest stuck out."

Considering that this new patient was a U.S. Army officer who commanded others in his unit, Sperry understood immediately this client's need to establish himself as a man of authority. The patient liked to be addressed by his rank, colonel, so Sperry accommodated him with the appropriate respect. It should be noted that he was a "full" or "bird" colonel, not the lower-ranking lieutenant colonel.

"So, Colonel, what seems to be the problem?"

"Well, Doctor, my wife and me. We been married for about six years."

"Yes," Sperry encouraged him to continue.

"We don't have children, just our work," the colonel explained. "And we're sort of going through a hard time."

This was an understatement. Both the colonel and his wife, Millie, seemed to be going through a midlife crisis at the same time. While the colonel's anxiety had been played out in the demands of his new command, the wife had recently been flirting with a male acquaintance. So far, this consisted merely of meeting the man for coffee on two occasions, but it was enough to make the colonel insane with jealousy.

"The colonel became extremely depressed," Sperry said, "to the point where he had gotten some antidepressants from his family physician. He had taken them for about two weeks and just had some annoying side effects, so he stopped the treatment. Although there was no prior history of psychiatric problems, the colonel was now acting progressively more desperate, suspicious, and paranoid. He was not only jealous about what he suspected was an affair, but he believed that his wife and her supposed lover were plotting against him."

THE COLONEL TAKES A FIELD TRIP

Sperry saw the colonel over a period of several weeks, and at each visit the man appeared more and more agitated, more obsessed about his wife's affair. This relationship between the wife and her colleague was not only improbable because they were hardly more than acquaintances but also because of her large size. The colonel's wife was rather massive, towering at least six inches above her husband.

The colonel began losing sleep worrying about what his wife might be doing. He worked long hours and was for all practical purposes on call twenty-four hours a day. Over the next three weeks he became progressively more fatigued. He was still unable to sleep at night—more accurately, he was unwilling to sleep. Sleep deprivation can have a profound impact on a person's perceptions, thoughts, and actions. It certainly did with the colonel. He believed that as long as he stayed up and kept an eye on her, his wife would be unable to get into mischief.

No matter what the wife said to reassure her husband, the colonel still maintained his suspicions. "What if I fall asleep?" the colonel said to Sperry quite sincerely. "Then she could sneak out in the middle of the night and meet the guy." He was convinced that as long as maintained his twenty-four-hour vigil, he could keep his marriage safe.

On top of his marital problems, the colonel was forced to take on additional responsibilities at work. One of these obligations involved attending a conference out of town, a prospect that sent him into a tailspin. How would he ever keep an eye on his wayward wife if he wasn't even in the same city? The colonel made up excuses for why he could not leave and finally pleaded with the major to let him stay home.

"It was at this point," Sperry said, "that I became increasingly concerned. I had been working in the Midwest, where it is relatively easy to get someone hospitalized and even to get the person committed. In California, however, it is very, very difficult to commit a person or get inpatient admission for someone who needs it. This is because there are so few inpatient beds available and very few people who have admission privileges."

About the time that Sperry decided he would have to begin commitment procedures, he got an emergency call late one night.

"Doctor?"

"Yes," Sperry answered in a sleepy fog, having just been awakened.

"Is this the doctor?"

"Yeah, who is this?"

"It's the colonel."

"Yes, Colonel," Sperry said in his calmest voice. "Where are you?"

"I'm at a pay phone."

"Very good, but where is this pay phone?"

Sperry heard the receiver drop and bang against the side of the glass. He figured the colonel was trying to get a fix on his position. Finally he came back on the line.

"I'm in the desert," he said in a small, quiet voice.

"OK, Colonel, may I ask what you are doing in the desert in the middle of the night? And why you are calling to tell me this?"

"Well, Doc, I'm sort of in a little bit of trouble. But don't worry—it's all going to work out."

Trouble indeed. It turns out that the colonel's suspiciousness had gotten so out of control that he had taken his wife out to the edge of the desert and tied her to a tree. He had quite a sizable gun collection, as you might expect from someone in the military and especially from someone so self-conscious about his small size in relation to others—especially his own wife. Now he was threatening to kill her.

"He was telling me all this," Sperry said, "at the same time that he was keeping watch on his wife tied to a tree five hundred feet away. He had wanted to check in with me because I had told him that if anything came up he should call me. This certainly qualified."

Sperry managed to calm the colonel down and convinced him to untie his wife from the tree.

"Colonel," Sperry asked the colonel, "how is it that she got tied to the tree?"

"Well, Doc, I wanted to get her attention when I talked to her. Otherwise she gets so distracted and starts walking away. I feel like an idiot following after her trying to say what's on my mind."

"It appears you've gotten her attention this time," Sperry observed mildly.

"Yeah. I think she's scared to death that I'll do something foolish."

"What are the chances that might happen?" Sperry wanted to be very careful to assess whether he was truly a danger.

"Pretty slim. I can't believe that I actually did this. What if my C.O. [commanding officer] finds out about this?"

"Colonel, there may be some other way we can come up with to improve communication between you and Millie."

"Doc, I think I should untie her, but I don't know what I'd say to her."

"Yeah. Untying her makes sense. You might say that you talked to your doctor and that he'd be happy to see you both in his office first thing tomorrow."

The colonel agreed and said they would both come in first thing that morning. Up until this point, Sperry had not yet seen them as a couple, mostly because of the wife's refusal to participate in therapy. After their "field trip" the previous evening, she was now a lot more motivated.

THE COLONEL FINDS A SOLUTION

"Once I saw them together as a couple," Sperry explained, "it became clear to me that there was this pattern of pursuer-distancer that very much characterized their functioning. But unlike the typical version of that configuration where the female pursues the male, it was the colonel pursuing his wife. Often, the pursuer believes that the other person is rejecting him or her. To ward off this perceived rejection, the pursuer will literally follow or 'shadow' the distancer around, pleading and demanding that his needs be recognized. Not surprisingly, the colonel's wife was overwhelmed by his emotional neediness. She had wanted to marry someone who was strong and could take care of her. Instead, she found herself pursued by a sniveling pantywaist of a man. She found his demands that she take care of him both repulsive and troubling.

Sperry wasn't particularly surprised to learn that Millie was ten years older than the colonel. He asked her what attracted her to the colonel when she first met him.

"Oh, he was so handsome in his dress uniform, with all that brass and braid. You know he's a 'bird' colonel. The real thing. And he's got a lot of people under his command."

"So," Sperry responded, "you find his presence and power particularly attractive."

"I sure did. And, at the same time, there was a softness and tenderness about him which made him even more irresistible."

As the session continued, the dynamics of the pursuer-distancer pattern became clearer. As long as Millie found the colonel strong but also tender, she couldn't resist being around him. But when she saw him as weak and frightened—which is the way he tended to act when under considerable stress—she was repulsed by his whiny and demanding pursuit behavior, so she distanced herself from these demands.

During their second session together it became more evident that this couple really cared about each other and wanted to stay together, if only they could find healthier ways of relating to one another. Despite the colonel's recent paranoid thinking and erratic behavior (as well as his access to guns), Sperry felt that the likelihood of his acting in a dangerous manner seemed slim.

"Why did I think that? Mainly because the colonel appeared to have shown reasonably good judgment and impulse control throughout his life, even when under considerable job and relationship stress. It was only during the past three weeks, when considerably sleep deprived, that his judgment and impulsive control were somewhat compromised. With increasing sleep deprivation, the colonel's suspicions about his wife and coworker escalated, creating a vicious cycle: continued sleep loss fueled his suspicions and jealousy, resulting in more pursuit, which lead to more distancing, which culminated in the desert 'standoff.'"

Fortunately, because of his Baptist upbringing, the colonel didn't drink. If alcohol—which can have a significant disinhibiting effect—had been a factor in the equation, it is doubtful that the colonel would have called Sperry, and he might very well have decided to shoot his wife.

The therapeutic challenge for Sperry was to figure out how to help Millie stop distancing herself from the colonel. "I basically reframed the situation," Sperry explained, "as an opportunity for the colonel to focus on the strengths and attractions in their relationship. I asked them to find some way to have a relationship that would build on their initial love for each other."

THE COLONEL GETS FIXED

For the next session, the colonel came in by himself—Millie had been unavoidably delayed by an accident that had stranded her on the freeway. He seemed a completely changed man. He no longer appeared agitated and paranoid. There were no indications of agitation nor suspiciousness. Rather, he looked rested, relaxed, and confident and was quite pleased with himself because he came up with what he believed was a solution to his problems.

"So, Colonel," Sperry observed, "you look quite pleased with yourself today."

"Doc, it's going to all work out." Then he smiled like a little Buddha with his ruddy cheeks and little belly sticking out of his small frame. "Seriously, Doc, everything is going to be fine."

"I see." Sperry did not feel completely reassured, as these were exactly the same words he had used when he had his wife tied to the tree with his arsenal of guns displayed around her.

"I mean it."

"I know you do, Colonel. But I'm not sure what you mean."

The colonel smiled again. "Well, tomorrow I go under the knife."

Sperry's face signaled his continued puzzlement, but the colonel was enjoying the attention. With repeated prodding, the colonel disclosed that he had scheduled an appointment at one of those little ambulatory surgery centers, doc-in-the-boxes, to have a vasectomy. He believed with all his mighty convictions that his main problem was being too potent sexually and that his wife was threatened by this. He had told her, and more likely convinced himself, that if he got himself "fixed," his wife could feel more comfortable around him.

"You are just the best, Doc," the colonel told Sperry. "You really helped me."

"I did?"

"Yeah, your idea about us finding a way—I think you said—to relate to each other differently. This is going to make all the difference. Trust me."

Sperry was speechless, unsure what to do next, so he just waited to see where this would lead.

"So, Doc, do I need to come back anymore, now that things are going to work out?"

The colonel had never been in therapy before, so he wasn't sure what the rules were. And this was a military man who was used to following rules to the letter. Sperry tried hard to dissuade his patient from trying to fix things through a simple incision inside his scrotum, but the colonel was insistent that this was the answer. Sperry finally suggested that it would be a good idea to meet again in a few days.

THE COLONEL NEEDS A SHOPPING BAG

"I was in the middle of a session the next day," Sperry said, "when I was interrupted by an emergency phone call from the colonel's wife."

"Doctor," she said in a panicked voice. I was certain that he had killed himself or someone else. "I'm at the hospital with the colonel"—even she addressed him that way—"and it doesn't look good."

"What's the problem?" Sperry asked, genuinely frightened by the fear in her voice.

She told him that they had botched the vasectomy at the little clinic. Instead of cutting the correct cord, they had accidentally severed lymphatic tissue. This is not uncommon when the surgeon is unskilled or inexperienced. The testicles become so swollen that the condition can actually become life threatening, which was why the guy was rushed to the emergency room.

"The poor colonel had a scrotum that was as big as a ten-pound watermelon. This is called elephantiasis. It's an inflammation that's caused by bacterial infection that we don't have much here but is common in Africa, hence the name elephantiasis. In this case, the little colonel's balls were literally the same size as an elephant's. His wife needed to encase them in a large shopping bag just to get him to the hospital."

The colonel was kept in the hospital for two days until the swelling went down and the infection was controlled. He became somewhat depressed realizing that his plan to sterilize himself had not worked out as he had hoped. But he didn't snivel, and he didn't pursue her. After all, he had a hard time moving those large balls around!

As fate would have it, an interesting turn of events took place. The more helpless the colonel became, the more his wife closed the distance between them. She appeared to enjoy the role of caretaker.

Somehow she had equated those large testicles with strength and power. He was strong and tender, and he needed her help and emotional support. He was her man, and she would stand by him. She would give him all the emotional support he needed. Millie spent more time with him as she realized finally how much she was needed.

Because the colonel had accumulated more than enough years in the military to qualify for retirement, he soon separated himself from the service so that they could begin a life anew somewhere else. He believed that once they moved out of that military community, the memories of these past months would fade, and they could get back to the way it was when they were first courting. As it turned out, this proved to be the case, at least the last time Sperry checked on them.

"Symbolically," Sperry explained, "this insecure little guy finally felt potent with his larger, more imposing wife. He felt like an elephant instead of a mouse or a bird. He was no longer a just a bird colonel but a giant elephant in Millie's eyes."

LESSONS FROM THE COLONEL

Sperry has spent a lot of time thinking about the meaning of this case in his work and his life. The colonel and his wife are especially memorable to him, not only because of the nature of their unusual behavior but also because of what he learned as a result of working with them. This was the first time that he witnessed so clearly the power of assigned roles in relationships, how an alteration in the pursuer-distancer pattern can change the whole structure of a couple's intimacy.

Instead of trying to change the colonel's personality, or even his behavior, it was the subtle alteration in the relational pattern that made all the difference. It had been so easy yet so unhelpful to think of the colonel in terms of his individual psychopathology. Once Sperry began looking at the larger system, both he and the couple felt empowered. "This case was a turning point," Sperry summarized, "in the way I understand people."

～— The Authors

Jeffrey A. Kottler is one of the most prolific authors in the fields of psychology and education, having written fifty books about a wide range of subjects. He has authored a dozen texts for counselors and therapists that are used in universities around the world and a dozen books each for practicing therapists and educators. Some of his most highly regarded works include: *On Being a Therapist, Compassionate Therapy, Bad Therapy, Making Changes Last, Beyond Blame, Travel That Can Change Your Life, The Language of Tears,* and *The Last Victim: Inside the Minds of Serial Killers.*

Jeffrey has been an educator for twenty-five years. He has worked as a teacher, counselor, and therapist in preschool, middle school, mental health center, crisis center, university, community college, and private practice settings. He has served as a Fulbright Scholar and Senior Lecturer in Peru (1980) and Iceland (2000), as well as worked as a visiting professor in New Zealand, Australia, Hong Kong, Singapore, and Nepal. Jeffrey is currently Chair of the Counseling Department at California State University, Fullerton.

Jon Carlson is Distinguished Professor of Psychology and Counseling at Governors State University, University Park, Illinois, and a psychologist with the Wellness Clinic in Lake Geneva, Wisconsin. In addition to serving as the long-time editor of *The Family Journal,* Jon is the author of twenty-five books in the areas of family therapy, marital enrichment, consultation, and Adlerian psychology. Some of his best-known works include *The Intimate Couple, The Disordered Couple, Brief Therapy with Individuals and Couples, Health Counseling, Theories and Strategies of Family Therapy,* and *Time for a Better Marriage.*

Jon has also developed and produced over a hundred commercial videotapes that feature the most prominent leaders in the field (including the professionals featured in this book) demonstrating their theories in action. These videos are used to train the next generation of practitioners.